THOMAS O. DORR

Pottery Technology

MANUALS ON ARCHEOLOGY · 4

POTTERY

TECHNOLOGY

PRINCIPLES AND RECONSTRUCTION

OWEN S. RYE

AUSTRALIAN NATIONAL UNIVERSITY

TARAXACUM WASHINGTON

THE MANUALS ON ARCHEOLOGY

are guides to the excavation, preservation, classification, analysis, description, and interpretation of special categories of archeological remains. The authors have drawn upon their experience and the contributions of other experts to formulate instructions for dealing with delicate, complicated or unobtrusive kinds of phenomena. Their intent is to enable those who are not specialists in the particular subject matter to classify and describe finds in a useful manner and to observe details easily overlooked during excavation or analysis. The manuals will be revised periodically to incorporate new information. Suggestions for improving the clarity or completeness of the instructions, illustrations, and data are welcome, as well as recommendations of topics appropriate to the series.

Dedicated to KHAN ZADA

only he and I know why

and

In memory of CLIFFORD EVANS

friend and colleague

First published 1981 by
Taraxacum Inc.
1227-30th Street
Washington, D.C. 20007

ISBN-0-9602822-2-X
Library of Congress Catalog Number: 80-53439

Designed by John B. Goetz
Cover motif by George Robert Lewis
Printed in the United States of America

Preface

I agreed to write this book because my personal experience with archeologists left me with the impression that many are not familiar with the principles of pottery making. My main aim has been to outline the technological processes and to call attention to the kinds of features useful for their reconstruction from archeological remains. Limitations of space prevent elaboration of many relevant aspects, but I hope enough has been included to alert the user to the potential and the problems of making inferences from technological data.

A strong bias has been introduced in that I have drawn heavily on my personal interests and experience, perhaps sometimes at the expense of general archeological concerns. Having been a potter for some 15 years, I have a very direct interest in the way potters in the past made and fired their wares. My approach is simple; if I am able to replicate their results, I feel I have successfully deciphered their behavior.

I have also done ethnographic studies among traditional potters in Pakistan, Egypt, Palestine (occupied Jordan and Gaza), and Papua New Guinea. As a result, I have been influenced personally as well as intellectually by the approaches, attitudes, and personalities of some 150 traditional potters. This manual provides the opportunity to integrate some of that experience with the concerns of archeology, in which my field experience is limited to ceramics from Palestine and Papua New Guinea.

Many people have contributed to this book, directly or indirectly. Among the indirect contributors, the many potters who have provided me hospitality and instruction are foremost. This includes my first teacher, Ivan McMeekin, who still seems to be looking over my shoulder and finding something that needs improvement.

Others directly involved in archeology have contributed to whatever knowledge and experience I have in this field. These include Clifford Evans, Betty Meggers, and others at the Smithsonian Institution; Albert Glock of the Albright Institute for Archaeological Research in Jerusalem, and various members of the Department of Prehistory, Australian National University. Among the latter, Jim Allen read parts of the manuscript and Jack Golson the complete text. The Department of Prehistory gave me freedom from other responsibilities during its preparation.

All drawings are by Winifred Mumford. Dragi Markovic did much of the printing of my negatives and also studio photography. I wish to thank Clifford Evans, Principal Investigator of the Ethnotechnology of South Asia Research Program, of the Department of Anthropology, Smithsonian Institution, for permission to use photographs taken in Pakistan during several seasons of fieldwork sponsored by that Institution.

Initial typing of the manuscript was done by Carol Joyce and Maureen Johnson, and Carol then retyped the corrected draft. Both will no doubt have finished their champagne long before this appears in print. Angela Drakakis-Smith undertook sub-editing of the original draft.

Brenda asked me to say that without her company this may well have been finished in half the time. Thanks for all the help and for managing to survive.

As for the rest, what is enlightening, what is boring, what is present or absent is my responsibility, although my Islamic friends would allocate at least part to the will of Allah. To judge that is most certainly not my responsibility.

Contents

Figures

Tables

1 Introduction

Pottery making, like metallurgy and the manufacture of glass, plaster, and cement, involves applying heat to manipulate and modify a class of inorganic materials. These activities have been collectively labeled "pyrotechnology" (Wertime 1973) because they make use of reactions taking place at elevated temperatures and require control of temperature, the rates of change in temperature, and the gaseous atmosphere surrounding the reacting materials. The development and increasing sophistication of techniques of pottery making seem likely to have occurred in conjunction with explorations in the use of these other materials.

This book has two aims: (1) to explain the techniques by which pottery is produced and the physical, chemical, and mechanical principles involved, and (2) to describe the features and methods for reconstructing techniques from archeological remains. I will deal only with a small portion of the total ceramic spectrum: pottery made by ancient peoples and traditional potters, who continue to use pre-industrial methods. I also will limit the discussion to more universal aspects of production and analysis; limitations of space prevent elaboration of the vast range of variations likely to be encountered by archeologists.

Analytic techniques developed in physics and chemistry have become popular among archeologists in the past few decades. Virtually all involve instruments that require operation by skilled technicians or specialists. While they are useful for specific types of analysis, they have distinct limitations in range of accuracy and application. Details of such techniques will not be presented, but some of their past and potential applications will be noted. For details of specific analytical procedures, works such as that by Aitken (1975) should be consulted.

Archeologists and ceramic technologists tend to speak different languages when referring to pottery. The terminology in this book is basically "potter's language." Although the concepts are derived from ceramics (the study of materials and techniques) rather than from archeology (the study of products), most will be familiar to archeologists. Specialized terms are defined in the text or glossary.

The perspectives of the technologist and the archeologist also differ. The former deals with the process of manufacture, the latter with the remnants of the product. Many details of the process cannot be differentiated in archeological specimens. I have included some of these to emphasize that culturally significant variables may be obscured and that similar effects can be produced by different methods. As with other kinds of scientific investigation, the validity of the results depends on the care with which the evidence is analyzed and interpreted.

I do not consider the approach outlined in the following pages to be the only one valid for studying ancient pottery. On the contrary, I believe that the maximum knowledge about people of the past is obtained from a number of lines of investigation, each supplementing the other. The technological approach provides knowledge of past attempts to deal with both natural and cultural environments, and increases understanding of varying "solutions" developed by different cultures.

The science of ceramic studies provides ordered knowledge of the behavior of materials at high temperatures and their suitability for various functions. It establishes the most efficient methods of producing ceramics. There is a danger in attempting to apply this knowledge to the work of ancient potters, whose information was not ordered in the same conscious structures. For example, a technologist can identify the "best" combination of materials available in an area for producing vessels with a specific function, such as cooking. Identification of those actually used may show that the potters used this blend, an average blend or even the worst materials possible. Worst, that is, from the framework of *our* knowledge. With the knowledge they possessed, the blend may have seemed best. Or it may have been employed because of ignorance of the properties of other available materials. Scientific awareness can become cultural bias if used uncritically. It will show us how *we* see past cultures, not how the people saw themselves.

PREVIOUS LITERATURE

Although writing and clay were associated in the ancient Near East, none of the cuneiform tablets mention pottery making. This is not surprising when one considers that even today the makers of village pottery learn their craft through oral traditions and "on the job" training. Some documentation does exist, however, particularly records of trading and other kinds of transactions. A sketch from a wall painting at Thebes shows Canaanite jars being brought into Egypt (Amiran 1969: Pl. 43-3). Egyptian tomb paintings depict kilns, forming of vessels, and other scenes of great value in tracing changes in technology (Lucas 1962:367–385). Representations of pottery making, decorating, and firing also appear on ancient Greek vessels.

Contemporary accounts of pottery manufacture are extremely rare prior to the past two or three centuries. One written in 1301 by Abu'l-Qasim, a member of a potter's family from Kashan in Persia, is a classic (Allan 1973). The production of Italian Maiolica was described in the sixteenth century by Cipriano Piccolpasso (1934). At the beginning of the eighteenth century, Père d'Entrecolles outlined Chinese porcelain making in Ching-te Chen (Burton 1906). All three studies were essentially descriptive and made technological information available to a wider audience than the craftsmen themselves.

Technological studies were stimulated by the beginnings of the industrial revolution in ceramics, led by people such as Josiah Wedgewood in England during the early eighteenth century. Publication began to increase and ceramic technology became an organized scientific discipline. Professional societies were founded and began to produce journals, such as the Transactions of the British Ceramic Society, the Transactions and Bulletin of the American Ceramic Society, and other national equivalents. Recent trends in ceramic science have been summarized by Budworth (1970).

The study of archeological pottery was initially oriented toward its artistic value. Much digging occurred, especially during the nineteenth century, to procure objects for sale to museums and private collectors rather than for scientific reasons. In keeping with this objective, emphasis was placed on criteria useful for verifying authenticity. A body of knowledge of stylistic and decorative attributes was accumulated that allowed the identification of place of origin and time of manufacture. Eventually, these data became sufficiently formalized to be used by archeologists for classifying pottery and establishing relative chronologies. The goal was to achieve conclusions about culture; there was little interest in level of technological accomplishment or the problems faced and solved by the makers.

A blending of cultural and technological questions was pioneered by Anna Shepard, a geologist who became interested in the study of pottery during the 1930's. Her contributions included the use of thin sections. Her book, *Ceramics for the Archaeologist* (1968), has been an important reference since its publication in 1954. Another major figure, Frederick Matson, concentrated on technology in earlier work (1943, 1951, 1952, 1956, 1960a, 1960b, 1963). The publication in 1965 of *Ceramics and Man*, which he edited and to which he contributed two papers (1965a, 1965b), marks a significant change to a broader cultural, biological, and environmental perspective. More recently, he has examined power and fuel resources in the ancient Near East (Matson 1966) and undertaken ethnographic studies directly related to archeological excavations (Matson 1972).

The writings of early travelers sometimes offer insights into the work of local potters and numerous accounts have been published by anthropologists. A bibliography of studies of traditional potters would contain some 10,000 entries, but unfortunately such a compilation does not exist. Many, if not most, of the reports describe practices in a single village or community. A few deal with a broad geographical area. The classical work of Linné (1925) on South America was an early contribution of this kind; others cover parts of the Mediterranean region (Hampe and Winter 1962), India (Saraswati and Behura 1966), Afghanistan

(Demont and Centlivres 1967), and Pakistan (Rye and Evans 1976). Other recent ethnographic research has focused on the solution of a particular problem rather than on pottery making as such. These studies deal with trade (Lauer 1970; Ellen and Glover 1974), use and distribution of pottery in households (Stanislawski 1977), and the effects of the environment on pottery making (Arnold 1975).

A significant development during the past 25 years has been the archaeometry approach. The application of physical and chemical analytical techniques has been facilitated by the use of computers for rapid analysis of statistical data. A brief review of the development of archaeometry has been provided by Peacock (1970).

A source of information sometimes overlooked by archeologists is publications aimed at modern craftsmen. Much of this literature gives practical guidance in using raw materials, and in forming and firing pottery. The best known work is *A Potter's Book* (Leach 1962), but Cardew (1969) and Sanders (1972) also provide general background for understanding the behavior of traditional potters. The most useful single volume for archeologists is by Hamer (1975), who gives a very complete outline of all aspects of pottery making. Fournier (1973) has published a similar, slightly less comprehensive work.

THE PRODUCTION SEQUENCE

A basic concept throughout this book is the pottery production sequence. The general sequence for any industry involves obtaining raw materials, refining and blending them, manufacturing a "product" or artifact by a succession of operations, and distributing the product to users. The sequence can be extended beyond production and distribution to include the use of the object by the consumer, its eventual breakage or obsolescence, and its disposal or recycling when no longer useful. If recycling occurs, such as crushing sherds for tempering clay, the artifact becomes part of another sequence.

From the viewpoint of technology, some operations are essential and some are not. The chronology of essential operations is fixed, whereas non-essential operations may be introduced at varying points or skipped. In pottery making, the essential operations include discovering sources of raw materials, choosing those to be used, extracting and transporting them to the site of manufacture, and preparing them for use; forming, drying, firing (including choosing fuels and methods of controlling heat), and distributing vessels to users; using them and, finally, disposing of them. In some situations, two kinds of feedback may affect the process. One is the user's assessment of the product, which enables the potter to make appropriate choices of raw materials, vessel forms, etc. The second is economic feedback, which eliminates processes and materials that make the product unsalable.

Non-essential operations include burnishing, applying paint or slip, and all other forms of decoration. These are non-essential because they do not affect the serviceability of the product. They are capable of much wider variation than essential steps and thus provide the most easily observed evidence of differences. For this reason, they have been widely used by archeologists for classification and comparison.

The reason for emphasizing the production sequence, with essential and non-essential operations, is to provide a pragmatic basis for identifying the important elements of pottery technology that will permit reconstructing the behavior of potters in the past. A potter operates within a realm of interactions controlled by physical and chemical laws and within a framework of choices that must be reevaluated constantly even by the most conservative artisan. As a simple example, natural clays vary in composition. If the potter exploits a vein of clay different from that he previously used, many vessels may be damaged during firing. Should new materials be sought or should the firing procedure be changed? The moisture content must be monitored constantly because it controls the working properties of the clay. The pottery-making process thus involves input to the potter (environmental, economic, cultural, physical), decisions about this input, and actions aimed at establishing equilibrium in the process. Ceramic technology is also directly affected by changes in other aspects of culture. The potter must consider new ideas (technological, economic, esthetic) and decide whether to incorporate or reject them. Other kinds of events, such as loss of territory in warfare, affect availability of raw materials and require experimentation with new sources.

Cultural traditions can exercise a strong conservative influence on the production process. For example, all potters working in a particular culture may be expected to use certain tempering materials and forming techniques. If they move to a new area, they may attempt to carry on this tradition. This can be investigated archeologically, provided the choice of materials made by the potters can be evaluated in terms of the range of materials available locally. The roles of innovation and conservatism in pottery making have been discussed in some detail by Nicklin (1971).

Cultural pressures can affect the choice of materials in other ways. Some techniques of decoration, such as carving or incising, are more successful when the clay contains no coarse inclusions that obstruct the path of the tool. Intricate decoration of this kind is thus usually associated with fine-textured materials. The functional requirements for vessels determine the suitability of shapes and this, in turn, affects the choice of techniques. In short, all the elements that contribute to the making of a vessel are interrelated and a change in any one will lead to changes in one or more of the others. Selection of materials, forming techniques, decorating techniques, firing methods, functions of vessels, and so on are all part of the potter's craft. In order to understand the latitude of choice within any stage, all must be examined.

Given that changes occur in pottery making, the archeological problem is to explain them. The approach advocated here is to establish the technological relationships that explain the choice of materials, forming techniques, and steps in production. If some of the changes remain unaccounted for when this analysis is complete, other hypotheses can be formulated and tested. Two applications of this approach are illustrated by the case studies in Chapter 7.

BASIC UNITS OF ANALYSIS

The basic units of analysis in pottery technology are: (1) attributes, (2) techniques, (3) process sequences, and (4) technological traditions. These are cumulative rather than independent. Attributes reveal techniques; a series of techniques constitutes a process sequence; one or more process sequences define a tradition. These relationships are important and should be kept in mind when judging which aspects of a piece of pottery or which actions of a potter are most relevant for describing a technology.

Attributes

These include observable, repetitive, physical phenomena such as color, minerals and assemblages of minerals, markings (e.g., fine lines, ridges), porosity, and details of size, shape, and decoration. Only attri-

butes present on several vessels are relevant. Unique examples may signify innovation or reflect inadequate sampling; they do not contribute to the reconstruction of a ceramic process sequence or tradition.

The attributes observable on sherds are not related. "A series of fine lines," for example, has no technological relationship to inclusions consisting of "10 percent quartz." Each belongs to a different set associated with a particular technique.

"Discriminatory attributes" are those implying differences in technique, such as illustrated by step 5 of Table 1. "Common attributes" are those shared. Any assemblage of vessels or sherds can be sorted using discriminatory attributes, common attributes being ignored.

Techniques

These are the repetitive human actions that produce the attributes. They are not observable archeologically, but must be inferred from the nature of the attributes. The principal techniques are: (1) preparing the body, (2) forming the vessel, and (3) firing.

Process Sequences

These are the successions of techniques necessary to produce vessels. Vessels that are identical are produced by a constant process sequence; those with distinct attributes are produced by different process sequences. The degree of relationship between

Table 1. Two forming process sequences for bowls. They differ only at Step 5.

Steps	Process A	Process B
1	Form ball of clay	Form ball of clay
2	Dig thumb into ball and pinch out bowl shape between thumb and fingers	Dig thumb into ball and pinch out bowl shape between thumb and fingers
3	Smooth rim between thumb and fingers while rotating bowl in other hand	Smooth rim between thumb and fingers while rotating bowl in other hand
4	Allow bowl to dry to leather hard	Allow bowl to dry to leather hard
5	Scrape base of bowl with sharpened wooden tool to thin base	Smooth base of bowl with ball of wet cloth
6	Allow to dry completely	Allow to dry completely
7	Paint line of pigment on rim	Paint line of pigment on rim

process sequences is indicated by the similarity in techniques at comparable stages. The process sequences on Table 1 differ only at step 5, where one bowl was scraped and the other was smoothed.

Technological Traditions

Technological traditions are recognized from high correlations between process sequences. The correlations are judged subjectively. Although employing statistical techniques for this purpose should be relatively straightforward, no attempt has been made to my knowledge.

Technological traditions may not be synonymous with typological traditions, which are usually defined in terms of vessel shapes and decoration. Different process sequences can be used to produce vessels with similar form and decoration. Conversely, a single process sequence may be used to produce distinct vessel forms.

It is conceivable that potters working in the same place at the same time could produce vessels that an archeologist might assign to separate technological traditions. For example, untempered clay may be used for large water containers and shell-tempered clay for cooking vessels. The relationship between the two "traditions" might be established by other criteria, such as co-distribution of the vessels in many households.

Whereas techniques and process sequences should correspond to the behavior and sequence of actions of the original potter, technological traditions recognized by archeologists may not conform to the conceptions of the potter.

Technological Patterns

The concept of a technological tradition implies transmission of ideas within a region or between regions. Similar traditions can develop independently, however. As a hypothetical example, a potter in India might produce cooking vessels using calcite-tempered clay; form them by coiling, scraping, and smoothing,

and fire them in an open fire. A potter working in a different time period in Melanesia might use the same materials, forming techniques, and firing procedures to produce vessels with similar functions. This independent recurrence of process sequences has been termed a technological pattern. The study of technological patterns sheds light on the evolution of ceramics by revealing the specific combinations of materials and methods that best fulfill the functional requirements of certain kinds of products (Rye 1976).

STABILITY AND CHANGE

All parts of the process of pottery production are susceptible to alteration, but not equally so. Changing the shape of a rim from vertical to slightly outflared is relatively easy, as is producing a vessel half as large but with the same proportions as others already in use. Substituting three concentric circles for a painted representation of a gazelle on the side of a vessel is also technologically simple.

Changes in materials can be made relatively easily if the properties are similar, but substituting materials with distinct behaviors will require altering the entire manufacturing process. For example, a successful change from quartz temper to beach sand containing shell would necessitate considerable experimentation with new firing techniques.

If forming techniques were studied through time in various areas and cultures, I predict they would be the most stable aspect of the production process. New vessel shapes will tend to be those that can be formed using the established basic techniques. Firing will also tend to be stable. Fuels may be changed relatively easily if their combustion characteristics are similar, but new methods are likely to be resisted. Firing is a very difficult process and potters become very sensitive to the events in a "normal" firing. Changing the approach removes the subtleties of control the potter has developed and a long period will ensue before an equivalent level can be reestablished.

2   Fieldwork

In addition to the data collected during survey and excavation of archeological sites, technological studies on pottery involve sampling the raw materials that may have been employed. If traditional potters are still working in the region, observation of their materials and techniques may aid in reconstructing those used in the past. Accumulation of data is pointless, however, without a specific research goal. Too often, archeologists hand a few sherds to specialists after their own examination has been completed and ask for comments. This chapter will specify the kinds of data required for technological analyses.

ARCHEOLOGICAL FIELDWORK

Site Surveys and Surface Collections

Scatters of sherds and other artifacts on the surface of the ground are a common indicator of an archeological site. Surveys usually involve mapping such locations and collecting a representative sample of the sherds. In regions where the characteristics of the pottery are well known, the collection is usually restricted to "diagnostic" sherds, such as rims, bases, and fragments with decoration.

To be useful for technological studies, the sample should be enlarged to give an indication of the range of materials, forming techniques, and firing techniques, as well as the range of vessel forms and decorations. This is accomplished by including sherds exemplifying the range of color, fabric, porosity, and hardness, along with any unusual features. If the number of sherds in a surface scatter is small (less than 100), it is best to collect them all. Their distribution over the surface should be recorded in as much detail as practicable. A small-scale map can be prepared using either surveying techniques or a compass and measuring tape. The map should indicate whether sherds are uniformly distributed or whether concentrations occur. In the latter event, the locations and frequencies of sherds in each concentration should be recorded.

Excavations

The principles and methods of stratigraphic control in excavations are well established and the following discussion assumes that good excavation technique has been used. No responsible specialist is interested in working on material that has not been excavated properly. If technological analysis of the pottery is planned, the person doing the analysis should take part in the excavation if possible.

Even a large excavation can produce only a portion of the original ceramic assemblage. Vessel types manufactured at the site and traded, especially those made for trading, will be under-represented or absent from the occupation debris, but may occur at workshops or in manufacturing waster dumps. Kinds of vessels often damaged during manufacture or most commonly used and hence broken at a more rapid rate are likely candidates for recycling. Underfired or low-fired vessels may disappear through processes of erosion. Small vessels, such as flasks, may be dispersed during seasonal use away from the settlement; others may be associated with preparation and consumption of food away from the site.

The first step in deciding on a sampling strategy is establishing the type of data required from the pottery. If technological analysis is anticipated, the obvious procedure is for the excavator to consult with a specialist long before excavation begins. This consultation should involve considerations such as the proportion of sherds to be returned for laboratory analysis and what is to be done with those discarded. To permit correlating stylistic classifications with technological classifications, the sample of pottery should contain the range of variation in attributes required for analyses of decoration, vessel shape, materials, forming techniques, firing techniques, etc. Sherds selected for technological study must be assignable to a stratigraphic context as precise as those employed for stylistic analysis.

If sampling is done during excavation, the sherds selected should represent:

(1) The range of mineralogy; freshly broken cross sections should be examined using a 10x hand lens to facilitate recognition of variations.

(2) The range of forming techniques; all sherds with marks on either surface should be kept.

(3) The range of decorative techniques; the full range of surface coatings, as well as painted and plastic decoration, should be represented.

(4) The range of vessel forms; rim and base sherds, plus any restorable vessels, should be saved.

(5) The range of firing techniques; examples of all variations in the color of the surface and structure of the cross section are desirable.

In addition to the sample exhibiting the range of variation in technological attributes, it is desirable to keep all large sherds. These are extremely useful for studying forming technique, because the large surface area allows the orientation of inclusions to be observed, and for chemical analyses, where it is desirable to establish the variation in composition over a small area. They also provide dilatometer samples for studies of firing temperature, which cannot be cut from small sherds.

In addition to samples of pottery, samples of soil should be taken from each stratigraphic layer. Each sample should weigh at least 500 grams and should be placed in a plastic bag immediately after extraction so that any moisture present is retained. These samples permit evaluation of the degree to which the composition of the pottery has been modified subsequent to burial.

Manufacturing Sites

From a technological standpoint, the most useful find in an archeological site is a potter's workshop. If preservation has been adequate, all the data necessary for reconstructing the procedures used by the potters can be obtained. Obviously, a "potter's workshop" is a variable entity. Where vessels were made in the household for use only in that household, evidence of pottery making will be scant compared with what may be left by fulltime professional potters who worked in special locations. The survival of a few itinerant seasonal potters in the Chitral Valley of Pakistan (Rye and Evans 1976) exemplifies a situation that would be unlikely to produce work areas recognizable archeologically. Several kinds of features may be preserved and should be watched for during survey and excavation.

Raw Materials. A stockpile of clay encountered during excavation would be an extremely valuable find. Mineralogical and chemical analyses can establish whether the clay was used to make the pottery with which it was associated. Samples of the raw material facilitate locating the sources. Unless the site has been disturbed, a stockpile of potter's clay or tempering material would be recognizable by its homogeneous composition and structure.

Facilities for Preparing Materials. Pits or vats used to prepare clay, hardened areas (surfaces) produced by the process of footkneading, and other kinds of features associated with pottery making may be difficult to detect or to identify unless accompanied by more specific types of evidence.

Tools. The likelihood of identifying an object as a potter's tool may decrease as the degree of specialization in manufacture decreases. Specialized equipment, such as the potter's wheel and instruments associated with its use, is easy to recognize. Natural tools, such as shells, sticks, and rounded stones, may be overlooked even if they are preserved at a site. If the pottery is carefully studied to reconstruct forming processes, the nature of the tools may be inferred to a limited extent. The marks on vessels can suggest what kinds of natural objects were employed.

Evidence of Firing. The more specialized the technology, the more easily recognizable is the evidence of firing. Open firing may leave only a patch of burned soil, indistinguishable from the effects of a cooking fire. Pits, especially if lined with stones or baked clay, may have been used for firing pottery. Kilns (Fig. 1) may be mistaken for other kinds of industrial installations, such as metallurgical furnaces,

Fig. 1. Partially excavated ceramic kiln constructed and used during the 12th century B.C. The firebox is divided by an arch that formerly supported the chamber; remnants of two other arches are adjacent to the interior of the right wall. The entry to the firebox was at the narrow front end. Scale in 10 cm units. Tell Jemmeh, Israel (Courtesy Gus W. Van Beek).

especially if similar structures have not been recorded previously. They can be distinguished, however, by the composition of the slag. Pottery kilns have siliceous slags with high potassium and possibly sodium content; metal furnaces have slags with significant metallic content, often iron or copper. Associated features, such as raw materials near the kiln or furnace and waster dumps or metallurgical slag dumps, also facilitate differentiation. Techniques for detecting magnetic anomalies can be used to locate buried kilns (Aitken 1975).

Wasters are sherds and vessels showing evidence of damage during firing. Wasters occur wherever pottery was made, irrespective of whether the site represents itinerant, home or workshop organization of production (Fig. 2). They may be discarded in "waster dumps," especially if production is centralized, or may be put to other uses. In Pakistan, for example, vessels or sherds damaged in firing are a common building material for domestic dwellings. It is unlikely that wasters will have enough value to be transported far from the site of manufacture, even if they are used.

Fig. 2. Firing wasters associated with an updraft kiln (upper right). Gaza Strip.

Workshops. The association of all or several artifacts and features strengthens the interpretation that the assemblage represents a workshop or manufacturing area. Firing usually creates a nuisance and potters are often banished to the edge of the settlement. They may work at their homes on all stages of the process until the vessels are dry and then remove them from the residential area for firing. I have observed this behavior in present-day Papuan coastal villages and on the northwest frontier of Pakistan (Rye and Evans 1976: 16). This creates a spatial separation between evidence of forming and evidence of firing.

In more specialized industries, the whole process is carried out in one location. Other activities that cause unpleasant odors, such as metallurgy, tanning leather, and dyeing cloth, may be concentrated in the same area. Discovery of evidence of one of these activities warrants searching for the others in the vicinity.

Even an experienced archeologist would not be wise to excavate a pottery manufacturing site without the assistance of a specialist. Such a site is a primary source for studying ancient technology and a nonspecialist would be unlikely to recover all the information potentially available.

CONSERVATION

Any artifact that has survived burial for hundreds or thousands of years can be assumed to have reached chemical and physical equilibrium with its environment. Excavation immediately places it in a different environment, where a new equilibrium must be attained. For some artifacts, this means very rapid deterioration. Fortunately, ceramics are composed of silicates and oxides that are stable in a wide variety of contexts. This accounts for the preservation of ceramics where other kinds of materials have decomposed. This stability also means that the conservation of pottery excavated by archeologists is seldom a problem.

The following discussion emphasizes aspects relevant to excavators. Special problems should be resolved in consultation with an experienced conservator. Other data on conservation of pottery are provided by Leigh et al (1972), Plenderleith and Werner (1971), and various papers in *Conservation in Archaeology and the Applied Arts* (I.I.C. 1975).

Four general rules should be observed:

(1) Conservation should stabilize rather than change an artifact.

(2) All treatments should be reversible.

Fig. 3. Destruction of the surfaces of vessels from exposure to salt after burial on the coast of Peru. **a,** Mochica. **b,** Nazca.

(3) All chemical or physical treatments should be recorded, specifying adhesives or impregnating mediums as well as simpler procedures, such as removing soluble salts from the pores.

(4) Unstable specimens should be kept in an environment similar to the one from which they were removed; if wet, keep wet; if dry, keep dry.

Exposure to Acids

High-fired, non-porous (fully vitrified) wares, such as porcelain, are resistant to acids except hydrofluoric. Low-fired, porous wares are attacked by some acids, such as concentrated sulphuric acid. These reagents are unlikely to be used, but exposure to even very dilute acids should be avoided because some components of the body, such as $CaCO_3$, are rapidly affected. Detergents should also be avoided.

Removal of Salts

If porous specimens are excavated from a wet saline environment, they will contain soluble salts. This is invariably true for pottery removed from marine contexts, but many terrestrial sites are also saline. Problems arise immediately if the pottery is allowed to dry, because the salts crystallize, expanding their volume, and creating internal pressures sufficient to cause disintegration (Fig. 3). Such pottery must be kept wet until stabilization can be undertaken by expert conservators.

Treatment of Unfired Objects

Unfired clay can be recognized by its friability and lack of strength. Small pieces can be detached from its surface easily with a fingernail. If placed in water, such specimens will slake or rehydrate, breaking down and regaining the original plastic properties of the clay. Obviously, unfired material will only survive in dry sites. If objects of this kind can be removed without fracturing, they should be kept dry and handled with extreme care because of their fragility. If broken, all fragments should be kept because they provide valuable data on the raw materials used by the potters.

Consolidation of Underfired Pottery

If underfired pottery cannot be excavated without fracturing or crumbling, it can be consolidated temporarily. Leigh et al (1972) recommend first attempting to stabilize a vessel by wrapping it with bandages. If this is insufficient protection, a consolidating substance can be painted or sprayed on the wrapping. When proper conservation can be guaranteed soon after excavation, applying a ten-percent solution of polyvinyl alcohol dissolved in water is a suitable temporary measure. When no additional treatment is likely to occur, the following procedures are appropriate: (1) if the specimen and surrounding soil are dry, apply a 10 percent solution of polyvinyl acetate dissolved in toluene; (2) if the specimen and surrounding soil are wet, apply a 10 percent solution of polyvinyl acetate dissolved in water.

If the condition of an underfired sherd or vessel is so poor that no useful morphological or stylistic data are likely to be obtained, the best procedure is to avoid any form of consolidation or treatment and to remove it for mineralogical and chemical studies. If the piece is destined only for this kind of analysis, all adhering soil should be carefully cleaned off before packing and kept in a separate bag.

Washing Stable Pottery

Pottery should be washed using water and a brush with soft bristles that remove only loose deposits from the surfaces; hard encrustations should be left for later examination because they may provide clues for reconstructing methods of production or use of the vessel. Washing should be done in such a way that no scratches whatsoever are produced by the brush or by grit dragged over the surface. Studies of manufacturing techniques and functions of vessels make use of scratches on the surface and those added during washing can confuse or destroy important evidence. During washing, the water should be changed frequently to eliminate suspended particles of grit.

The person doing the washing should be alert for the following phenomena:

(1) Organic coatings on the surface, especially fugitive materials such as resins or other plant derivatives.

(2) Decoration or coating added after firing and thus easily removed with a brush, such as pigments filling incisions and clay painted on the bottoms of cooking pots to enhance resistance to thermal shock.

(3) Variations in color between the inner and outer surfaces, which may offer clues to the use of the vessel.

(4) Deposits resulting from usage, such as carbon on the exterior indicative of cooking and accumulations on the interior resulting from heating hard water.

(5) Residues on the interior that may permit identification of cooking or storage functions.

(6) Fragile surfaces resulting from application of a friable slip or use of materials containing soluble salts.

(7) Decoration that may be visible only when the surface is wet because of destruction by erosion.

In all cases, washing should stop at the point where removal of any of these substances is likely and their presence should be noted.

Mending and Restoration

Most excavated pottery is in the form of sherds. The attempt is commonly made to fit pieces together into larger sherds and to reconstruct vessels. This procedure has several advantages:

(1) If enough sherds fit together, the shape of the vessel can be reconstructed more accurately and morphological comparisions will be more precise.

(2) Even if only a few sherds fit together, a larger area is provided for studying technological and stylistic attributes.

(3) If sherds that fit together are from different layers or units of the excavation, they imply the deposit may have been disturbed, whereas if they are close together they suggest the vessel has remained in situ.

Whether sherds that fit together should be physically joined by glue is a separate decision. Specimens destined for technological studies are more useful if kept separated. In studying the forming techniques of closed vessels, the most relevant attributes are on the interior because the exterior receives additional treatment at a later stage. Because the interior is seen neither by the potter nor by the user, it is allowed to retain the earlier markings. These will not be visible if the vessel is fully restored and the analyst will also be deprived of tactile evidence obtained by feeling the walls and attempting to locate marks left by tools or the fingers of the potter. One solution, if restoration is required, is to leave some sherds out so that the interior of the base, the sides, and the neck or upper part of the wall remain clearly visible. This recommendation applies less to open vessels, such as dishes or bowls, where both interior and exterior surfaces normally remain exposed to view.

For petrographic and chemical analyses, it is necessary to make thin sections and to reduce sherds to powder. Cross sections of vessel walls must be examined to reconstruct firing practices. As a minimum, several small sherds from each restored vessel should be set aside for these purposes.

Because a significant amount of information is lost by restoration, this process should be reversible. A glue such as duco, which is soluble in acetone, should be used. Cellulose nitrate or polyvinyl acetate adhesives are also suitable because both can be dissolved when necessary. A sandbox is convenient for holding pieces during drying. One sherd is partly buried upright in the sand so that the one being glued to it is held in place by its own weight. If additional support is required, rubber bands, spring clothes pins or small "C" clamps can be used to hold the fragments together until the adhesive sets.

SUPPLEMENTARY STUDIES

If studies of ceramic technology are planned, two kinds of data should be collected during archeological fieldwork. First, the area surrounding the site should be surveyed to locate all sources of materials potentially exploited in making the pottery. Second, the work of any traditional potters surviving in the area should be studied. With careful planning, both can be combined with the archeological program.

Identifying Sources of Materials

The chemical and mineralogical characteristics of sherds are often analyzed to obtain groupings that employ materials obtained from different sources. This type of study is simpler than attempting to locate the sources, which requires fieldwork that may be expensive and extensive analytical facilities. Attributes of the pottery are compared with attributes of the raw materials, and either a high or a low correlation may be obtained. The results may be difficult to interpret if all potential sources in the region have not been sampled during fieldwork and if the correlations are not significant statistically.

Fieldwork is facilitated if the locations of potential sources can be predicted either from theoretical considerations or from characteristics of the pottery. The non-plastic mineralogy of the clay is usually a more reliable indicator than the clay-mineral remnant fraction. If the assemblage of minerals consists of volcanic-rock weathering products or river-gravel deposits, for example, areas likely to possess these materials may be identified using geological maps.

Sources of Clay. Broad-scale (regional) geological maps are of little use for locating small-scale deposits of specific composition because sediments are described in a generalized manner, such as "sandy clays and conglomerates." Detailed local reports may be more useful, but geologists are mainly concerned with recording deposits with economic or industrial importance. Unfortunately, clays significant for modern industry were seldom those valuable to ancient potters. Conversely, the fusible and highly plastic, colored clays most suitable for making low-fired, unglazed pottery are of little economic significance to modern industry, although some may be appropriate for making bricks. Occurrences of shales, slates, and igneous rocks, such as granites, which can weather and form clays, are clues to potential primary deposits. Secondary deposits may be found in alluvial and lacustrine contexts. Creek and river banks, road cuts, and eroded gulleys provide opportunities to observe buried deposits.

Because natural occurrences of clay are likely to be far more numerous than those actually worked by ancient potters, it is desirable to narrow the search. Local residents are often good informants. In parts of the world where pottery continued to be made until recently, older people may remember where the clay was obtained. Others who use the land, such as farmers and road workers, may possess useful knowledge. Brickmakers will know what deposits are suitable for their purposes. If any drilling has been done, such as bore drilling for water, the personnel involved may possess useful information.

A thorough discussion of sampling procedures is beyond the scope of this manual, but four general considerations are important:

(1) The principle of least effort implies that the deposits exploited will be those most accessible to the manufacturing sites. Thus, if the source is known, the general location of the manufacturing site can be inferred; conversely, if a manufacturing site has been encountered, the general location of sources of raw materials can be predicted.

(2) The samples collected from the region surrounding a known manufacturing site should represent the full range of materials used. If the chemical and mineralogical composition of the pottery is known, the range of potential sources can be narrowed by eliminating those not compatible.

(3) The samples collected from each deposit and outcrop should represent the full range of vertical and

horizontal variation. In small localized deposits, this requirement is easy to fulfill. Sedimentary deposits that extend over a large horizontal area may be impossible to sample adequately.

(4) When a potential source has been found, its coordinates should be recorded with sufficient accuracy that it can be relocated by other workers. Topographic features useful for identifying its location should be described.

Before samples are collected, tests of workability and observations of inclusions should be made and the results recorded. If the deposit is not wet enough, a handful of clay can be moistened and kneaded until it is sufficiently plastic that a coil about 1 cm in diameter and 5 to 10 cm long can be formed by rolling the ball between the hands. This should be bent and the outer side examined for cracks. If the clay is very good, the coil can be bent completely and tied into a knot without cracking. A very "short" (not workable) clay will break into two pieces when treated this way. Another method of testing workability is to form a small ball of clay, about 1 or 2 cm in diameter, and to flatten it between finger and thumb. The clay should be rerolled into a ball and reflattened repeatedly until it cracks and becomes too dry to continue. A very poor clay will crumble on the first flattening, indicating that it could not have been used for making pottery. A very plastic clay will survive 15 to 20 cycles of rolling and flattening before becoming unworkable.

The suitability of clay for making pottery can also be evaluated by observing the quantity and sizes of "accessories" or contaminants. If mineral grains, root fragments, and other inclusions are abundant, the clay is unlikely to have been used because such materials are difficult to extract. In general, if a high proportion of the inclusions is larger than about 5 mm, the clay is also unsuitable. A clay containing a small proportion of accessories finer than about 0.5 mm is suitable for most ancient pottery-making processes if its other properties are satisfactory.

Sample size is dictated by the laboratory procedures to be used. Chemical and mineralogical analyses require no more than 500 grams of clay, but if more extensive studies are anticipated each sample should weigh at least 5 kilograms. This amount is sufficient to permit compounding several bodies, to make test pieces for firing trials, and to conduct most other kinds of experiments.

The specific methods of collecting samples vary with the nature of the deposit. A profile, such as a river bank or road cut, is best sampled by digging a channel vertically from top to bottom at least 10 cm deep and 10 cm wide. The material removed should be discarded and the channel deepened another 10 cm. The content of this second cut constitutes the bulk sample. If the deposit shows stratigraphic variation, the material from each unit should be kept separate so the chemical and mineralogical differences can be assessed. Contamination can be prevented by placing each sample on a large sheet of plastic film, about three by one meter, as it is removed.

If a sample is larger than required, it can be decreased by quartering. This involves mixing the material thoroughly, heaping it into a conical pile, and dividing the pile into four equal portions. Three are discarded and the fourth retained. This process of mixing, heaping, and quartering can be repeated until the desired size is obtained.

Clays overlain by soil must be sampled by coring. A hand auger or core sampling tool is used to drill through the overburden and into the clay deposit. The hole should be drilled in increments of 15 to 30 cm. The soil of each successive increment should be removed carefully from the tool and laid on a plastic or canvas sheet where it can be examined for stratigraphic differences. Each stratigraphic unit should be bagged separately. Auger or core samples can be reduced to suitable size by the quartering procedure described above.

Samples of clay should be placed inside a strong plastic bag. Because paper tags are vulnerable to damage from dampness, a metal or aluminum foil label should be enclosed. Descriptive and locational data can be written on foil with a ballpoint pen. After the tag has been inserted, the top of the bag should be sealed with a plastic-coated wire. Ideally, each plastic bag should be inserted in a canvas bag, tied again at the top, and provided with another label. Double labeling insures identification of samples, even if the outer tag is lost. Samples that cannot be identified with certainty are useless.

Sources of Tempering Materials. Most tempering materials and natural inclusions are sufficiently large to be identifiable in thin sections. If the material added by the potter can be distinguished from accessories present naturally, mineralogical analysis of sherds provides the best clues for discovering the source of the temper. If the composition is distinctive, it may permit identifying a specific location. For example, crushed basalt was used by potters in the Middle East. Details of the size and type of crystals can not only identify the flow, but may even differentiate the margins from the interior. Obviously, studies of this technical nature are outside the expertise of most archeologists and require the collaboration of mineralogists and geologists.

Ethnographic Studies

Descriptions of surviving traditional potters contribute to our knowledge of ceramic technology in ways that no reconstruction from archeological evidence can achieve. A traditional potter is one who uses materials, tools, techniques, and firing methods that are not demonstrably of recent introduction. Usually, the antiquity of a particular practice can be established only for one or two generations, using the potter's own testimony and literary sources. By contrast, it is often easy to recognize recent innovations, such as machinery, types of kilns, and application of glazes. If change has been extensive, the value of a study for the history of ceramic technology and archeological interpretation will be minimal.

Because traditional pottery making is disappearing in many societies, any archeologist or anthropologist in a position to do so should record the procedures of potters still working. It is not only important to take notes and photographs; it is also necessary to collect samples both of all materials used and of the products. Such samples serve as controls for laboratory studies of archeological specimens. An ethnographic collection can be used, for example, to ascertain the variation in composition of vessels made by the same potter. These data can be compared with the variation in archeological specimens assigned to the same group. Descriptions of forming techniques combined with X-ray studies of the vessels will show the orientation of inclusions that results from the specific techniques used. These standards can be applied to excavated sherds, facilitating reconstruction of the ancient forming techniques.

Interviewing

Guidelines for recording ethnographic information, based on my field experience in Pakistan, Egypt, Papua New Guinea, and among Palestinian Arabs, are presented in the Appendix. They were developed to insure no significant aspects of technology were omitted.

In practice, I have found that the best approach is to ask permission to watch a potter at work. This is almost invariably given. The time of initial contact may not coincide with initiation of the process, so whatever stage is underway becomes the first focus of study and questions can be asked during the work. If time is available, the entire sequence can be observed. Potters are often willing to demonstrate specific techniques if requested, once rapport has been established.

Familiarity with pottery processes is the primary requirement for an observer. This knowledge permits distinguishing aspects that are of interest from those commonly known. For example, it is useless to spend hours recording details of the construction of a kiln if these data have been published. Familiarity conveys another advantage by improving communication with the potter. The most productive results in my own work have derived from exchanges of information, in which the potter supplied data on techniques of preparing clay, for example, and then questioned me on techniques of glazing, for which he had difficulty obtaining facts. This type of exchange has immediate benefits and increases the probability that future investigators will be welcomed by the craftsman.

It is usually easier to obtain technological information in a short time than to study the role of the potter in the cultural or economic setting. Questioning on the micro-economics of production may be useless or elicit false information, because the craftsman wishes to avoid taxes or inflates the prices of wares in anticipation of sales to the questioner. No data that cannot be cross-checked should be considered reliable.

Equipment

The following special equipment is required for studies of traditional pottery making:

(1) Two measuring tapes, one 5–10 meters long and one 50–100 meters long.

(2) Strong plastic bags of several sizes for samples and aluminum tags for labeling.

(3) Instruments for measuring temperature during firing. There are two principal kinds. Temperature-sensitive paints, pyrometric cones, and fusible pellets react at one fixed temperature or over a narrow range; they are consequently of limited use unless the approximate temperature is known. Thermocouples and a portable indicator are more suitable.

Thermocouples contain two metal wires of different compositions, which are welded together at one end. When this welded couple is heated, a difference in electric potential is generated that is proportional to the temperature. This current is registered on a scale graduated so that the temperature can be read. A chromel/alumel couple is suitable for most ethnographic work, since temperatures are unlikely to exceed 1200° C.

Thermocouple wires are susceptible to corrosion or changes in composition in some atmospheres with consequent loss of accuracy, so they require protection by a sheath. Ceramic tubes are broken easily, making a metal sheath preferable. I have used Inconel-sheathed thermocouples successfully for a number of years and find that a one-meter length is most versatile (Fig. 4). When ordering an instrument, the maximum working temperature (1200° C) and the atmosphere anticipated should be provided to the manufacturer. A sulphur-containing reducing atmosphere should be specified if the exact conditions are not known.

At least three meters of compensating cable will be required for each thermocouple to keep the indicator far enough from the fire (Fig. 5). Several thermocouples can be used with the same indicator if the switch has the appropriate number of junctions. The compensating cable should be covered with an insulating material, such as fiber glass. Any jacks or couplings should be ceramic rather than plastic.

An optical pyrometer performs the same function as thermocouples and indicators. This is not recommended for open fires because it is difficult to obtain a consistent reading. It is often inappropriate for kilns because there is no opening to provide the necessary visibility. Thermocouples can be inserted while the kiln is being set and left for the duration of the firing.

Fig. 4. Thermocouple inserted in the top of an updraft kiln. Only 15 cm of the sheath are visible; the thermocouple extends 80 cm down into the kiln chamber. The cable leads to an indicator.

Fig. 5. Recording temperatures registered by the thermocouple during firing of the updraft kiln shown in Figure 4.

3   The Production Sequence

Pottery making requires expertise in materials, forming, and firing. Chapters 4, 5, and 6 discuss each of these stages in detail. Here, the production sequence is outlined to provide a background for placing the more detailed data in perspective and to call attention to some of the general principles underlying the manufacturing process.

MATERIALS AND THEIR PREPARATION

Clay is the basic material for all pottery. In their natural state, all clays contain minerals other than clay minerals and usually also organic materials, such as plant fragments and finely divided remains. These are known as "accessories." The sizes of the grains or crystals of accessory minerals are seldom as small as those of clay minerals unless the clays have been deposited under very specialized conditions (such as deep-sea sedimentation).

To a ceramist, the significant characteristic of clay is the presence of clay minerals. The distinction between clay and clay minerals is important. Clay is a naturally occurring, fine-grained sediment or erosion product, which becomes sticky or plastic when wet and shrinks when it dries. Clay minerals have specific compositions and crystallographic structures. The individual crystals or "particles" are so small (kaolinite crystals, for example, are usually smaller than 2 microns) that they can only be seen using an electron microscope. In the absence of these minerals, clays would have no plasticity and would not shrink or harden on drying.

The suitability of naturally occurring clays for making particular kinds of wares varies considerably. Almost any natural clay can be used for low-fired (below ± 800°C) pottery, although with varying degrees of success. As firing temperature increases to the stoneware range (between 1150° and 1300°C), many natural clays become unsuitable because vessels made from them fuse or warp when fired. A very narrow range of materials is suitable for producing the highest fired porcelains. Other qualities of the clay must also be considered by the potter. A natural clay that fires satisfactorily may not have sufficient plasticity for forming. Alternatively, a clay may be too plastic, with high shrinkage that causes cracking during drying.

The high plasticity characteristic of many natural clays provoked one of the first major technological advances in pottery making; that is, blending of materials or "tempering." In archeological usage, temper refers to any material other than clay minerals in the fabric, but this is not a very useful concept when studying technology because all clays contain accessory minerals. The archeologist must attempt to differentiate natural inclusions from those added by the potters. The methods for accomplishing this are often complex and arduous, and differentiation may be impossible in some cases.

Obtaining Materials

Assuming the potter knows what blends to use, his first task is to obtain the materials (Fig. 6). These may be gathered by the potter or an assistant, or traded or purchased, depending on the cultural context. Even at the simplest levels of technology, variations in natural deposits become obvious to potters. They will not collect their materials at random even within a single deposit, but will select that portion having the most appropriate properties and the least variation.

The selection of materials may be restricted by extraneous factors, such as ownership or control of land, seasonal access, depth of overburden, and distance of transport. Land ownership or control may be impossible to establish archeologically. The output of labor and cost of transport make exploitation decreasingly viable economically as distances increase, except for specialized materials required in small quantities. The materials are usually delivered to the workshop or production area without treatment apart from removing the most obvious impurities, such as large rocks. If specialized equipment is used for processing, the most efficient arrangement is to have the equipment at the location where subsequent activities will be performed.

Preparing Materials

Initial processing of the raw materials involves removing particles of coarse matter, including fragments of rock and remains of plants. The decision as to what is "too coarse" will depend to a large extent on the wall thickness of the vessels to be made; the thinner the walls, the finer the particle size required.

At the simplest technological level, the clay is commonly dried in the sun and crushed into small lumps so the unwanted inclusions can be seen readily and picked out by hand (Fig. 7). A more sophisticated means of removing coarse fragments is sieving. The most efficient approach is to add water to the clay until it forms a fluid, which passes through a sieve readily. Particles larger than about 0.2 mm can be removed with modern equipment, but the slowness of this procedure makes a mechanically driven vibratory sieve desirable when materials are being prepared in large amounts. Traditional potters were seldom able to make sieves with an aperture less than about 1 mm unless they used non-durable materials such as cloth. Another common method of separation is settling. The clay is made into a liquid slip, which is poured into a vat or container. After the coarser grains have settled, the uppermost finer fraction can be transferred to another vat or container.

Among non-mechanized cultures, air separation or winnowing is not feasible for refining clay because of the amount of time required to crush it to the fineness necessary and the difficulty of collecting the fine fraction. Winnowing may be employed when the

Fig. 6. Obtaining raw materials. **a,** Digging clay from a hillside deposit. **b,** Selecting cobbles suitable for additive from a riverbed. Pakistan.

Fig. 7. Crushing clay with a wooden pestle. Note the sieve at the right. Pakistan.

a

b

Fig. 8. Preparing additive. **a,** Crushing a cobble with a hammerstone. **b,** Sieving crushed stone to remove excessively large particles before blending with clay. Pakistan.

coarse fraction is desired and the light fraction can be allowed to blow away. Air separation techniques are used in some modern industries.

Levigation is a sophisticated process of settling that removes everything but the clay fraction and larger particles of very low specific gravity, such as charcoal. The clay is prepared as a slip, which flows slowly down very gently sloping channels. The fine fraction flows over a lip at the end of the channel and the coarse fraction settles behind the lip.

Separation techniques are usually not used with non-clay materials in simple technologies. Instead, non-plastic minerals are selected with the appropriate particle size distribution, such as naturally graded sands. If these are not available, the non-plastic materials are crushed or ground and excessively coarse fragments are removed (Fig. 8). Crushing can be mechanized relatively easily, as attested by the Oriental stampmills driven by water power. Crushing becomes impractical when very fine powders are desired because of the time required for pulverization. Grinding methods are used to produce the fine powders needed for glazes and pigments. Querns or handmills are still used for this purpose in some parts of the world. Mortars and pestles are more often employed for preparing pigments.

PREPARING THE BODY

In the literature on ceramic technology, the term "body" designates the blend of materials used for forming pottery, whether before or after firing.

"Body" is used in this general sense though this manual; "paste" and "fabric" are synonymous with fired body.

Blending

The methods of physically mixing materials vary widely. Probably the simplest is to wet the clay until it becomes plastic or soft plastic, then to sprinkle the non-plastic or organic additives over the surface and mix them in by kneading. A process used by some potters in simple economies, and presumably very widely in antiquity, is foot kneading. The body is formed into a pile and the potter systematically treads around it, kicking down material from the top to blend with that at the bottom (Fig. 9). Foot kneading is a quick, if laborious, way of mixing additives into clay in large batches (50–100 kilos). For smaller amounts, the same result is achieved by hand kneading. Hand kneading is a universal pre-forming operation, even if foot kneading is used for initial mixing (Fig. 10).

In more sophisticated body-preparation techniques, the clay is first converted into a slip. Additives are then sprinkled over the surface or shoveled into the container and the liquid is stirred with a paddle. After it is uniformly blended, it is poured into shallow stone, brick, plaster or cement vats, or over a flat area of hard-packed ground, and allowed to dry to a plastic condition (Fig. 20). Sun-drying is used in simpler industries, and is most effective in warm climates or at least warm seasons. It is generally used in conjunction with wheel-forming techniques, where large amounts of body can be consumed in one day. Preparing body as a slip is not well suited for blending some kinds of additives. Organic materials float, whereas heavy minerals sink and accumulate as sludge at the bottom of the container.

Preparing for Forming

The body must be brought to workable consistency before vessels can be formed. If it has been stored for any length of time under moist conditions, it

Fig. 9. Foot kneading. Sand used as a parting agent to prevent the clay from sticking to the kneading platform can be seen at the left. Pakistan.

Fig. 10. Rolling clay into a lump for hand kneading after preliminary foot kneading. Note the parting agent spread on the platform. Pakistan.

may need to be dried slightly before use. The potter must also insure that moisture and inclusions are evenly distributed. One method of accomplishing this is wedging. In this technique, a lump of clay is cut in half using a wire and one half is picked up, inverted, and slapped down onto the other half. This procedure is repeated for 10 to 20 cycles, when the mass has been converted into a series of very fine laminations and is quite uniform.

Hand kneading is another mixing technique, in which the clay is rotated systematically or rolled and unrolled. The cycle is repeated until the potter judges from the feel and appearance that the moisture and inclusions are evenly distributed. A secondary but very important side effect is elimination of pockets of air trapped during earlier stages of preparation. Finer air bubbles that remain become uniformly dispersed.

FORMING OPERATIONS

Water Content

In considering forming operations, it is necessary to appreciate the significance of the water content of clays or bodies and its effect on their properties (Fig. 11).

Slip and Slurry. When enough water is mixed uniformly with clay, it forms a suspension that acts as a liquid. For most clays, about 50 percent water by weight is sufficient, but some require up to 100 percent. As the proportion of water rises, the properties of the suspension increasingly resemble those of water rather than clay. Concomitantly, the rate that accessory minerals settle accelerates. When the process is reversed and the water content is reduced, viscosity increases.

A suspension that flows readily is termed a "slip." When viscosity is sufficient to impede flow, the mixture is known as "slurry." Slurry can be used in various ways. For example, it can be applied to a vessel by hand to give a rough surface. It can also be applied to the region where a handle is to be attached, so that the handle will bond firmly rather than crack away during drying. Slurry is commonly used to repair cracks that develop during drying before firing and to fill pits on the surface.

Workability. With further loss of water, the clay becomes plastic. Its properties are intermediate between a viscous liquid and a solid. When pressure is applied to plastic clay, it yields; when the pressure is removed, it retains the new shape.

With clay bodies, "workability" is preferable to "plasticity" for designating this property. Plasticity is defined in terms of a series of physical criteria and can be specified by quantitative relationships between these criteria. Workability, by contrast, is a human or subjective quality, defined by the potter's judgment of how well suited a particular clay or body is to the

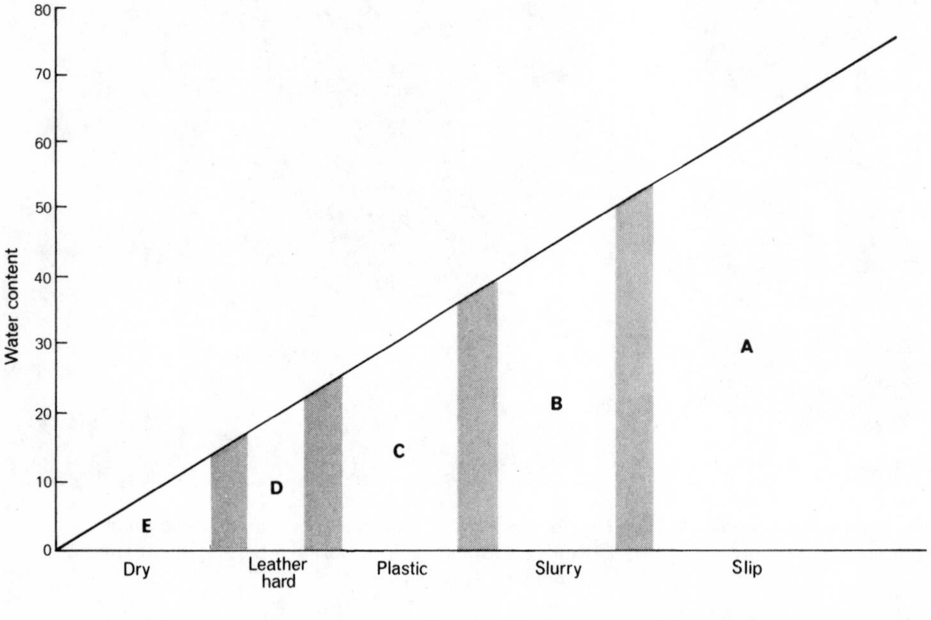

Fig. 11. The properties of a hypothetical clay body as a function of water content. a, Liquid range or slip. b, Semi-liquid range or slurry. c, Plastic range. d, Leather-hard range. e, Dry range.

processes he envisages using. The universal criterion for judging workability is feel. The subtle change in workability as clay dries is well known to potters and is the basis of all plastic forming operations. At one extreme, which may be called "soft," the clay responds readily but vessels can deform under the pressure exerted by their own weight. At the other extreme, which can be called "stiff," the clay is more difficult to work, but vessels are very stable and retain their shape despite being moved, picked up and set down or even inadvertently bumped or knocked.

The proportion of water required to maintain plasticity or the "plastic range" extends from about 15 to 50 percent. The plastic range for pottery bodies usually varies between about 20 and 35 percent.

Techniques

A multitude of techniques has been devised for applying pressure to plastic clay to form vessels. The simplest and most obvious is pinching between fingers and thumb. Throwing on a potter's wheel is related to pinching in that pressure is applied inside and outside a hollow lump of clay. The function of the wheel is to revolve the piece so that fresh working faces are presented continuously for the pressure to act upon. Other techniques, such as coiling and slab building, exploit the ability of plastic clay to form a permanent bond when pieces are pressed firmly together. They may be used independently or in combination (Fig. 12).

In some forming techniques, operations are performed at different stages of the plastic range. The rough shape of a vessel may be produced using soft clay and the form refined using a beater and anvil when the clay has become stiffer. In constructing coiled vessels, coils formed from quite soft clay are used to build the lower walls. The partly completed vessel is then allowed to dry sufficiently that it can support the weight of coils added to form the upper walls. The fact that thickness of walls affects the rate of drying can also be exploited to schedule finishing operations. A section of a vessel with thin walls can be finished first; when it has dried, the thicker portions will still be soft and can be finished while the vessel is held by the less easily deformed drier section.

When the water content drops below the minimum for the plastic range, the clay loses its plastic properties and behaves as a solid. In the first stage of this transformation, it is generally known to potters as "leather hard" and has a consistency similar to stiff cheese. Vessels at this stage of dryness will break rather than deform under pressure, but still can be cut with a knife or fine wire.

Turning, which involves removing excess material from the base of wheel-thrown vessels, is done at the leather-hard stage. Applying handles is usually done at the very stiff plastic or incipient leather-hard stage, when the vessel is not easily deformed by the pressures exerted in applying the handle, but subsequent shrinkage of vessel and handle will be relatively similar. A handle or other addition to a drier vessel would crack off because of differential shrinkage.

Many decorative processes are most successful when the vessel is leather hard. Incising and combing tend to throw up an unattractive sharp edge when performed on plastic clay, but leave a clean cut on a leather-hard surface (Fig. 47). Seals and roulettes make clear impressions on leather-hard clay, but produce distorted ones on soft plastic surfaces. Burnishing is most effective when the clay is leather hard, although the optimum stage of dryness varies for different bodies.

Slips, especially those applied by dipping, are often added when the surface is leather hard. Some glazes are also applied at the end of this stage, when the rims and other faster-drying areas are just beginning to change color. Leather-hard or plastic clay is darker than dry clay, and the transition in color is obvious.

DRYING

It is apparent from the preceding discussion that drying is an integral part of vessel forming and must be controlled to achieve the properties of clay most appropriate for specific techniques. A vessel must not be allowed to lose all its moisture before it is complete.

Different clays and bodies dry at different rates when exposed to standard conditions. Clays with coarser clay minerals, such as kaolins, tend to dry more quickly; very plastic clays, such as those containing montmorillonite, tend to dry more slowly. The drying rate is related to the nature of the packing of minerals, which governs the size and distribution of capillaries through which water reaches the surface where it can evaporate. Because clays and bodies shrink during drying, stresses are created when one

a

c

b

d

Fig. 12. Forming a vessel using a combination of throwing, coiling, and beating techniques. **a,** Clay being flattened on a turntable previously sprinkled with parting agent. **b,** Lifting to form the walls while rotating the wheel with the right foot. **c,** Adding a coil to heighten the wall. **d,** Thinning the coil and smearing the lower edge over the pre-existing wall. **e,** Refining the walls by beating, using the other

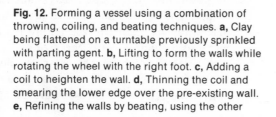

e

g

f

hand as a support on the interior. **f,** Flaring and refining the rim. **g,** Applying decoration to the finished wall. **h,** The finished portion has been removed from the wheel and attached to a flattened disk of clay to form the bottom, which is being rounded using a paddle opposed on the interior by an anvil. **i,** Refining the exterior of the bottom. Pakistan.

h   i

Fig. 13. Vessels drying in the sun prior to firing. Pakistan.

part dries more quickly than another and cracks develop.

Potters become aware of appropriate drying rates for the materials they use and employ this knowledge in conjunction with observation of microclimate to minimize damage (Fig. 13). They are careful to place vessels where they will not be exposed to drafts or direct sunlight at early stages of drying. The relationship between the drying rate of the body being used and the local climate will to some extent determine the nature and layout of the workshop. In a very hot dry climate, vessels made from clays that dry rapidly must be put in an open space sheltered from the sun. Clays or bodies that dry slowly may require special drying rooms or well insulated buildings, which are kept cool. In a cool damp climate, specially heated rooms may be needed to speed up the process.

Drying rate also affects the output or rate of production. When vessels can safely dry in one day, a potter capable of producing 100 vessels a day can achieve this output. If they take a week to dry, how-

ever, a potter able to form 100 per day may be restricted to making only 20 unless a very large space is available to store the accumulating drying vessels. In many parts of the world, potters work seasonally, producing at their full capacity during hot drier months and slowing down or suspending production during cold wet months because of the difficulty of drying vessels at a sufficiently rapid rate.

SURFACE TREATMENTS

Some decorative techniques are best executed when vessels are completely dry. Potters who apply slip by wiping do so at this stage because the moisture is absorbed and the slip dries almost immediately. If this were done earlier in the drying sequence, the slip would remain wet and be wiped off in some areas as it was applied to others.

Dry surfaces are most suitable for many types of painted decoration. If a pigment suspended in water is deposited on a plastic or leather-hard pot, it tends to flow, run or spread unevenly. If applied on a bone-dry vessel, however, the water in suspension is absorbed and the pigment dries immediately with a sharp edge. Pigments mixed with water may have a little clay added so they flow more easily and adhere more firmly.

Whether glazes are applied to leather-hard or to dry vessels is determined by the clay content in the glaze mixture. If a glaze contains about 30 percent or more clay, it should be applied at the white-dry stage because its shrinkage will match that of the vessel. If a glaze has a low content of clay (less than 10 percent), it can be applied successfully to a bone-dry surface. It is common practice in modern industry and among studio potters to heat vessels to 950° C, cool and apply the glaze, and then refire to the maximum temperature desired.

FIRING

It is essential that vessels be completely dry during the initial stage of firing, especially if heating is rapid. Otherwise, the moisture trapped will convert to steam, creating sufficient pressure to rupture the vessel. This process can be verified by throwing a piece of moist clay into a fire (provided good eye protection is provided) and observing the resulting dramatic explosion.

The main aim of firing is to subject vessels to sufficient heat for a long enough time to insure complete destruction of the clay-mineral crystals. The minimum temperature varies between about 500° and 700°C, depending on the type of clay. When heated above these temperatures, clays take on the characteristic properties of pottery: hardness, porosity, and stability under a wide range of chemical and physical conditions.

The principal variables controlled by the potter during firing are the rate of heating, the maximum temperature, and the atmosphere surrounding the objects.

Temperature

The rate of heating is important because chemical reactions are not instantaneous and sufficient time must be allowed for completion of desirable reactions. Reactions take place at specific temperatures; for example, the critical temperature must be exceeded to insure destruction of the clay minerals. Overfiring is undesirable for most ceramics, however, because it produces various kinds of damage. For example, warping results when vitrification reactions are allowed to proceed too far.

In practice, the maximum temperature that can be reached is governed by many variables, including the type of fuel, the amount of heat produced by the fuel, and the insulation surrounding the objects being heated. Kilns allow greater maximum temperatures to be achieved than open firing, which does not produce temperatures above about 1000°C.

Atmosphere

The atmosphere or gas surrounding the objects influences all types of ware, whether fired at low or high temperatures, by reacting with constituents of the body. The three principal atmospheres — oxidizing, reducing, and neutral — are distinguished by the predominance of oxygen (oxidizing), carbon monoxide (reducing), or carbon dioxide (neutral). The atmosphere is controlled by the amount of air available to burn the amount of fuel supplied. If insufficient air is provided, reducing conditions are produced. If the ratio of air to fuel is sufficient to allow complete combustion without excess of fuel or air (the stochiometric ratio), neutral conditions are produced. If excess air is provided, oxidizing conditions result.

Methods

The two principal methods of firing pottery are open firing and kilns.

Open Firing. Although open firing involves little or no building and maintenance of structures, it requires a high degree of skill and observation. The fuel and vessels are set together and fired to a maximum of 1000°C. To reduce loss of heat, potters often use some kind of insulation, such as placing large sherds over the top of the setting. Some control over rate of firing can be achieved through choice of fuel. Animal dung, for example, burns slowly and uniformly, raising the temperature gradually, whereas grass, straw, and twigs burn very quickly causing a rapid rise. Potters using quick-burning fuels usually preheat the vessels to eliminate all free moisture and minimize the risk of shattering during heating. Some control over atmosphere can be achieved by the placing of fuel and vessels so as to regulate the flow of air through the setting. With all forms of open firing, it is virtually impossible to control the atmosphere after firing has begun.

Kilns. Kilns do not always represent an advance over open-firing techniques. Some limit temperatures below 1000°C, have as wide a range of variation in temperature at the peak of firing, and use more fuel to heat an equal number of vessels because the kiln structure must also be heated. Only about 10 percent of the heat generated is available to the ware being fired. Heating the kiln requires 30–40 percent and the rest is lost in waste gases and conduction and radiation from the kiln structure (Rosenthal 1954:108).

Ancient kilns and modern traditional kilns can be classified into two basic types: (1) those in which the fuel and vessels are set together and (2) those in which they are separated. In the latter, the fuel is burned in one space (the firebox) and the heat passes through openings or flues into another chamber where the vessels are placed. This arrangement usually permits good control over the firing atmosphere because the supply of both fuel and air to the firebox can be regulated. It also allows the highest temperatures to be achieved. Kilns where fuel and vessels are set together (Fig. 87) represent a transitional stage between open firing and sophisticated updraft and downdraft kilns.

POST-FIRING TREATMENTS

Many traditional vessels are not completed by firing. Unglazed vessels that will be used to store liquids may need to be made impermeable by applying a coating to the surface. Permeability is a different property from porosity, porosity being a measure of the volume of pore space in a ceramic and permeability a measure of the rate at which liquids can pass through the wall. A vessel can have high porosity but low permeability if the pores are not connected. Sealing the surface has only a slight effect on porosity, but a very significant one on permeability.

A variety of plant extracts has been used as sealers, especially resins, gums, and pitches. Usually, they are brushed or rubbed on while the vessel is still warm or after it has been reheated. Containers for storing expensive liquids, such as oil, wine, and perfume, are likely to need sealing. Treatment of vessels for storing water varies with climate. In hot climates, it is desirable for water to permeate to the exterior where it can evaporate and promote cooling; sealing would inhibit this process. Cooking pots are unlikely to have sealers applied to the exterior because they would burn off when the vessel was placed on a fire. It is common for the interior to be sealed, however, often by the user rather than the potter by boiling a food that has an acceptable taste and leaves a permanent residue.

Unless the potter markets and distributes his wares, his role in the production process generally ends here. Some form of testing the fired ware may be done, although there is little mention of this in ethnographic descriptions and no means of determining whether or how it was done in the past. A common test is to tap the vessel with knuckles or a stick. A clear sound indicates a well fired vessel; a muffled or uneven tone indicates a cracked one.

From the archeological point of view, the pottery process is far from complete at this stage. Vessels are used, broken, discarded, reused, or buried, and subjected to alterations from natural and cultural agents. Interpreting the clues left by the potters and users, and recognizing post-depositional effects are the challenges that face the ceramic technologist.

TECHNOLOGICAL CONSIDERATIONS

The nature of the materials and the functions of vessels are interrelated variables. The materials (combined with forming methods and firing techniques) contribute the physical properties that insure the vessel can perform a particular function. If it can be established that specific materials are usually correlated with specific functions, the presence of these materials can be used to infer function. The analyst should keep in mind other kinds of variables in making such interpretations, however.

Functional Requirements

Domestic functions can be divided into three categories: (1) cooking or heating, (2) storage of solids, and (3) storage of liquids. The requirements are different. Vessels used for cooking must have good resistance to thermal shock in order to withstand repeated heating and cooling without fracturing, and also low permeability so the contents do not seep through the walls. High thermal conductivity would permit faster heating, but also promote faster cooling after removal from the fire, so intermediate thermal conductivity might be most desirable. To minimize permeability, it is necessary to control porosity.

The properties of vessels used for storing drinking water vary with climate. In cold climates, low permeability is desirable to minimize loss by seepage. In hot climates, by contrast, permeability should be sufficient that water can percolate to the outer surface, evaporate, and thus cool the contents. Storage of solids presents no special problems, so a very wide range of materials is suitable. Vessels for storing liquids other than water may require low permeability to minimize loss.

To produce a range of vessel types with properties appropriate to different functions, potters have several options: (1) to use different materials and firing procedures for each type, (2) to use the materials most appropriate for one type, recognizing that vessels destined for other purposes will not have optimum properties, or (3) to use the same materials for all kinds of vessels, choosing those that offer the best compromise. The second alternative is likely to predominate among traditional potters, but instances of the first have been observed.

Another solution is to reduce permeability by applying an organic coating, such as gum, resin or pitch, to the surface after firing. This procedure makes it possible to employ the materials and firing procedures best suited for cooking vessels for manufacturing both cooking and water storage containers without sacrificing the optimum requirements of either function.

Resistance to Thermal Shock

One of the most difficult properties to achieve is resistance to thermal shock, which causes cracking during repeated heating and cooling. Cracks develop because the outer wall, exposed directly to the fire, expands more than the inner wall, which is kept cooler by the contents. Tensile stresses on the inner surface are relieved by fissures. At first, these may be barely noticeable. Eventually, they become so large that the vessel may collapse. Cracks can also form on the outer surface as the vessel cools, if the interior is hotter than the exterior.

The principal variables affecting resistance to thermal shock are: (1) porosity, the number and sizes of pores; (2) mineral inclusions, their type, quantity, and size distribution; (3) thermal expansion, the extent to which clay matrix and inclusions expand on heating, and (4) shape of the vessel (Rye 1976).

Porosity. For maximum resistance to thermal shock, large pores or voids are desirable because when the crack reaches a void its propagation is arrested. The simplest means of achieving large voids is by using organic temper, which burns out during firing. Since large voids significantly increase permeability, it may be necessary to apply a slip or other coating to compensate for this effect.

Mineral Inclusions. The effects of thermal expansion of inclusions have not been studied, but the best results would be expected when the rate is close to that of the clay matrix (Rye 1976). Calcite, plagioclase, and several heavy minerals have expansions similar to average fired clays (Skinner 1966). Grog has the same index as fired clay because it is fired clay. Quartz, one of the most common inclusions, has a relatively high expansion.

Vessel Shape. The shape of a vessel can affect its resistance to thermal shock. Thermal gradients, which cause cracking, are minimized by uniform thickness of the wall and absence of sharp angles or changes in direction. For this reason, most cooking pots have rounded bottoms and simple body contours.

Size of Inclusions

In general, the size of inclusions varies with the size of vessels and thickness of the wall. If the wall is 2 mm thick, inclusions larger than 2 mm in diameter will weaken it. If large, thick-walled vessels are being formed, larger inclusions are needed to prevent the vessels from collapsing under their own weight during forming. Potters making small, medium, and large vessels could thus be expected to use tempers with different particle sizes. The type of material may be the same, especially if it is crushed by the potters, as it is easy to separate the particles into several grades by sieving or settling.

Variations in particle size may correlate with variations in hardness and porosity. During firing, reactions such as fusion begin on the surfaces of crystals or grains and penetrate inward gradually. The surface area provided by a given weight of temper is greater if the particles are fine than if they are coarse, so that using the appropriate size can permit achieving reactions more rapidly or at a lower temperature.

Sizes of inclusions can also affect technique of decoration. For example, coarse inclusions increase the difficulty of producing fine incisions because grains dragged by the tool will distort the margins of the cuts.

Effects of Firing

The behavior of materials during firing varies considerably. Some are refractory, which means that they withstand firing without fusing and are generally stable at elevated temperatures. Others fuse, forming glass, or vitrify. If too much fusible material is incorporated in a body, it can collapse during firing.

Below 900°C, no fusion occurs regardless of composition. Some materials are unstable and either decompose, volatilize or burn out (oxidize) below 900°C; these are not considered either refractory or fusible. Above 950°C, some kinds of materials begin to fuse and form glass, but most remain refractory. Most rocks and sediments fuse as the temperature increases to about 1300°C.

VARIATIONS IN PROPERTIES

The generalized nature of the preceding discussion must be countered by emphasizing the range of variation that can characterize every stage in the production process. It is all too easy unconsciously to project our familiarity with standardized, mass-produced products into the analysis of archeological and traditional ceramics and consequently to attach too great importance to variations in their properties.

The classificatory and control devices used by potters in the past have usually been far less precise than our facilities for analyzing their results. Materials that vary widely according to our physical and chemical measurements may have been considered identical or interchangeable. Methods of measurement were also less sensitive. Materials for blending, for example, were often calculated by volume rather than weight. Potters using clay and sand mixes might judge that "two handfuls of sand is enough for this much clay." Although our measurements might determine that the proportion of sand varies between 20 and 45 percent, this variability might be viewed by the potter as within the normal range; he would consider a body with 20 percent sand identical to one with 45 percent sand. Similarly, firing temperatures, whether in open firings or kilns, can vary not only between firings and within settings, but over parts of a single vessel by as much as 400°C. The same latitude applies to the shapes of vessels; the criteria used by a potter to judge that two vessels are the "same" may be difficult or impossible to reconstruct. Thus, the parameters for defining a technological tradition cannot be specified until the range of variations encompassed within the tradition can be differentiated from characteristics that are outside the "normal" range.

4   Materials and their Preparation

Materials for ceramics have two distinct sets of properties: those before firing and those during and after firing. At the simplest technological level, only clay and two other ingredients are required. These are water for mixing with the clay to render it plastic and fuel for firing the vessels. The development of ceramic technology has involved widening the range of materials, increasing understanding of their properties, expanding the diversity of forming techniques, and improving the efficiency and control of firing.

This chapter reviews the materials used to make pottery and their methods of preparation, and describes the types of analyses appropriate for reconstructing the behavior of the potters.

CLAY

Clay is a naturally occurring, earthy, fine-grained material that becomes plastic when mixed with a limited amount of water (Grim 1968:1). Its plasticity allows it to be deformed by applying a force and to retain the new shape when the force is removed. Another important property of clay is its hardness and durability when heated. The combination of ease of shaping and permanence on heating makes clay an important material to man.

The main factors controlling the properties of clays have been described by Grim (1962:2) as follows:

(1) The clay-mineral composition; the identity, relative abundance, and nature of crystallinity of the clay minerals present.

(2) The non-clay mineral composition; the rela-

tive abundance, identity, shape, particle size, and distribution of non-clay minerals.

(3) The organic content; the kinds and amounts of plant remains or organic molecules absorbed on the surface of the clay-mineral particles. All natural clays contain one or both types of organic matter.

(4) Exchangeable ions or salts present; identity and amount.

(5) Texture; the size distribution and relative orientations of particles and the forces tending to bind them together.

Clay Minerals

Natural clays are almost always composed of several clay minerals (Carroll 1962), and non-clay minerals are always present as accessories. The specific assemblage is determined by the process of formation and extent of subsequent disturbance. Secondary clays, which have been reworked by erosion and transportation by wind, water or other agents, generally have complex compositions owing to the mixing of minerals during transport. Primary clays, which have remained where they were formed, have more uniform compositions.

To some extent, the availability of primary and secondary sources determines the types of pottery that can be produced. White-bodied wares and high-fired wares, such as stoneware, require specialized materials. Low-fired red earthenwares can be produced from a great variety of clays, and suitable sources can be found almost anywhere.

Principal Groups. The main groups of clay minerals, each of which has a number of "species," are kaolinites, halloysites, allophanes, illitites, chlorites, smectites or montmorillonites (smectite being the more recent and preferred name), vermiculites, and attapulgite-palygorskite-sepiolites. The properties of those most important for making pottery will be summarized. More detailed discussions are provided by Grim (1962:7–51; 1968:31–50).

Chlorites generally have poor workability and fire to dark colors.

Halloysites have a chemical composition similar to kaolinites but a distinct crystal morphology. They may have poor workability, expressed in cracking during forming and drying, and must be heated slowly to prevent fracture during firing.

Illites (also known as hydrous micas) have variable compositions. The crystal structure usually contains potassium; iron and other colorants may also be present. Vitrification begins at relatively low temperatures (below 1000° C). Color after firing is rarely white. Workability is usually poor.

Kaolinite has a crystal structure that does not allow substitution of fusible elements in the crystal lattice. Kaolinitic clays are therefore often refractory and withstand high temperatures. They are stable during firing and can be heated relatively rapidly without damage to vessels. Pure kaolinites fire white because of the absence of colorants in the crystal structure. Plasticity varies with particle size and shape; well formed, large crystals have less plasticity than small irregular crystals.

Montmorillonites have very fine particle size and allow a range of substitutions in the fusible elements composing the crystal lattice. Plasticity and shrinkage during drying are very high. Because cracking usually occurs during drying, montmorillonitic clays cannot be used alone. A low proportion (less than 10 percent) may be advantageous because it improves workability. The fired color is usually brown, red or gray. Their strength when dried and their capacity to form films make small amounts of montmorillonites beneficial constituents of pigments, slips, and decorative coatings.

Techniques of Identification. Clay minerals have crystals of distinctive sizes and shapes, but they are too small to be seen with an ordinary light-transmitting microscope. The most common technique for identification is X-ray diffraction, which reveals the crystal structure (atomic spacing). Details are provided by Grim (1968:126–164; see also Searle and Grimshaw 1959:229–243). The electron microscope offers another approach (Grim 1968:165–184). Scanning electron micrographs of standard clay minerals and references to earlier microscopic studies are provided by Borst and Keller (1969).

Supplementary techniques for identifying clay minerals include differential thermal analysis (DTA), in which samples of the unknown material are heated and the exothermic and endothermic changes are plotted against temperature. Thermogravimetric analysis (TGA) measures changes in the weight of a sample with increasing temperature. The DTA technique has been discussed by Grim (1968:285), who has published DTA curves for the common clay minerals (1962:91–93).

The clay-mineral composition of clays is difficult to determine from fired pottery. This follows from the nature of pottery, whose permanence is insured by destroying the clay-mineral structure during firing. Obviously, if the clay mineral has been destroyed, it cannot be identified. There are two circumstances, however, where identification may be possible. The first is if the pottery was not originally heated to a high enough temperature or for a long enough time to decompose the clay minerals completely. The second is if the firing temperature was not much above that at which decomposition occurs. In these cases, the decomposition products can rehydrate with time to some extent (Grim 1962:95), and the restored crystals may be identifiable by X-ray diffraction.

Even if no rehydration occurs subsequent to firing, the original form of certain clay minerals may be observable with the scanning electron microscope. Kaolinite, for example, does not become amorphous immediately after decomposition. Instead, it forms metakaolin, which retains the hexagonal outline of the original kaolinite particles. Metakaolin does not break down until around 950° C, providing a range of temperature between about 500° C and 950° C when the shape of the original mineral crystals can still be observed. Other clay minerals also retain their outlines in the range above that producing decomposition but below that at which new minerals begin to form. The conditions have been specified by Grim (1962:98–121). These temperatures are within the ranges used to fire much unglazed ancient pottery.

The time required for these identifications, along with the necessity of access to very expensive equipment, makes clay-mineral composition an impractical basis for classifying pottery. Applied to samples taken from groups or classes established by other criteria, it provides useful information because the properties of the clay minerals influence the tempering, forming, and firing processes.

Workability

The pre-firing property of greatest importance to the traditional potter is workability; that is, the general suitability of the materials for forming pottery. The workability of clay bodies derives from the blend of clay minerals and non-plastics, which are other inclusions naturally present or added by the potter. Workability is not synonymous with plasticity. Plasticity is the property that allows a material to be deformed and to retain its new shape. A highly plastic clay has poor workability when used alone.

Of the materials used for a pottery body, the clay minerals contribute most to plasticity. If a clay is not plastic enough to be workable, its plasticity can be increased by several methods. Plasticizers, such as tannic acid and vinegar (acetic acid), can be added. Animal dung was used for this purpose in Tarsus during the Early Bronze Age (Matson 1956). Another remedy is to sour the clay by leaving it stored in a plastic condition for a long period. Algae, bacteria, and other agents multiply, increasing both the workability and the odor. Some clays that have been soured smell very bad and connoisseurs of soured clay employ stench to judge workability.

An alternative to using plasticizers is to mix two or more clays together. Usually, a clay having good workability but high shrinkage and poor firing qualities is mixed with one having poor workability but low shrinkage and good firing characteristics. Arnold (1971, 1972) noted mixing of clay by Peruvian and Yucatecan potters, and Rye and Evans (1976:20) reported this practice by a Pakistani potter.

NON-PLASTIC ADDITIVES

Many secondary clays become hard and strong after firing to relatively low temperatures, but are too plastic for forming vessels. Such clays also tend to crack during drying or firing. Their workability can be improved and their susceptibility to cracking decreased by non-plastic additives. As implied by the name, these are stable (non-soluble) materials, which do not develop plasticity in contact with water. Many other terms have been used, such as "opening materials," "aplastics," "backing," and "fillers," but "non-plastics" is preferred. Non-plastics can be mineral (such as quartz and calcite), organic (seeds, plant stems, root fragments), bio-mineral (shell, burned bark, coral, sponge spicules) or man-made (crushed pottery).

Another class of additives commonly used in modern ceramic industries is colorants, such as ochers and oxides. These have little effect on workability and fired properties, apart from fired color. In ancient pottery, these materials were commonly used in surface coatings on vessels, but not as body additives.

Inclusions

The term "tempering" is generally used in the archeological literature to denote non-clay additives, but there is no equivalent term in the field of ceramic technology. The reason is a difference in focus. Ceramic technologists attempt to explain the behavior of materials, whereas archeologists use materials to reconstruct human behavior. If a sherd is examined closely, it will be seen to have inclusions; rock fragments, minerals, pieces of organic matter or other particles are distinct from the finer clay matrix. To say that the sherd has inclusions is a description of the sherd, a material object (inclusions being "attributes" as defined in Chapter 1). To say that the sherd is tempered is a statement about human behavior at some time in the past. To infer this merely from the observation of inclusions is unwarranted because inclusions can originate from non-human activities, such as transport of eroded materials in rivers and co-deposition of clay and non-clay minerals. The most useful discussion of tempering is by Arnold (1974).

Potters may remove minerals, organic materials or other undesirable inclusions from clays (Fig. 14). They may add inclusions to enhance workability or to improve properties after firing. Obviously, neither removing undesirable materials nor using clay containing natural inclusions falls within the definition of "tempering," yet both are important aspects of the treatment of inclusions.

To infer from sherds whether the behavior described as tempering has occurred requires distinguishing inclusions already present in the clay from those added by the potter. This may be difficult or impossible for certain kinds of materials. All naturally occurring clays (as opposed to those processed by man) contain grains of minerals, such as quartz, feldspar, micas, and many others. If mineral grains or rock fragments are present in a sherd, even a skilled sedimentary petrographer may not be able to determine whether they are natural or artificial in origin. Other kinds of inclusions, such as "grog" (crushed sherds), can be readily

Fig. 14. Natural inclusions in clay. This clay was made into a slip and sieved to give the three fractions shown. All the clay minerals are in the pile on the right; large minerals and plant remains are in the pile on the left.

identified as added by man because the material does not occur in nature. Because of these uncertainties, unless there is clear evidence of human behavior (tempering), non-plastic additives should be labeled inclusions rather than temper. If necessary, they can be qualified as "mineral inclusions" or "organic inclusions."

Principal Types

Characteristically, modern industrial ceramic materials are highly refined to attain constant, repeatable properties. By contrast, the materials used by ancient potters were usually variable from one batch to the next, as well as between one potter and another. Because of this variability and the relatively low firing temperatures employed, ancient ceramics have re-

ceived little attention from industrial technologists.

The data in the following summary of the properties of the principal kinds of inclusions do not permit complete evaluation of the technological reasons for the choices made by ancient potters. Further research comparing the behavior of different materials before, during, and after firing would facilitate our understanding of this aspect of ceramic technology.

Calcium Carbonate (CaCO₃). Calcium carbonate occurs naturally in a variety of forms (Fig. 15). Limestone rocks extend over large regions, and some clays (marls) have a high calcareous content. Crystalline calcite is found in limestone formations. Marine shell is available on most beaches and freshwater shell is also widespread. Coral fragments may be mixed with shell on beaches near coral reefs.

All forms of calcium carbonate act as non-plastics

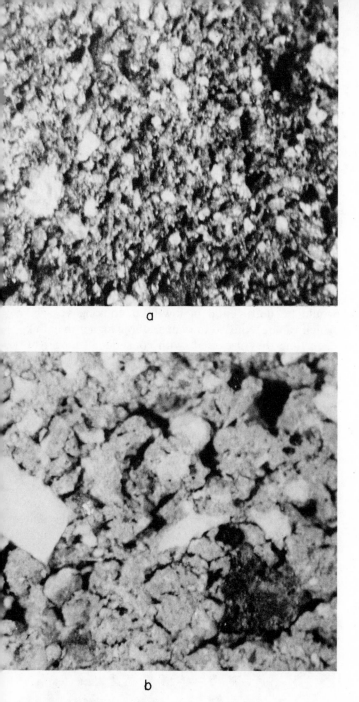

Fig. 15. Calcium carbonate inclusions. **a,** Beach sand containing shell fragments. **b,** Crushed shell; the large white particles are conch. Photographed using 40X magnification (Courtesy R. Christopher Goodwin).

When heated above 750° C, calcium carbonate begins to decompose into CO_2 and CaO. The decomposition becomes increasingly rapid as temperature increases. Pottery fired in the range between about 750° and 1000° C is subject to disintegration after firing due to hydration of CaO. This difficulty can be overcome by adding sodium chloride and possibly other salts to the clay or by using material containing salt naturally. Hydration damage is more extensive when the original grains of calcite are large than when they are very fine.

At higher temperatures or when very finely powdered $CaCO_3$ is used, CaO reacts with silica to form calcium silicates. These are stable. With still further temperature increase, and especially in a reducing atmosphere, the calcium can combine with sodium and other fluxes and silica to form glass. Vitrification commences at about 950° C.

The presence of calcium carbonate in sherds can be detected easily by its reaction with hydrochloric acid. A drop of the acid placed on a grain of $CaCO_3$ will effervesce vigorously, whereas other common white-colored inclusions show no reaction.

Grog (Crushed Sherds). This man-made material has several advantages over natural types of non-plastic additives. Pottery damaged during firing becomes a source of temper, rather than a useless waste product. The material is available at the manufacturing site, eliminating need for transport. Sherds are easier to crush than most rocks and minerals. Because the grog is already fired, it is stable during refiring and possesses the same properties as the fabric into which it is incorporated.

Some of the advantage is lost if most firings at a particular site are successful, because damaged vessels are too few to supply the necessary quantity of temper. In this case, sherds from refuse deposited during previous occupation of the site or vessels broken during use may be substituted. Any difference in composition has no noticeable effect on the properties of low-fired pottery. Grog can always be inferred to be temper rather than a natural inclusion (Fig. 23 b).

Organics. There are two separate categories: fine and coarse. Very finely divided organic material, partly plant remains and partly organisms such as algae and bacteria, helps improve the plasticity of clays. If converted to solid carbon rather than fully burned out during firing, it may decrease the permeability of the vessels.

Coarse organic material may be either plant fragments present naturally in the clay or chopped plant materials added by the potter (Fig. 16). Added material

when mixed with clay. Their behavior during and after firing varies with temperature. Up to 750° C, they remain relatively inert and pottery fired below this temperature is stable. Shell and crystalline calcite have been used in many parts of the world as temper for cooking ware and thus may be assumed to have beneficial properties in this application. Since the thermal expansion of calcite is similar to that of average fired clays (Rye 1976), stresses due to differential expansion of clay matrix and temper are minimal when the vessels are heated and cooled during use in cooking.

Fig. 16. Organic inclusions. Pottery tempered with straw from Southern Arabia (Courtesy Gus W. Van Beek).

may be agricultural waste, such as straw or stems from crop plants. Use of this type of temper may be more common where pottery making is a seasonal activity, coinciding with the end of harvesting. The presence of coarse plant material reduces shrinkage and improves the workability of clays that are too plastic. Much of it burns out during firing, leaving relatively large voids. These voids are advantageous in cooking vessels because they interrupt cracks that form as a consequence of thermal stress during use.

Plant fragments naturally occurring in clays can be differentiated from those added by potters by their form and the type of plant. Natural inclusions vary considerably in size and tend to have irregular shapes, whereas chopped plant materials are likely to be relatively regular in size and shape.

Adding animal dung may improve the plasticity of clays and, because it is consumed during firing, can increase the permeability of vessels (Matson 1963). This temper can be recognized by comparing the organic residue in the sherds with samples of dried animal dung.

Silica (SiO₂). A great diversity of forms of silica exist in nature. Quartz, which occurs in most rocks and unconsolidated sediments, can be expected to be present in all pottery except that originating from regions with calcareous formations. In ceramics, it is refractory unless glass-forming elements (such as sodium, potassium, calcium, and magnesium) are present to act as fluxes. These combine with silica at temperatures above 950° C to form glass, making quartz an indispensible ingredient of whiteware bodies used for modern domestic wares.

Quartz undergoes a crystalline inversion at 573° C, changing its molecular structure and increasing the size of crystals. This suggests that quartz inclusions would be detrimental in low-fired cooking vessels, which can be exposed to temperatures higher than this each time they are used, with consequent danger of fracture.

Many other forms of silica have been identified in pottery (Fig. 17). Hydrated forms, such as flint and chert, occur naturally in some clays. Along with quartz, these minerals are very hard and difficult to crush. Crushing is facilitated by calcining or preheating the mineral to about 800° C, which causes fracturing. Sand, composed of rounded or angular particles of silica, is frequently used as temper (Fig. 17 a).

Another source is living organisms. Examples are diatomaceous earth, formed from the coatings and skeletons of siliceous organisms; spicules of certain kinds of tropical freshwater sponges, and bark of several tropical trees that deposit silica in the cells (Fig. 18; Linné 1925, 1931; Meggers and Evans 1957). These forms of bio-silica are characterized by a highly porous structure, which allows easy crushing, and create a

Fig. 17. Siliceous inclusions (rounded sand) and crushed basalt (black particles). Photographed using 40X magnification (Courtesy R. Christopher Goodwin).

Fig. 18. Siliceous inclusions obtained by burning bark of trees and extracting the silica deposited in the walls of the cells. **a, c,** Elongated pits on leached surfaces. **b, d,** Fibrous appearance characteristic of this temper.

tively low temperatures. Such materials can thus produce very strong hard pottery at temperatures as low as 1000° C. The fusion temperature of rocks can be established by heating samples in a small furnace and noting the temperature at which fusion begins.

Felspars are used as fluxes in modern industrial white wares, fired to temperatures above about 1150° C. Their fluxing action is negligible below this temperature, so they function as inert fillers in low-fired traditional wares.

Micas occur naturally in many clays and their crystal structure is closely related to those of the clay minerals. Poorly crystalline micas can improve the plasticity of clays. Some micas fuse at relatively low temperatures, but little useful fusion can be expected below 1000° C. Mica is unlikely to have been intentionally added as a tempering material in the past; where it occurs in sherds, it is likely to have been a natural inclusion in the clay. Micas were used as fluxes in high-fired Chinese wares, stonewares, and porcelains.

Soluble Salts. The composition of the water used to wet the clay can have a significant effect. Fresh water, with only traces of mineral content, alters the workability of clays but has no influence on fired properties because it is removed during firing. Water from saline sources, especially seawater, contains dissolved salts that can significantly affect vitrification (and hence hardness and porosity) and color. Experimental studies of these effects, particularly of color variations with temperature, have been reported by Matson (1971).

Significant amounts of soluble salts may be present in some natural clays and minor amounts occur in all clays. Salts may also be added by the potter. Working from sherds alone, it is possible to determine that soluble salts were present, but not whether they were natural constituents of the clay or water or were added consciously.

Soluble salts are carried in solution to the surface of vessels during drying and remain when the water evaporates. Salt concentration is much greater, therefore, on the surface than in the center of the wall,

stress-absorbing network in the fired pottery particularly desirable for cooking wares.

Other Minerals and Rocks. Most heavy minerals, such as zircon and rutile, have low thermal expansions and thus are desirable additives for vessels to be used for cooking. The heavy minerals are refactory in the temperature range used for firing traditional pottery.

Fusible rocks, such as basalt, form glass at rela-

and forms a layer after firing that is recognizable in thin section. Salt may also crystallize at or near the surface and volatilize during firing, leaving distinctive cavities or voids. Voids with a cubic form and having a yellowish rim, caused by the formation of iron-calcium silicates, may be detectable near the center of the cross section, especially if granular salt was added to the clay. The most characteristic indication that salt was present is the range of colors on the surface (Matson 1971).

The presence of significant amounts of shell, calcite or other forms of $CaCO_3$ as inclusions makes it probable that salt was incorporated in the body. The reason is that firing to temperatures over 800° C causes $CaCO_3$ to decompose, forming CaO. After firing, CaO combines with water vapor from the air, forming $Ca(OH)_2$, which has larger crystals. These create pressures that can fracture the vessel. It has been demonstrated (Chapter 7; Rye 1976) that adding salt water rather than fresh water to the clay inhibits this damage and allows firing to higher temperatures. Clays with a naturally high salt content produce the same effect (Arnold 1971).

PREPARATION OF BODIES

Preparing a body to the stage where vessels can be formed involves achieving the correct size distribution of the particles in the materials to be used and blending these materials in the correct proportions. The simplest procedure is to obtain naturally plastic clay from a waterlogged deposit, knead, and use it. This method would be successful only if the size distribution of the inclusions happened to be suited to the forming processes. Blending waterlogged clay with natural sand possessing particles of suitable size distribution is a slightly more advanced procedure. More complicated measures are generally employed for preparing the clay, preparing the temper, blending the body, and preparing and applying surface coatings.

Preparing Clay

Naturally occurring clays usually have a water content lower than required to give optimum workability. This means water must be added. Placing lumps of damp clay in water or pouring water over the clay are not practical methods because the water will not penetrate. The clay must be dry before it will take up water

uniformly. If it can be spread in the sun, it will dry in a day or two. In cool or wet climates, where the clay must be dried under shelter, the drying time will be much longer. Thorough drying is insured by breaking large lumps into smaller pieces. No evidence of these activities is obtainable from excavated pottery.

Coarse fragments of rock, plant or other undesirable kinds of material must be removed. These can be picked out by hand if lumps are pulverized using a hammerstone, mortar and pestle or other instrument (Fig. 7). Sieving is ineffective for removing non-organic inclusions from dry clay, but practical if the clay is converted into a slip. Plant remains are also more effectively removed by sieving slip. Soft parts, such as fragments of leaves, can be left in the clay but harder pieces of stem and root cause problems during vessel forming.

In order to prepare slip, the clay must first be slaked. Slaking results when water is added to dry clay. The lumps gradually disintegrate as the water penetrates the pores (Fig. 19). Some clays slake much more readily than others; a few, such as montmorillonites, do not slake because the clay minerals at the surface of lumps swell and prevent penetration of water to the interior. Slaking may be accomplished in a few hours, but usually requires several days.

Fig. 19. Slaking clay. The dry clay has been mounded and a depression formed in the center to hold the water and provide a large surface for penetration. Peshawar, Pakistan.

Fig. 20. Slip method of preparing clay. Foreground: slaking and settling pit; background, slip that has dried to a plastic state.

After the clay has been slaked, enough additional water is added to place it in suspension when stirred. Slaking and stirring may be done in the same vat or pit. A flat-bladed wooden paddle may be used or the potter may get into the pit or vat and stir the clay with legs and hands. This procedure is employed by present-day Palestinian potters.

Once the clay is uniformly in suspension, coarse particles can be removed. Pouring the slip through a sieve is theoretically feasible, but traditional potters seldom have access to sieves with apertures smaller than about 1 mm. Sieving is thus unsuitable if it is desired to eliminate smaller particles. It also has the disadvantage of being slow and tedious. A more practical method is settling (Fig. 20). When the slip is allowed to stand, the larger particles and those of high specific gravity settle to the bottom most rapidly. The suspension can be drained off through an outlet slightly above the bottom, leaving the residue in the pit or vat. Alternatively, the finer fraction can be removed using a bucket.

Whether sieving or settling was performed may be detectable from sherds. If light and heavy minerals are present in the same particle sizes, the material is more likely to have been sieved. If heavy minerals are absent, then settling is more probable (provided, of course, that heavy minerals are known to occur in the original materials).

The finest fractions of clay are obtained by a process known as "levigation" or "elutriation." Clay slip flows slowly through a relatively long shallow trough before entering a vat or pit. Baffles or low walls (which may be less than 5 cm high) placed along the bottom of the trough cause coarser or heavier particles to settle and be trapped, whereas the finer material remains in suspension. Levigation processes can be recognized from sherds by the extremely fine sizes of the mineral particles, which are generally less than 50 microns (although temper may be coarser).

Preparing Temper

Tempering materials require no special preparation if they are in the form of sand with suitable particle-size distribution. Rocks, sherds, shells, and other compact materials require crushing; if crushing is not thorough, large particles may be removed by sieving (Figs. 8, 21). Organic substances may need chopping or other special treatment.

Evidence of preparation may be recognizable in sherds. Sharp angular fragments suggest crushing, whereas round forms do not. Angular grains occur in recently deposited sands, however, so sand deposits in the vicinity of a site should be examined to ascertain the nature of their particles. The shape of organic fragments may suggest how they were prepared.

Fig. 21. Sieving temper to eliminate excessively large particles. Pakistan.

a

b

c

d

Fig. 22. Plastic body preparation. **a,** Slaked clay.
b, Forming moist clay into a ball.
c, Kneading. **d,** Body ready for forming vessels. Pakistan.

Blending

After the clay and tempering materials have been prepared, they must be combined and the mixture brought to a workable stage. The two principal ways of achieving this are plastic body preparation and slip preparation.

Plastic Body Preparation. This method involves adding sufficient water to the clay to bring it into a plastic condition and then incorporating the temper by kneading (Fig. 22). Traditional potters often use part-

ing agents to keep the sticky clay from adhering to the surface on which it is being prepared. The parting agent may be sand, ash, dry powdered clay or another similar material. This is sprinkled on the ground, house floor, wooden preparation dish or whatever surface is used. During preliminary kneading, the parting material will be incorporated. If it has the same composition as the temper, it may be indistinguishable. If the composition is different or no temper has been added, it may be recognizable because of its relatively minor occurrence. Its abundance rarely exceeds 5 percent by volume, whereas temper is usually present in significantly larger proportions. Parting materials used before kneading is complete become incorporated homogeneously throughout the body, whereas those used while molding vessels appear only on the surface (Fig. 67 c).

If temper is added, it can be sprinkled over the clay and mixed in by kneading. The extent of kneading can be inferred from archeological pottery, but there is no way to identify the process.

Slip Preparation. Slip or wet preparation involves adding sufficient water to the dry clay to form a slip before any blending occurs. This sophisticated process is more likely to be used by full-time specialists producing relatively fine wares. ·

After the clay has been through the appropriate separation process (sieving, settling or levigation), tempering materials can be mixed in by stirring. The slip can then be converted to a solid state by draining it into drying beds, shallow pits or built-up vats, where the water can evaporate. Drying is much quicker if the beds are in direct sun.

A variation of the slip-preparation technique used by some Palestinian potters involves adding sand to the clay slip and pouring the mixture through a sieve, thus removing coarse particles simultaneously from the clay and the temper. Other variations are possible, but would probably be difficult to recognize from examining sherds. Additional evidence of preparation procedures may be obtained from excavating a potter's workshop and observing the facilities for preparing clay.

Assessing Correct Proportions. Ethnographic observations suggest that potters judge the proportions of materials by volume rather than weight. Regardless of the method used to measure relative volumes, some variation can be expected between batches. If a potter uses standard containers (such as pottery vessels) for measuring, the range of variation may be relatively small. If he or she dumps a pile of clay on the ground and sprinkles temper over it, the range of variation between batches could be relatively large.

The amount of temper needed varies according to the kind of clay minerals. In general, non-plastics are added to pure clays to reduce shrinkage and improve workability. For kaolinite, a suitable proportion is between about 20 and 50 percent non-plastics, whereas for montmorillonite, which is very plastic, up to 80 percent may be needed. Non-plastic additions comprising less than about 10 percent of the volume of a body have little observable effect on the working properties of any kind of clay. The normal ratio will vary between about 20 and 50 percent. If non-plastic inclusions are present naturally in the clay, the amount of material added will be correspondingly less.

The potter must be able to determine whether sufficient temper has been added. If the workability of the clay is affected, correct workability is best assessed by its feel. In the words of Salmang (1961:67): "for the old hand-forming processes the thumb of the worker is the most sensitive instrument for measuring plasticity. By its aid the best working body can, after a little practice, be judged with such precision that the thumb will always retain its value as a plasticity meter." Potters also learn to judge whether the clay is too sticky or too stiff, and can accurately assess the size and amount of grit.

Other methods of evaluating clays include taste, which will indicate whether soluble salts are present. Biting moist clay can reveal fine grit undetectable by touch. Characteristic minerals can be identified visually; color will give some indication of plasticity and constancy of composition, as well as reveal the presence of organic materials. When clays have been soured, their suitability can be judged by their smell.

Skilled potters experienced in working with a range of materials can determine from the appearance of fired vessels whether the clay was very plastic or difficult to work. Curvature, wall thickness, forming markings, and shape are clues to the rapidity with which the vessel was formed. Highly plastic clays allow extreme curvatures, relatively thin walls, and rapid forming.

Storing

When the materials have been mixed to the proportions required and dried to the plastic stage, the body may be used immediately or stored for varying periods. Workability can increase during storage as a consequence of the growth of bacteria and other micro-organisms. This "souring" can be promoted by adding organic acids (such as acetic acid, vinegar or stale wine), alginates, tanning derivatives or fine, decomposing organic material. No evidence of the use of such materials is likely to be recognizable in sherds.

Kneading

The final stage of body preparation is kneading. This involves manipulating the clay until the moisture

Fig. 23. Two types of fabric containing voids caused by air bubbles, indicating insufficient kneading. **a,** Fine texture with natural (?) inclusions. **b,** Grog (crushed sherd) temper. Photographed using 40X magnification (Courtesy R. Christopher Goodwin).

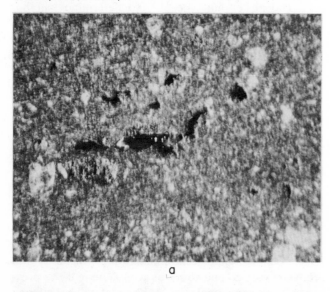

a

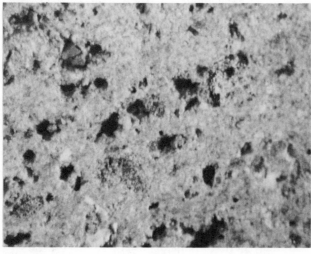

b

and inclusions are uniformly distributed and the air bubbles and voids are eliminated. Various methods have been described by Rye and Evans (1976), but they cannot be distinguished from excavated specimens. The extent of kneading can be inferred from the presence of voids (Fig. 23); many voids of varying sizes indicate that little kneading was done, whereas a limited number of fine voids indicates thorough kneading. Voids created by trapped air should not be confused with those left by burning out organic materials, such as plant remains. Their shapes serve for differentiating these two types in most cases.

SURFACE COATINGS

The principal surface coatings are slips, pigments, paints, washes, colorants, and glazes. All involve a material or materials obtained by the potter, prepared and mixed if necessary, and applied to the vessel. These treatments are distinct from the unintentional effects of firing, such as colors produced by oxidation or reduction, "firing clouds," and deposition of carbon. They are also distinct from modifications caused by materials incorporated in the body, such as efflorescence of salt.

Terminology

The terms used to describe intentional surface coatings can be defined as follows:

Colorant. The chemical element or elements from which a color is derived. The main ceramic colorants are metallic elements, such as iron, manganese, cobalt, copper, nickel, chromium, tin, cadmium, selenium, arsenic, and vanadium. The results vary depending on their combinations and on the temperatures and atmospheres of firing. Carbon can also be considered a colorant because of its blackening effect. The specific color produced by the same elements changes dramatically and the range of hues increases when they are in a glass (vitreous) rather than a crystalline state (Table 2).

Glaze. A coating of glass fused to the surface of a pottery vessel. Glazes and glasses have similar structures and respond similarly to differences in rates of cooling from high temperatures. When cooling is sufficiently rapid, no crystals can form; if the same material is cooled more slowly, a crystalline structure results. Glazes are sufficiently distinct from other types of surface coatings to be discussed in more detail below.

Paint. A material added before or after firing to decorate the surface of a vessel. Slips, pigments, and a variety of other substances can be used. This term describes the potter's action rather than a particular kind of material.

Pigment. An assemblage of colorants and substances that may modify the color, increase adhesion before or after firing, and improve flow or brushability. Examples include natural ores, oxides of metallic colorants, and natural and man-made mixtures. Organic pigments, such as vegetable dyes, can be applied before firing but decompose and lose their color at high temperatures. The only color that can be produced by organic materials is black or gray. The use of organic adhesives to bind pigments to vessels after firing and methods of their identification have been discussed by Shepard (1968:177).

Slip. A fluid suspension of clay in water. By definition, slip contains clay minerals, but no useful purpose is served by setting an arbitrary limit on clay content. Slip can be an intermediate stage in the preparation of clay bodies, as well as a surface coating. Its fluidity can be readily changed by adding or removing water. Slips used for decoration are commonly a different color than the body. White slips result from the absence of metallic colorants in the clay; colored slips contain colorants, most commonly iron. The term is generally used in archeological literature to refer to a fired coating, but it applies equally to the fluid raw material.

Wash. This term has been used for a variety of distinct treatments. In the Middle East, it has been applied to post-firing coatings such as lime. In other regions, it has been defined as a very thin coating of pigment covering all or part of the surface of a vessel, added before firing.

Methods of Application

The diversity of techniques for applying surface coatings is great and only a few of the better known ones will be reviewed, with emphasis on slips. Many surface coatings acquire their particular character from a specific combination of materials, method of application, technique of firing, and treatment of the vessel after firing. Even after all these procedures have been analyzed, some effects cannot be fully understood.

Slip. There are three principal techniques for applying overall coatings: (1) dipping, (2) pouring, and (3) wiping. Dipping or immersing a vessel in a container filled with slip suspension produces a more uniform and even coating than the other methods. Because the coating will separate from the surface if the vessel is dry (Fig. 24), it should be applied while it is sufficiently moist to minimize differential shrinkage. If the coating covers the vessel, the marks of the potter's fingers may remain at the base or rim, depending on how it was held during dipping. Dipping produces several diagnostic effects. The slip penetrates recesses, grooves, and incisions. If the vessel is partly submerged, a straight line divides slipped from unslipped portions. The part submerged longest takes on a thicker coating, which may run when the vessel is removed.

Fig. 24. Slip exhibiting flaking and spalling, indicating it was applied to the vessel when the surface was too dry. Otowi, New Mexico.

Pouring is accomplished by putting the slip in a container and emptying it over or into the vessel (Fig. 25). This method allows less control over coverage than dipping and is used particularly for vessels that are too large to be dipped or that are to be coated only on the interior. The vessel must be turned as the slip is poured and the line of termination becomes a series of arcs if the revolution is not uniform. A heavier coating develops on the portion of the vessel that was lower during pouring; otherwise, thickness is uniform. Runs are common and may cross unslipped areas.

The third method is wiping the surface with a sponge, cloth, or ball of grass or similar plant material soaked in the slip (Fig. 26). Wiping applies the coating to smooth surfaces, but does not force it into deep grooves, such as occur where a handle joins the wall. The margin of the slip may be regular, but is more likely to be irregular. Fine grooves produced by the applicator correspond to the direction of wiping.

Pigment. Common ores or earthy materials used as pigments may not adhere when applied with a brush. Adherence is generally better if the vessel is completely dry, because the water used as a suspending medium for the pigment is immediately absorbed into the body. Painting on a completely dry surface also has the advantage that clear, crisp margins are produced (Fig. 27). If the surface is leather hard or plastic, the pigment will tend to run at the edges and may dribble if applied thickly (Figs. 28, 65 c). These consequences may be used intentionally for decorative effects. There is danger that paint applied to a wet vessel will crack or peel off when the vessel dries and shrinks.

Several advantages result from adding clay to the pigment: (1) it settles more slowly, (2) it flows more

Fig. 25. Applying slip and glaze by pouring. **a,** Pouring liquid slip over a jar held above a large basin to capture the runoff. **b,** Glazing the interior of a bowl by pouring in the suspension and sloshing it around. **c,** Undulating margin indicative of the pouring method. Pakistan.

Fig. 26. Applying slip by wiping. **a,** Coating the upper part of a jar. **b,** Coating the bottom. Note the striations left by the cloth applicator. Pakistan.

Fig. 27. Lines with sharp and even edges, indicating that the design was painted when the surface of the vessel was dry. Zuni, New Mexico.

Fig. 28. Lines exhibiting uneven density, irregular margins, and dripping, indicating painting was done when the surface was still sufficiently moist to allow the pigment to flow.

readily, allowing more uniform brushwork and longer strokes, and (3) it adheres more firmly. The variation in hues of the clay and pigment enhances the range of colors that can be produced by varying their proportions. The content of clay can be relatively high provided the resultant shrinkage is not excessive. If it is, or if the mixture is applied too thickly, it will crack during drying, forming a fine network of more or less hexagonal lines. Such high-clay pigment can be designated "slip."

Pigments and slips can both be applied by brushing. Finely spaced alternations in thickness are characteristic of this method and are caused by drag of the bristles through the medium. The coarser the brush, the more pronounced the unevenness of the coating. The shape of the brush dictates the type of stroke and its size determines the length of a continuous line that can be drawn. If slips are used for line work or complex patterns, application by a brush is the most appropriate technique.

Resist. Any material applied to the surface to prevent adhesion of other materials applied over it may be termed a resist. Wax, which can be melted and painted on with a brush, is used in Japan (Sanders 1972:174–5). Pigments, slips, and glazes will not adhere to waxed areas. Paper, leaves, and other solid materials can be shaped as desired and stuck to the surface, being removed after painting over them is completed. Modern resists include latex, which can be peeled off before firing.

Droplets of paint may adhere to waxes, oils, varnishes, and natural resins used as resists; these can be wiped off if desired while still wet. The margins of lines and areas may be somewhat irregular and the width of bands may be variable. Portions of leaves, paper, and other solids do not allow any adhesion of the paint, provided they are not porous. The edges of decorated areas may show signs of lifting if the resist was removed before firing rather than left in place to burn off.

In general, resists are applied after the vessel has

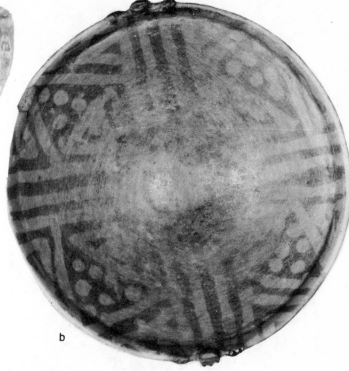

Fig. 29. Resist decoration. **a,** Zoomorphic design on the exterior of a tripod vessel. Chiriqui, Panama. **b,** Geometric design on the interior of a red-slipped bowl. Pillaro, Ecuador.

been fired, but may be combined with painting executed before firing. The pigment employed with the resist is carbon (or a material that carbonizes), giving this decoration its diagnostic gray to black color.

Techniques of resist decoration in the Americas have been discussed by Shepard (1968:206–213). Care should be taken not to confuse this effect (Fig. 29) with background painting, where color is applied so the design also consists of the unpainted portions of the surface (Fig. 108).

GLAZES

Glazes are glasses in the sense that their physical structures are similar. The glaze material applied to a vessel melts and fuses to the surface during firing at high temperature. On cooling, the glaze hardens and becomes stable. The temperature of melting of common glazes ranges between about 900° and 1450°C.

Glazes have both esthetic and functional roles. Esthetically, they provide a wide range of colors and a variety of reflectances and textures. Functionally, they

render vessels impervious to liquids, resistant to acids and alkalis, and easier to clean.

Constituents

Glazes have three groups of constituents: (1) network formers, (2) network modifiers or fluxes, and (3) intermediaries.

Network Formers. Glass cannot form from all combinations of materials. A "network former" is required. The network former common to most ceramic glazes is silica (SiO_2). Boric oxide (B_2O_3) and phosphorus pentoxide (P_2O_5) may be substituted, but although glasses based on these compounds melt at relatively low temperatures, they are impractical because they are soluble in water.

Network Modifiers. Although network formers can be used alone to produce glasses, they are unsuitable for glazes. Fused silica is not practical because its melting point is above 1700°C, whereas the highest temperature achieved in traditional kilns is about 1300°C (Chinese porcelains and stonewares). Temperatures in Islamic kilns probably never exceeded about 1100°C. In order to produce glazes at these lower temperatures, fluxes or "network modifiers" must be added to lower the melting point of the silica. Common fluxes are sodium, potassium, calcium, magnesium, and lead. Lithium, barium, and other elements are sometimes used. Iron acts as a flux under reducing conditions.

A glaze can be produced using a mixture of lead oxide and quartz, both finely ground, at firing temperatures around 800° to 1000° C. Unfortunately, its presence on food containers renders them poisonous, although almost certainly most traditional and ancient potters were not aware of this effect. Another deficiency of lead is that it becomes increasingly volatile as temperature increases, making it useless as a flux above about 1150° C. Sodium and potassium are suitable fluxes at intermediate temperatures (between about 1000° and 1200° C). They are relatively unstable used alone, but the addition of calcium and magnesium produces more durable results. Sodium and potassium-based glazes have high thermal expansions and during cooling shrink much more than the pottery body onto which they are fused, causing a network of fine cracks to develop. This "crazing" can be overcome to some extent by varying the proportions of flux and silica.

Intermediaries. Stronger glazes, less prone to crazing, are produced by adding "intermediaries," such as alumina. The presence of alumina is one of the principal differences between glasses and glazes. Fe_2O_3 also acts as in intermediary under oxidizing conditions.

Glazes can be formulated to mature at any given temperature by varying the compositions of each of the above groups of constituents, their amounts, the form in which they are introduced (i.e. the minerals in which they are combined), and their particle sizes. Transparency, opacity, mattness, and reflectance can be controlled by similar manipulations. Glazes must be fired at the temperature for which they are intended. A glaze that is underfired will be dull and crystalline in appearance because the constituents have not melted properly. An overfired glaze will be very shiny, will usually craze severely, and can become fluid and run off.

Describing Composition

Until relatively recently, glazes were compounded from "recipes" derived by trial and error over long periods of time. The potters often attempted to keep them secret by incorporating procedures that were unnecessary technologically to mislead potential competitors.

In the late 19th century, the ceramist Seger developed the standard method of defining composition in terms of the relative proportions of molecules of each element, expressed in three groups corresponding to network modifiers (fluxes), intermediaries, and network formers. For convenience and ease of comparison, the amount of network modifier is expressed as unity.

Using this method, the composition of a very simple lead glaze would be expressed:

Network Modifier		Intermediary		Network Former	
PbO	1.0	Al_2O_3	0.1	SiO_2	1.5

This means that the glaze consists of PbO, Al_2O_3, and SiO_2 in the proportions 1.0:0.1:1.5 molecules. To make a batch of this glaze, the molecular proportions must be converted into weight proportions. The resulting "recipe" is: PbO, 223 parts by weight; Al_2O_3, 10.2 parts, and SiO_2, 60 parts. Expressed in percentages, the composition is: PbO, 76.0 percent; Al_2O_3, 3.5 percent; SiO_2, 20.5 percent. In analyzing ancient glazes, the composition is determined first and provides the basis for calculating the molecular formula.

The compositions of complex glazes are expressed by the same rules. For a porcelain glaze, the formula is:

K_2O	0.3	Al_2O_3	0.4	SiO_2	4.0
Na_2O	0.1				
CaO	0.6				

Note that the sum of the flux group is still unity. Comparing the two formulas shows that the porcelain glaze has relatively higher contents of Al_2O_3 and SiO_2. The porcelain glaze is intended for firing at a much higher temperature (about 1250° C) than the lead glaze (about 900° C) and therefore relatively less flux is needed. Because molecular composition is correlated with firing temperature, the general firing techniques of ancient glazes can be inferred from their analyses.

General Types

Ancient glazes may, for convenience, be classified according to the principal flux used. The four principal types are: lead glazes, alkaline glazes, lime-felspar glazes, and salt glazes.

Lead Glazes. Lead ores, especially PbS, galena, and lead sulphide, are very widely distributed geographically and lead glazes may have been developed independently several times. For example, Shepard (1968:46) describes lead-glaze paint on prehistoric pottery from the southwestern United States. Their low firing temperature is well within the range employed for much unglazed pottery and they fuse readily to most clays. Their main disadvantage is that they are poisonous if not correctly compounded and are relatively fluid when molten, tending to dissolve underlying painting.

The compositions of ancient and modern lead glazes fall within the following ranges:

PbO   0.3-0.7 Al_2O_3 0.1-0.35 SiO_2 0.7-3.5
CaO   0.1-0.4
MgO   0.0-0.1
ZnO   0.0-0.3

Adding tin oxide to a lead glaze produces a white, opaque surface that is suitable for painted decoration. This additive was widely used by Islamic and European potters.

Alkaline Glazes. Alkaline glazes are usually clear (transparent) and shiny, although less shiny than lead glazes. A wide range of underglaze decorative colors can be used. Because of the high thermal expansion of their constituents, alkaline glazes tend to craze unless used on a highly siliceous body or with a siliceous slip.

The main fluxes in these glazes are sodium and potassium. The variation in composition among traditional potters in Pakistan (Rye and Evans 1976:150–151) is:

Na_2O 0.75-0.87 Al_2O_3 0.05-0.11 SiO_2 3.04-3.34
K_2O 0.06-0.10
CaO   0.05-0.14
MgO   0.01-0.03

In the Middle East, early glasses were made from a mixture of siliceous sand and ash produced by burning desert plants, along with other minor ingredients. Early alkaline glazes and many Islamic alkaline glazes can be presumed to have been compounded from a similar mixture of materials.

Lime-felspar Glazes. These are the hardest, most durable, and most resistant to chemical attack of the types discussed here. They would normally be fired in the temperature range between 1200° and 1350° C. Composition generally falls within the following range of variation:

K_2O 0.0-0.3 Al_2O_3 0.4-0.8 SiO_2 3.0-5.0
NaO   0.0-0.3
CaO   0.4-0.7
MgO   0.0-0.3

The earliest examples appear to have been caused by wood ash, which contains members of the typical flux group (especially K_2O, CaO, and MgO), moving through the kiln during firing, settling on vessels, and reacting with alumina and silica in the clay. Later, minerals of the felspar group were employed. These supply CaO, Na_2O, and K_2O, depending on their composition, and occur mainly in igneous rocks, which also supply other constituents of the glaze. Felspathic glazes were limited to China, Japan, Korea, and Thailand until the 18th century, when they became common in Europe.

Salt Glazes. These are a high-temperature form of alkaline glazes, whose distinctive feature is their method of application. Vessels are placed in a kiln and heated to between 1150° and 1300° C. Common salt (NaCl) is then thrown in the firebox. The salt immediately decomposes, forming Na and Cl ions. The sodium moves through the kiln, combines with silica and alumina in the body of the vessels, and forms a glaze on the surface. The glaze is characteristically very thin, but hard, durable, and resistant to chemicals. This technique originated in Germany around the 12th century and has been widely used by "colonial" potters.

Colorants

In the absence of colorants, glazes are either transparent or white. The effect of colorants varies with the composition of the glaze, the other colorants present, the temperature and atmosphere during firing, and the compositions of the body, slips, and other underlying materials. An almost infinite variety of colors can be produced, although some (such as red) were difficult for ancient potters. As a general rule, the potential range is much greater at lower temperatures. Some commonly used colorants and their effects are given in Table 2. Parmelee (1951) provides a detailed discussion of the means of producing a wide range of colors in ceramics.

METHODS OF IDENTIFYING MATERIALS

Attempts to determine what materials were used and why usually employ two kinds of approaches: (1) chemical analyses and (2) mineralogical identifications. Erroneous interpretations can result, however, unless replication experiments are conducted because

Table 2. Differences in the reactions of colorants in glazes exposed to oxidizing and reducing atmospheres during firing.

Colorant	Oxidizing	Reducing
Iron	Buff, pink, yellow, brown black	Gray, blue, green
Copper	Green (lead glaze), tur- quoise blue (alkaline glaze)	Purple, red
Cobalt	Blue	Blue
Manganese	Purple, black	Unstable
Tin	White (opacifier)	Volatilizes
Nickel	Gray	Brown
Chromium	Green	Yellow

clays with very similar chemical compositions may differ greatly in workability.

Before any analytical work begins, it should be decided whether chemical or mineralogical techniques or a combination should be employed. Considerations include the uniformity of rock types in the source areas; time and specialized labor required to prepare samples for specific techniques; time and level of skill needed for the analyses, and availability of computer time and suitable programs for processing the data. The fact that quantitative mineralogical analysis is a very slow procedure, whereas quantitative data can be obtained quickly using chemical techniques is also relevant to the decision.

Analytical procedures should be discussed with the person who will undertake the studies. Although choice is usually restricted by the facilities available, it is also partly determined by the problem. Williams and Jenkins (1976) compared three methods of classifying pottery and identifying the sources of materials: (1) thin-section petrography, (2) heavy-mineral analysis, and (3) arc spectrography. They found that petrographic analysis was most useful in regions with diverse types of rocks, whereas trace-element analysis was preferable in regions of geological uniformity.

Chemical Analyses

Whereas 20 years ago, a major-element silicate analysis by wet chemistry methods required up to a week to complete, current methods allow analyses of up to 1000 samples per week, determining 20 or 30 major and trace elements for each sample. The computer permits very rapid processing of the data. These speeds can be expected to increase, making classifica-

tion of pottery on the basis of composition ever more practical.

If chemical analysis is selected, the specific approach needs planning. All elements are not identifiable on a routine basis by any single technique (Hughes, Cowell, and Craddock 1976), so several may be required. Among the possibilities are neutron activation (Al Kital et al 1969), X-ray fluorescence, and atomic absorption spectroscopy (de Bruin et al 1976; Hughes, Cowell, and Craddock 1976). The X-ray isoprobe, a portable instrument, has been discussed by Hall, Schweizer, and Toller (1973). Neutron activation has been widely used; its main advantages are that the concentrations of many elements can be determined by a single analysis, a large number of samples can be analyzed efficiently on a routine basis, and damage to the artifacts is slight.

Although chemical analyses appear to offer an objective basis for differentiating pottery, there are many pitfalls both in obtaining the data and interpreting them. In order that procedures can be evaluated by other workers, publications should specify sampling methods, analytical precision in the techniques of analysis, element concentrations, variability within and between samples, and statistical procedures used to group the data.

Selecting Samples. The aim of identifying variations is to provide a basis for inferring cultural practices. Before any inferences can be attempted, it is essential to know the amount of variation within a single sherd. How does this range compare with the variation between sherds known to belong to the same group? What is the compositional variation between vessels an archeologist would consider identical? Does this represent variation from one potter to another? Does it represent groups of potters, one producing compositionally consistent ware (that is, using consistent materials consistently) and the others producing compositionally inconsistent wares (that is, using variable materials or selecting materials from a variety of sources, but being consistent in other aspects of production)? What variations were introduced during the "life history" of the sherd?

Possible sources of variation within a sherd or vessel include: (1) incomplete mixing of clay and temper (imperfect kneading); (2) using different mixtures for different parts of a vessel, such as adding more temper when making handles; (3) processes affecting the homogeneity of the cross section, such as volatilization of elements from the surface, adding slips, and differential temperature during firing; and (4) uneven distribution of minerals, so that a small sample may include a large grain that does not represent the "normal" composition.

Minor variations in the concentrations of elements may occur among vessels of the same shape, made by the same potter from the same materials, prepared and fired in the same way. Larger variations may be produced by trivial causes. For example, a group of potters who work consistently in all aspects of production may obtain their clay from fallow agricultural land, whose location (and therefore composition) changes annually (Rye and Evans 1976:39). A similar kind of variation would occur among potters using clays from floodplains. Failure to recognize the origins of such variations can lead to erroneous conclusions. Sampling must thus take into account the known variations in composition within and between sherds or be done in such a way that this variability will be measured during the analysis.

With the exception of the isoprobe and some X-ray fluorescent techniques, chemical analysis cannot be used for whole vessels or even sherds. The sizes of the samples and methods for taking and preparing them differ for each technique. Those appropriate for atomic absorption studies are described by Hughes, Cowell, and Craddock (1976), for X-ray fluorescence by Poole and Finch (1972), and for neutron activation by Perlman and Asaro (1969).

Selecting Significant Elements. It is generally impossible to predict which elements will give meaningful groupings within a collection of pottery; indeed, their identification is the principal aim of the analysis. If the results are to be compared with data from previous studies, it will be necessary to test for the same elements and to use similar equipment.

The elements in traditional ceramic materials are generally divided for convenience into two categories: major elements and trace elements. Major elements are those likely to account for one percent or more of the total. Nine are invariably present in traditional ceramics. Trace elements are usually expressed in parts per million. An intermediate category, minor elements, is sometimes used to identify the range between major and trace elements.

The major elements are conventionally calculated as their commonly occurring oxides. Thus, instead of reporting Si (silicon), Al (aluminum), Fe (iron), and so on, the analyst specifies SiO_2 (silica), Al_2O_3 (alumina), Fe_2O_3 (ferric oxide), and FeO (ferrous oxide). The oxides are usually listed in the order followed by geologists, which corresponds to their relative frequencies in the earth's crust:

SiO_2	silica
Al_2O_3	alumina
Fe_2O_3	ferric oxide
FeO	ferrous oxide
CaO	calcia or lime
MgO	magnesia
Na_2O	soda
K_2O	potash
TiO_2	titania

Among the elements that may occur in major or minor frequencies or as traces are P_2O_5 (phosphorus pentoxide), BaO (baria), SrO (strontia), Li_2O (lithia), MnO (manganese oxide), and S (sulfur). Glazes, pigments, and vitreous slips may contain As (arsenic), Sb (antimony), B (boron); Cd (cadmium), C (carbon), Cr (chromium), Co (cobalt), Cu (copper), Au (gold), Pb (lead), Ni (nickel), Se (selenium), Ag (silver), Sn (tin), U (uranium), and Zn (zinc). With the exception of lead, zinc, and boron, these constitute colorants or opacifiers in glazes.

Many other trace elements may be present, but unlike the major elements their occurrence cannot be predicted. This variability makes them more sensitive than the major elements as indicators of specific sources.

"Loss on ignition" is commonly included in chemical analyses of traditional ceramic materials. This is determined by heating a sample to between 900° and 1000° C and calculating the weight of volatile and combustible substances lost during firing. These include organic materials, water, and decomposition products, such as carbon dioxide.

In the absence of other limitations, the choice of elements can be guided by the anticipated or known variation in the raw materials. Concentrations of the nine major elements are unlikely to differ by more than about 20 to 30 percent even among clays from distinct sources, whereas the concentrations of trace elements may differ by a factor of 100 or more. Major elements have been used successfully, as in a study that differentiated Northern and Southern Chinese high-fired wares on the basis of the concentrations of SiO_2 and Al_2O_3 (Hall, Schweizer, and Toller 1973). For finer discriminations, however, it is usually necessary to use either a large number of elements (Harbottle 1970) or trace elements, which can vary significantly even in deposits that are mineralogically similar.

All elements are not equal in discriminatory value

because their concentrations can be altered considerably by conditions during and after firing. The element most affected by firing is carbon, which can be deposited or removed in widely varying concentrations on different parts of a vessel. Elements such as chlorine, fluorine, and bromine are volatile and their abundance may be a function of firing temperature rather than the original composition of the raw materials (Perlman and Asaro 1969). Some metals, such as copper and cadmium, tend also to be mobile, especially at higher temperatures. Although Attas, Yaffe, and Fossey (1977) concluded that firing to low temperatures has little effect on the composition of clays, their tabulations show decreases in the concentrations of a number of elements (Rb, Ce, Sm, Eu, Lu, Th, Ta, and Cr) after firing. Elements whose concentrations are altered during firing should not be used for comparison unless a correction can be applied. Discrepancies attributable to the effects of firing can be eliminated when comparing sherds with clays by firing the clays to a low temperature (700° C) before analyzing their compositions (Freeth 1967).

The concentrations of elements may also be altered during use of vessels. Carbon is prone to variation on containers used for cooking. Phosphorous content has also been correlated with function and may differ considerably over a single vessel (Duma 1972). The uptake of these elements during use depends on the porosity of the wall and the nature of surface coatings. Vessels with glazed surfaces should be affected less than vessels with slipped or uncoated surfaces.

Conditions during burial in a site can also affect composition. Freeth (1967) studied the variation in concentrations of elements with depth in the ground. He found that calcium was lost and the rate of loss decreased with increasing depth. Manganese content, by contrast, increased with depth. Beiber et al (1976) suggest that sodium and barium are likely also to be incorporated under certain conditions. Effects may be more pronounced on the surface than the interior (Poole and Finch 1972). Unless samples from both surface and core are used in analytical studies, groupings using any of these mobile elements as main discriminants must be viewed with scepticism. In addition to studying the variations within sherds, it is desirable to have data on soil conditions (Cornwall 1958). These can suggest whether deposition or leaching has occurred and which elements are most likely to have been affected. For example, highly calcareous soils favor deposition of calcium; well drained, wet soils facilitate removal of calcium

and sodium; acid soils promote leaching of iron.

Another source of variation, which need be considered only for fine wares, is levigation or settling of clays before use. The effects of this procedure appear to vary. Attas, Yaffe, and Fossey (1977) found significant differences in trace-element concentrations among the fractions they analyzed, whereas Freeth (1967) reported that variation in composition was not significant. If the fineness of the ware suggests preparation by levigation, and natural clays are being analyzed to identify sources, the effects of this method on the composition of the pottery must be taken into consideration.

Unless the variations introduced during manufacture, firing, use, and burial are recognized, vessels that originally had the same composition may be assigned to different groups and sources of raw materials may be identified incorrectly.

Interpreting the Data. If the distortions can be recognized and corrected or eliminated, the elemental concentrations obtained from analyses should represent the original composition of the body. To group specimens of like compositions, the first procedure is to determine the ratios of elements within each analysis. If the concentration of one element varies directly with another, only one of the covarying elements need be included in the statistical comparisions (or the ratio can be used), eliminating redundancy.

Concentration ratios can identify variations due to uneven mixing of the matrials. For example, if a temper containing only Si, Fe, Ca, and Mg were added to a clay containing only Si, Al, Na, and Fe, the constant ratios would be Ca/Mg (restricted to the temper) and Al/Na (restricted to the clay). These two ratios would remain constant irrespective of the proportions of clay and temper in the mixture, whereas the ratios of Si and Fe would vary. If the data are being analyzed by computer, the program can be written to calculate ratios for all the elements in each sample.

The validity of groups based on chemical analyses depends on the care exercised in sampling, analytical procedures, eliminating or controlling variables, and selecting appropriate statistical treatment for the data. Given thorough attention to all these, interpreting the groupings should be the simplest part of the process of investigation.

Mineralogical Identifications

The techniques chosen for mineralogical studies depend on the hypotheses under investigation and on the facilities and expertise available. For example, it may be suspected that a site was a center of pottery manufacturing and supplied non-manufacturing sites in the region. This interpretation would be favored if (1) the pottery at all the sites had the same mineralogical composition and (2) the raw materials available at the presumed manufacturing site possessed the appropriate composition, whereas those near the other sites did not. Such a hypothesis would be meaningful to a petrographer or geologist asked to undertake the mineralogical analyses.

A great diversity of analytic techniques has been developed by geologists (e.g. Carver 1971). Those most often used in archeological research are thin-section studies, electron microscopy, electron microprobe analyses, and heavy-mineral analyses.

Selecting the Samples. A sample of sherds is selected by direct inspection to represent the full range of fabrics in the assemblage. The important attributes are: (1) the appearance (color, size, amount, shape) of mineral grains, and (2) the sub-surface color, which is more diagnostic than surface color. Attributes such as the presence or absence of firing cores, surface coatings, decoration, and vessel form should be ignored in this sampling. Body sherds are of equal value to rims and bases.

An alternative approach is to select samples from each pottery type, defined by the archeologist on the basis of criteria such as vessel form and decoration. In this case, the aim of mineralogical analysis would be to examine whether or how the mineralogical classification correlated with the types. Whatever the basis for selection, the number of sherds in the samples must be determined by discussion with the petrographer or ceramic technologist who will make the study.

Relevant Attributes. The attributes useful for mineralogical description fall into two general categories: (1) texture and (2) composition.

Texture is a geological term that applies to the crystallinity, grain size, and fabric of rocks. In pottery, texture embraces the following attributes: (1) degree of vitrification (relative amounts of glass, crystals, voids, and groundmass or clay remnant), (2) grain size of crystalline material, and (3) orientation of minerals and voids.

Composition refers to the proportions and conditions of the minerals. The description should include: (1) an estimate or determination (by a method such as point counting in thin section) of the amount of each mineral present, (2) an indication of the degree of alteration from heating during the original firing of the

pottery, and (3) the presence of high-temperature minerals.

Macroscopic Studies. The first step is to identify the macroscopic inclusions useful for separating the sherds into groups. For example, some may contain mica; some may contain fragments of black basalt; some may lack both minerals. These characteristic minerals and any non-mineral inclusions must be recognizable by a non-petrographer; that is, the person who will later classify the whole assemblage of sherds. Cooperation between this person and the petrographer is vital to insure that the petrographer realizes that the aim of thin-section studies is to isolate easily recognizable "characteristic" inclusions, and the archeologist or assistant understands the difference between characteristic inclusions and other kinds.

The surfaces of sherds and edges fractured in antiquity usually have coatings, either applied by the potter or accumulated during use and burial, which inhibit examination of the relevant attributes. Identifications should be made using freshly broken edges. Tack hammers, pincers or pliers with jaws designed to remain parallel as they open and close permit removing a piece about 5 mm wide from the edge of each sherd. This fragment is used for identification, rather than the sherd itself. For convenience, these samples can be mounted on cards (Fig. 30).

Matson (1963:492) has recommended making standard cards using examples with known amounts of temper and known particle-size distributions. Comparing specimens of unknown composition with these standards permits rapid assessment of the amount and particle-size distribution of the inclusions. These quantitative data may be obtained more readily if the sample pieces are cut with a diamond wheel rather than broken off. The specimens should be about 5 mm wide and up to 2 or 3 cm long. They can be fixed to a card with any adhesive, labeled, and stored. Up to 50 pieces can be placed on a 4 by 5 inch card. The standards must be prepared in the same way as the samples. That is, if the samples have fractured edges, so should the standards; if the samples have cut edges, so should the standards (Fig. 31). Other uses for cut sections of sherds are discussed by Smith (1972).

Using direct inspection, hand lens or binocular microscope, or a combination of methods, the samples are sorted into groups by comparison with the standards. This second classification will reveal sherds incorrectly included in the groups established by the preliminary separation. Some will probably form new groups, but others may be unique. The unique sherds

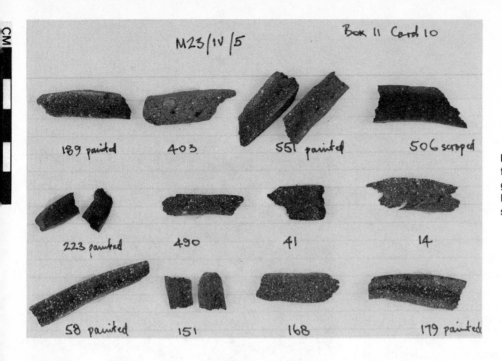

189 painted   403   551 painted   506 scraped

223 painted   490   41   14

58 painted   151   168   179 painted

Fig. 30. Sample chips broken from the edges of sherds and glued to a card to facilitate handling, reference, and storage.

and samples from any new groups should be thin-sectioned. In addition, as a check on the reliability of the classification of the total assemblage, several sherds can be selected from each major group for thin-sectioning. Study of these with a petrographic microscope will confirm or reject groupings and permit new groups discovered during closer examination to be described fully.

This sequence of analyses should be adequate to classify all materials in a sherd assemblage, although additional petrographic studies and visual inspection of complete groups may be required. The result will be a classification according to composition, which can be compared with classifications based on forming techniques, firing techniques, and other criteria.

A variation in the method described above is worth mentioning. If X-rays showing the orientations of inclusions are used in studying forming techniques, they should be consulted in selecting the initial samples for petrographic study. If large-sized X-ray film is used, a considerable number of sherds can be included on each exposure, making the technique suitable for large samples. Inspection of the radiographs allows rapid identification of the size, shape, and amount of normal and abnormal inclusions. Although the types of minerals cannot be distinguished, some kinds of inclusions (such as shell) can be recognized with practice.

Microscopic Studies.

Thin-section Studies. This widely used technique requires a specialized petrographic microscope, specialized facilities for preparing specimens, and specialized training for identifications. All these are available in geological departments, but despite having been used to study archeological pottery for almost a century (Peacock 1970) they are rarely encountered in archeological laboratories.

Thin sections cut from low-fired pottery show a

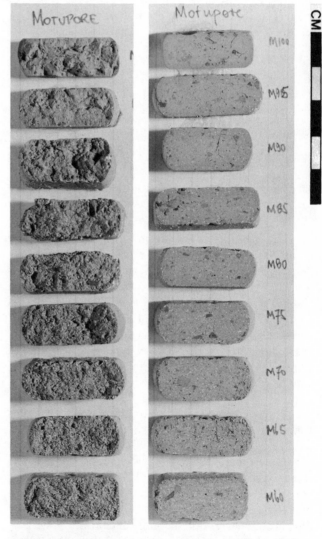

MOTUPORE   Motupore

M100

M95

M90

M85

M80

M75

M70

M65

M60

Fig. 31. Briquettes prepared using varying proportions of clay and sand to serve as standards for describing archeological ceramics. Samples with broken (left) and cut (right) faces have been glued to a card to facilitate comparison with sherds.

matrix or "background" of uniformly fine texture, which is the residue of the clay minerals. Even when their structures have not been completely destroyed by firing, it is difficult or impossible to identify specific clay minerals because of the very fine size of the particles. Fine pores and larger voids resulting from air trapped because of incomplete kneading always occur. Some glass may be formed, but very little is to be expected from firing temperatures below 1000° C. Minerals other than clay minerals are usually the most obvious visible component of the fabric and the one relevant to the mineralogical analysis (Fig. 32).

Skilled petrographers can estimate amounts of minerals to an accuracy of about 10 percent by simple inspection. Accurate determination of the relative amounts of clay matrix, glass, and specific minerals can be made using point-counting and photographic-contrast techniques, details of which can be found in texts on petrography. These techniques are relatively slow, but Peacock (1970:385) recommends their use because

the texture of a sandy potsherd is an extremely complex matter, depending on factors such as the proportion of sand to clay, roundness of the grains, their sphericity and the properties of the size distribution. If each of these were isolated, measured, and expressed in terms of mathematical parameters as is customary with sedimentary rocks, it would put the study of such wares on a much more objective basis.

Determining whether mineral inclusions are natural constituents of the clay or were added requires petrological detective work. Two physical properties of the particles are useful for differentiation: (1) shape and (2) size distribution. Grains with rounded edges have been subjected to natural erosion and transport, whereas grains with sharply angular edges result from crushing. Presence of the latter type generally implies addition by the potter. The presence of two sets of minerals of differing origins is also a definite indication of tempering.

The natural or artificial origin of rounded grains cannot be established from shape alone, but size distribution may permit their distinction. A poorly sorted sediment contains a wide range of particle sizes, whereas a well sorted sediment contains a very narrow range. All inclusions in a sherd should be measured using the Wentworth scale advocated by Shepard (1968:118) or the more recent phi scale conversion of the Wentworth scale (Folk 1968:25). If their frequencies show a normal distribution, use of a naturally graded (poorly sorted) silty clay is implied. In other words, the natural clay contained a mixture of

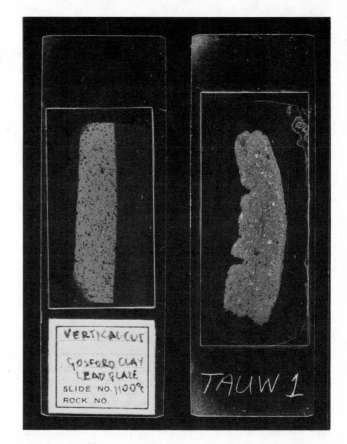

Fig. 32. Pottery thin sections. A slice of pottery was affixed to a glass slide and then ground to a thickness of 0.03 mm. A glass cover slip has been placed over the fragile section to protect it.

inclusions that made it suitable for forming vessels. A bimodal distribution of grain size, by contrast, indicates a well sorted mixture of inclusions and suggests that sand or coarse sediment (or artificially prepared "temper") was added. Care must be exercised in arriving at this interpretation, however, because of the many possible variations in preparing clay for pottery making. The evaluation of grain sizes in thin sections has been discussed by Textoris (1971).

Microfossils occurring in pottery may be characteristic of specific geological deposits or indicative of the age of the rocks from which they were derived. Both these clues serve to narrow the potential sources of the raw materials (Glock 1975:12).

Plant remains, especially seeds and their impressions, are worthy of study not only from the viewpoint of ceramic technology but also for data on agriculture (Fig. 33). Criteria for identifying many cultivated plants have been published by Renfrew (1973).

Electron Microscopy. Although the structures of

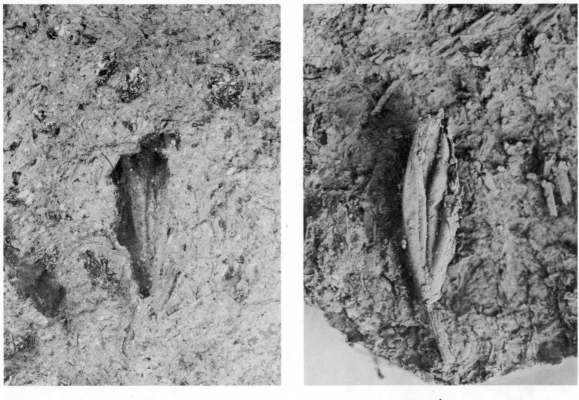

a   b

Fig. 33. Impression left by a barley seed on a piece of pottery from Hajar Bin Humeid, Southern Arabia, dating about 150 B.C. **a,** Impression. **b,** Cast made to facilitate identification. (Courtesy Gus W. Van Beek).

clay minerals are destroyed during firing, pseudomorphs remain when the temperature is low enough. These are identifiable using a scanning electron microscope. Although no studies of this kind have been made, they deserve consideration.

Electron Microprobe Studies. The electron microprobe can be used to identify the chemical compositions of minerals with grain sizes below the threshhold of other techniques, since it can focus on an area about 25 microns in diameter. Because access to this expensive equipment is limited and most identifications can be made using other methods, the electron microprobe is best restricted to specialized studies of the composition of slips and glazes.

Analysis of Heavy Minerals. Each mineral has a characteristic specific gravity. Two general groups are recognized, "light" and "heavy," the dividing line being a specific gravity of 2.9. Since sedimentary deposits differ in the types and amounts of heavy minerals, the identification of specific assemblages in pottery can aid in locating the deposits used by potters (Peacock 1967, 1970; Williams and Jenkins 1976).

The procedure involves crushing the pottery to free the mineral grains from the matrix. The grains are separated by immersing them in a liquid of specific gravity 2.9, in which the light minerals float and the heavy ones sink (Rye and Evans 1976:129). A trained observer can determine both the types and the size

distributions of heavy minerals using a microscope. Although well known in geology, this method has not been used extensively to study pottery. Because of the laborious nature of preparing samples, it is most appropriate for specialized problems where other techniques cannot provide adequate information.

SURFACE COATINGS

Two general categories of coatings may appear on pottery: (1) those resulting from intentional application or from physical or chemical processes during manufacture, and (2) those originating from use or post-burial conditions. Descriptions should specify: (1) origin, (2) composition, (3) stage of application, and (4) method of application.

Intentional Applications

Coatings may be applied before or after firing for decoration or to make the surface less permeable. Pre-firing and post-firing applications are most easily distinguished by reheating two samples of sherds to about 750° C, one sample in an oxidizing and the other in a reducing atmosphere. No change will occur in coatings applied before firing if the original firing con-

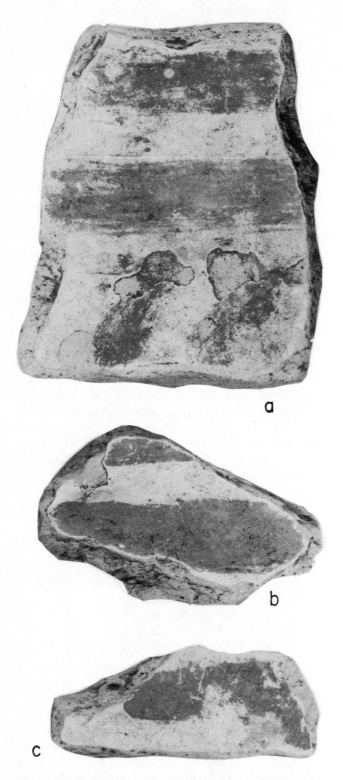

Fig. 34. White-slipped sherds. The slip forms a clearly defined layer on the surface that contrasts with the color and texture of the underlying fabric.

ditions are replicated. If the vessel was originally fired in reducing conditions, the reduced refiring will produce no change; if originally fired in oxidizing conditions, the oxidized refiring will produce no change. Most coatings applied after firing will show considerable change on reheating and organic coatings will be removed except in rare instances, such as when graphite is present.

Slips. Slips are generally a different color than the fabric and this color difference is the simplest criterion for recognizing slip coatings on unglazed pottery. The surface color should be compared with the immediate subsurface color on a freshly fractured edge (Fig. 34). When the color of a slip is close to that of the underlying fabric, other criteria must be employed. These include:

(1) Evidence of boundaries; for example, a slip may be present on only one surface or part of one surface.

(2) Thicker deposits with a fine network of more or less hexagonal fractures. Examination with a hand lens or binocular microscope should show that the fractures do not extend into the underlying fabric (Figs. 35, 98 b).

(3) Study of the cross section in thin section. The slip forms a clearly defined layer with strong orientation parallel to the vessel surface and is optically distinct from the fabric, especially in polarized light.

(4) Evidence of technique of application (Fig. 35).

(5) Determining whether or not the surface layer is distinct in composition from the subsurface fabric. Non-destructive chemical analytical techniques that allow determination of composition are suitable for all surface coatings, not only slips (Cesareo et al 1972; Hall, Schweizer, and Toller 1973).

Glazes. Glaze coatings are readily identifiable by their glassy appearance and general resistance to reagents except strong acids, such as hydrofluoric acid. With the exception of some alkaline glazes, glazes bond firmly to the body and are unlikely to be lost during use or burial. They are often applied over pigments or slips and, unless the glaze has weathered and become opaque, these are also readily identifiable by their appearance. Pigment coatings have no relief, whereas brushed slips require a considerable thickness to produce a uniform color and thus have a relief that can often be felt through the glaze.

The principal approach to studying the composition of ancient glazes is chemical analysis because complete fusion of all the original constituents leaves no minerals intact for identification. Crystals may occur,

Fig. 35. White slip applied by wiping, leaving striations or streaks, especially prominent at the right. Note the fine network of cracks developed during firing. Zuni, New Mexico.

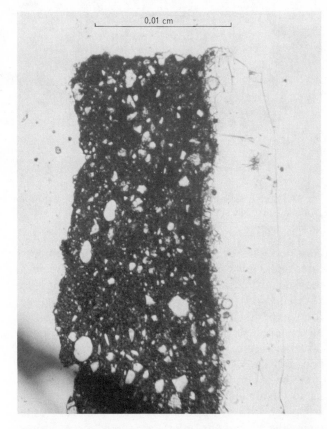

Fig. 36. Cross section of a sherd with a glazed surface ground to a thin section for electron microprobe analysis. The glaze is transparent (right). Note the crystal growth into the glaze at the interface with the fabric and the bubbles in the glaze.

but are produced during firing and provide little insight into the original composition.

If a potter's workshop were excavated, glaze raw materials might be encountered. If not, underfired vessels could provide samples; in extreme cases, many of the minerals remain unaltered and thus available for mineralogical analysis.

The development of new techniques of chemical analysis, using instruments such as the electron microprobe and X-ray fluorescent analyzers, permits far more detailed studies of composition than have previously been possible. X-ray fluorescent techniques can be used to analyze glazes nondestructively (Hedges and Moorey 1975; Hedges 1976; Cox and Pollard 1977) and the isoprobe analyzer allows rapid assessment of composition (Hall et al 1973). The advantage of analysis in situ is offset by the major disadvantage that composition at the surface may be unrepresentative. During firing, the glaze reacts with constituents of the

body, slips, and underglaze or overglaze decoration; the composition will thus be zoned according to distance from these materials. Some elements, particularly potassium and sodium, are leached inwards during burial. Another possibility for error is introduced if some minerals in the original batch of glaze do not melt.

The effects of zoning, the composition of crystals within glazes, and the composition of slips, bodies, and decorative materials over and under glazes can be measured using the electron microprobe (Rye and Evans 1976:147). Suitable samples can be removed from inconspicuous areas and the damage, which can be as small as 3 mm in diameter, can be repaired using epoxy resins with suitable colorants. The sample should penetrate into the body; when cut and mounted, the cross section of glaze and body is available (Fig. 36).

Although analytical techniques make possible

Fig. 37. Painted vessels given a coating of resin on the exterior after firing, while the surface was still hot, to produce a lustrous surface. Waiwai, Guyana.

educated guesses as to materials and firing temperatures and allow the calculation of appropriate recipes, they cannot reveal the composition of an ancient glaze with certainty. More accurate data can be obtained from experimental reconstructions. A batch can be mixed, applied to a suitable body, and fired to a range of temperatures in oxidizing, neutral, and reducing conditions.

The experimental samples that appear most similar to the ancient glaze under investigation should be compared with it in several ways. The glaze, and especially the glaze-body interface, should be examined with a binocular microscope to estimate bubble formation, degree of melting of the glaze constituents, and degree of recrystallization during cooling (Rye and Evans 1976:143). Loss through volatilization, enrichment through reaction with the body and decorative materials, effects of zoning, and composition of crystals in the experimental glaze can be measured using an electron microprobe. Differences in composition between the unfired and fired experimental samples can be specified quantitatively. Applying these corrections to the composition obtained from analyzing the ancient glaze permits much more accurate reconstruction, but does not achieve certainty. Absolute accuracy is attainable only in rare cases when contemporary information is available. A classic example is the Assyrian cuneiform texts on glass making, which Brill (1970) used to replicate the products of Mesopotamian artisans.

Pigments. Pigments are recognizable from their form (decorative lines, bands, symbols) and method of application, which is usually with a brush. Although the range of colors used on unglazed pottery is normally restricted to reds and browns grading into black, a considerable variety can be achieved (e.g. Nazca

pottery of southern Peru and Coclé pottery of western Panama). Manganese may be mixed with iron to produce deep black. Pigments are best characterized by their chemical composition, which can be identified using surface analytical techniques.

Whereas many studies have been aimed at determining the sources of pottery body materials, attempts to identify the sources of pigments and colorants are few. In part, this reflects the difficulty of obtaining samples without contamination from the body. A more significant handicap is the fact that decorative materials are used in such small quantities that they can be secured from diminutive deposits or considerable distances. For example, a Pakistani potter obtained clays within two kilometers of his village and slip material near the village, but imported a black pigment, which he used at a rate of about a kilogram a year, from some 60 kilometers away. Unless very detailed geological information is available or traditional potters using the ancient materials can be consulted, it is rarely possible to match decorative materials with ancient sources.

Miscellaneous Coatings. Other kinds of postfiring coatings include plaster, lime, organic dyes, resins, gums, waxes, varnishes, and mineral coatings (Fig. 37). The latter, unless fixed by an adhesive, are characteristically recognizable by their friability and will rub off easily. Because of their fugitive nature, the only evidence may be smudges of colors distinct from the body and the soil.

White coatings may be clay, plaster, lime, or burial deposit. Lime will effervesce when a drop of dilute hydrochloric acid is applied, but this is not a definitive test because white clay containing a small amount of calcium carbonate will produce the same reaction. Identification of other white coatings requires specialized techniques; most useful are thin sections and optical emission spectroscopy.

Effects of Physical and Chemical Processes

Probably the most commonly asked question about coatings on unglazed pottery is: "Is there a slip or not?" Effects simulating slips may be caused by firing, soluble salts in the raw materials, and techniques of finishing.

Firing Effects. The cross section on the freshly fractured edge of a sherd often shows a gray or black zone at the center. If this core extends almost to the surface, the intervening thin layer of contrasting color may look like a slip (Fig. 105 a). If this effect is due to firing, the layer will vary in thickness from one vessel to the next and even over different parts of the same vessel or sherd. Confirmation that the "slip" is really a thin layer of carbon-free body at the surface can be obtained by reheating a sherd to 600–700° C for half an hour. This will remove carbon from the gray core and the whole cross section will assume the color of the surface. From this, it can be concluded that the contrasting color is a consequence of rapid cooling, which allowed minimal time for penetration of oxygen. This occurs when vessels are removed from an open fire at maximum temperature and allowed to cool in air.

Soluble Salts. If soluble salts are present in the body, they will be carried to the surface in solution and deposited as the water evaporates. This deposit reacts with the body during firing and can form a distinct skin or layer that resembles a slip. The simplest method of identifying a surface layer as a salt "bloom" is by its color. A considerable variety of colors may occur, particularly pale brown to pink, white skin on pink body, white body, pale yellow, and olive green (Matson 1971:66–7). Combinations of these are commonly found on a single vessel where there was variation in temperature during firing. Sulphates and chlorides can be expected and their presences verified in thin sections.

Finishing Techniques. The so-called "self-slip" effect, where the surface appears to have a slip of the same color as the underlying fabric, results from smoothing and other finishing techniques. In contrast to a true slip, there are no signs of applications of a separate coating; there are no slip-like effects on sharp edges, carinations, rims, undercuts, or in incised and carved decoration (that is, the effect appears only on unbroken portions of the surface), and the layer is uniform in thickness, with no traces of runs, dribbles or buildups. This effect can be produced by wetting the hand and rubbing it over the surface. Fine grooves from the fingers can be observed either directly or under magnification. Because the hand cannot reach into grooves or rub smoothly over projections, these features remain unaffected. Alternatively, the moistened surface can be rubbed using a tool, such as a pebble.

EFFECTS OF USE AND BURIAL

Various kinds of coatings may accumulate during use or burial. Some closely resemble intentional applications and care must be taken to establish their origin.

Effects of Use

Coatings resulting from use are generally confined to one surface. Storage jars may have contents adhering to the interior; cooking pots may have carbon deposited on the exterior and food residues on the interior. Reheating sherds to about 600° or 700° C for half an hour should remove any organic coating, but will not indicate whether it was an intentional application after firing or an effect of use. The composition of organic coatings can be determined by optical emission spectroscopy and organic analytical techniques (Lucas 1962).

Effects of Burial

Burial deposits extend across the original fractured edge of a sherd, as well as across the interior and exterior surfaces. If the groundwater is calcareous, it may cause formation of a thin coating that cannot be removed by ordinary washing but will dissolve when painted with very dilute hydrochloric acid. Calcareous coatings may conceal pigments or slips, making their removal from a sample of sherds desirable for accurate classification.

Other kinds of post-burial deposits may be recognized by examining other porous materials, such as bone or stone, from the site. The presence of similar coatings is most readily explained by exposure to similar conditions subsequent to deposition.

5 Forming

GENERAL CONSIDERATIONS

The analysis of forming techniques is the study of the manner in which pressure was applied to the clay. This includes reconstructing the amount of the force, the area to which it was applied, and the condition of the clay (properties in relation to water content) when it was applied. It also includes determining whether the force was applied with the potter's fingers or a tool.

Forming techniques can be analyzed using little or no specialized equipment; hence, forming can be reconstructed more easily than materials or firing. Various writers, including Kelso and Thorley (1943) and Shepard (1968:53–57), have provided brief outlines, but the only comprehensive reconstruction of forming techniques for a complete archeological assemblage is by Franken (1969, 1974). Some of the concepts used here derive from his work.

In the study of vessel forming, two kinds of data are important: attributes and the sequence of execution. An attribute may be a marking on the surface, a particular form of fracture, an indentation, or any other characteristic of a vessel useful for reconstructing its physical genesis. Because of the plasticity of clay, spurious markings can occur with relative ease. A potter accidentally rubbing his clothing against a vessel will produce a mark that is unique and contains no information about forming techniques. Thus, unique or "accidental" attributes are generally ignored.

Two concepts are useful in establishing the sequence in which techniques were applied. The first is the "essential sequence." During analysis of attri-butes, it can be determined that some procedures must have occurred before others. For example, if a series of fine lines continues below the area of attachment of a handle, it can be inferred they were there before the handle was applied. The second is the "drying sequence." The clay proceeds from plastic at the beginning to dry at the finish of the sequence, so marks made in plastic clay are (with some exceptions) earlier than those at leather-hard or dry stages.

Some attributes correlated with specific techniques may not appear on vessels being analyzed, even though that technique was used. Attributes resulting from techniques used early in the forming process sequence may be obliterated by those used at a later stage. Surface evidence of early stages also varies with the form of vessels. It is likely to be preserved on the interiors of bottles and narrow-necked jars, because these are not visible and are relatively inaccessible when the shape is completed. It is likely to be obliterated on bowls and plates, because both interior and exterior are exposed and thus are refined for esthetic and functional reasons. Variables of these kinds can be assessed by using a wide range of attributes for the recognition of a specific technique.

It is necessary to assume that if a potter is making "identical" vessels using an "identical" sequence of processes, these processes and vessels can be grouped into a single category despite minor variations. Variations will be smaller if the potter is highly skilled than if he is less skilled. They also will be less for an "easy" form than for a "difficult" one.

Standardization of measurement in producing a given form is in terms of the potter's body rather than a uniform system, such as a ruler. Measurements are usually taken from the hand. The distance from the tip of the thumb to the cleft between thumb and index finger can be used in judging the height of a rim. Such measurements become unconsciously incorporated into the potter's mental template. Consequently, if two potters with slightly different hand sizes are producing "identical" forms, the dimensions as determined by an absolute measuring system will vary proportionately to the relative sizes of their hands. If measurements are being taken to assess the relative consistency of a given form, this inter-potter variation can be compensated by using a ratio, such as

$$\frac{\text{neck height}}{\text{total vessel height}}$$

Two prerequisites for reliable analysis of forming techniques are:

(1) A sample of sherds and complete or nearly complete vessels large enough to permit differentiating unique from representative procedures. Experiment has shown that reliable results can be obtained using a sample of at least 10 vessels of a specific form or the equivalent in sherds.

(2) Suitable standards against which the unknown assemblage can be compared. The most important are: pottery made by surviving traditional potters in the region, along with detailed observations of their methods of working; collections of pottery in museums, if descriptions of working methods are available; and replication experiments, using skilled potters to form vessels by various techniques and noting the attributes produced on the vessels.

CATEGORIES OF ATTRIBUTES

Selective Breakage

Vessels fracture selectively because of differences in shape, variations in wall thickness, and stresses produced by forming. If wall thickness is completely uniform, fracture is likely to be random. If the base is very thick, it may remain intact when the vessel is broken (Fig. 38). This selective fracture can become apparent in an assemblage of excavated pottery. Care must be exercised in postulating specific forming techniques as an explanation, however, because many other variables may contribute including manner of use, disposal practices, and reuse or recycling of broken vessels for secondary purposes.

Fig. 38. Selective preservation. These bases are from vessels of the same form; they have survived intact because they are thicker than the upper walls and display the same pattern of fracture where wall thickness has been decreased.

Surface Markings

The surfaces can have markings resulting from every operation during forming of the vessel. Some of the common varieties are:

Casts, depressions left by a tool or hand. Incision leaves a "cast" of the profile of the tool; wiping the fingers across the surface of soft clay leaves a series of fine parallel lines; throwing a vessel on a wheel leaves a series of throwing grooves or "casts" of the potter's fingers. In the paddle-and-anvil technique, the anvil leaves a series of casts on the interior. A vessel supported by a chuck or support ring will have a cast where contact occurred; a base placed on a flat surface when soft will have casts of that surface.

Ridges, left by the junctions between parts of molds (Fig. 39) and by tools moved across the surface when it was soft.

Facets or flat areas, produced by cutting with a straight tool, such as a knife blade or taut wire, or by using a flat paddle to beat the clay (Fig. 75).

Drag marks, caused when grit or hard inclusions are dragged across the surface; the grain may remain at the end of the line (Fig. 75).

Compression ridges, found only on wheel-thrown vessels. When a vessel has been narrowed in diameter by applying pressure to the outside only as it

Fig. 39. Vessel made in a two-piece mold. Note traces of the seam, especially on the face and neck. Chimu culture, Peru.

revolves, a series of rhythmic ridges form on the interior due to compression of the clay (Fig. 62).

Miscellaneous markings can result from abrasion and wear during use or from careless washing after excavation. Care should be taken to avoid confusing these with marks produced during forming.

In addition to describing all surface markings, their distributions should be noted. Consistent differences usually imply that distinct techniques were used on different parts of a vessel.

Opposing Pressure

Until vessels become leather hard, pressures applied to one surface (e.g., the exterior) will affect not only the surface but the entire wall. For example, when a seal is applied to the outside, it must be pressed firmly to deform the clay and leave an impression. If the interior is not supported, this pressure will dent the surrounding area. Thus, whenever it is deduced that pressure was applied, evidence that the whole wall is distorted or that opposing pressure was exerted should be visible. Such evidence is always present on thrown vessels (one hand inside, the other outside) and on

vessels formed by a beater and anvil (Fig. 116; beater outside, anvil inside).

Surface Finish

This category differs from surface markings in that the operations affect the reflectance of light and the texture or "feel" of the surface, rather than its contour. The attributes include luster (corresponding to operations such as burnishing and polishing) and overall texture (whether gritty or fine and smooth; irregular or regular).

The surface finish may be similar over the entire vessel or variable. Markings resulting from surface finishing usually are oriented in fixed directions (vertical, diagonal).

Surface Deposits and Segregation Effects

Coatings derived from specific forming techniques include dustings of sand, ash or powdered clay used as parting agents with molds, and material adhering to the base as a consequence of resting on a friable surface while still plastic.

Variations in Wall Thickness

Thickness of the wall may vary horizontally (around the circumference at any given height) and vertically (from rim to base). A skilled potter can infer much of the forming process by feeling subtle variations in thickness and reconstructing the finger and hand movements of the maker. Eccentricity of wall section (Fig. 74 f) and other characteristics of the relationship between the inner and outer surface should be recorded, such as whether a concavity on the exterior corresponds to a convexity on the interior. Such features indicate whether pressure was applied from one side or both sides.

Fracture

Three main categories of fractures can be distinguished: (1) cracks limited to the surface or extending through the wall and contained at one or both ends; (2) "normal" fractures, perpendicular to the wall, and (3) laminar fractures, parallel to the surface (Fig. 40).

A useful summary of the relation between fractures and the techniques of producing vessels has been

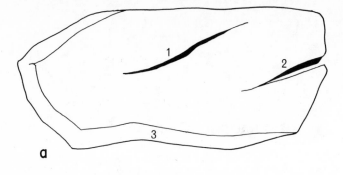

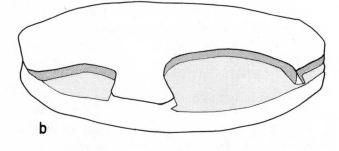

Fig. 40. Principal types of fracture. **a,** Cracks contained at one (1) or both (2) ends or perpendicular to the wall (3). **b–c,** Laminar fractures viewed from the surface (b) and in cross section (c).

Fig. 41. Schematic renditions of the principal orientations of inclusions in the cross sections of sherds. **a,** Perfect preferred orientation. **b,** Partial preferred orientation. **c,** Random orientation.

provided by Hamer (1975); briefer coverage can be obtained from Fournier (1973).

Preferred Orientation of Inclusions

"Preferred orientation" refers to the alignment of inclusions and voids in the walls and surface coatings. When pressure is applied to plastic clay, it causes the clay minerals and some accessories to become aligned perpendicular to the direction of the force (Fig. 41). This preferred orientation only occurs when the pressure is applied before the clay has become leather hard. Because different forming techniques involve different applications of pressure, the preferred orientation of particles varies with the technique. It is more easily observed for large clay minerals, such as illite and chlorite (Grim 1962:75).

The orientation of inclusions can be studied on the cross section of a sherd or vessel or using X-ray techniques (Fig. 51). Details of X-ray equipment and procedures are given by Rye (1977). Techniques used by geologists to quantify grain orientation may be applicable to sherds (Bonham and Spotts 1971, Jizba 1971).

Particle Size

The size range of inclusions, particularly mineral grains, is sometimes relevant to the study of forming techniques. It is difficult to throw vessels on a wheel if particles exceed about 2 or 3 mm. Certain types of plastic decoration, such as incision and impression, are difficult or impossible in the presence of large particles. Large vessels cannot be formed using clays having extremely fine particles. Although particle-size distribution is useful for establishing which techniques may have been compatible with a particular kind of clay body, it is a secondary or "checking" attribute rather than direct evidence that a particular technique was used.

Voids

In addition to solid inclusions, voids are common in ancient pottery, especially low-fired unglazed wares. Voids should be differentiated from pores. Pores are very fine interstices formed by the packing of materials in the body. Voids are hollow spaces, usually recognizable without magnification. Four categories of voids can be distinguished:

(1) Organic pseudomorphs. These preserve the shape of the organic material originally present; identification may permit differentiating accidental from intentional incorporation in the body (Fig. 33).

(2) Large voids, occurring randomly, visible to the unaided eye, and usually flattened. The long dimension is generally greater than 2 or 3 mm and may be greater than 1 cm. The long dimension is usually parallel to the surface of the vessel.

(3) Join voids. These occur between two pieces of clay that have been joined, as for example where a handle has been affixed to the wall. Such voids may also occur where a rim has been thickened by folding it over, or between coils in vessels constructed by coiling.

(4) Fine voids, less than about 1 mm in the longest dimension. These cannot be differentiated from pores and can only be recognized using a microscope (Fig. 23).

Distinguishing join voids and large voids is important because join voids result from specific forming operations, whereas large voids imply inadequate kneading of the clay. The orientation of voids is one of the clues for inferring forming operations. Orientation of large voids may be recognizable from the sherd, but fine voids can be observed only in thin sections. The orientation of voids may be described as "random," "parallel," (long axes parallel) or "intermediate."

Vessel Shape

Some vessel shapes are incompatible with some forming techniques. For example, square or oval vessels cannot be formed on the wheel (although they can be modified to these shapes by later operations). Vessels with round or sharply pointed bases require specialized techniques; footed vessels usually require a special stage for forming the foot.

Indirect Evidence

Evidence for reconstructing forming techniques may be recovered in excavations. Depictions in Egyptian tombs and on Greek vessels are extremely valuable. Discovery of a workshop or tools and equipment is even more useful, provided they can be assigned to a specific time period.

GENERAL PROCEDURES

The distinction between primary and secondary forming techniques, the support of vessels and method of removal from their supporting surface, methods of rotation, influence of drying, and effects of tools must all be considered in assessing the significance of attributes.

Primary and Secondary Forming

Because clay body is wedged or kneaded to insure uniform consistency before forming operations begin, the process usually starts with a ball or lump of clay. It is useful to distinguish three main stages of conversion: primary forming, secondary forming, and surface modification. The first two are sequential; the third may occur during either of the other stages, after them, or both.

During primary forming, a lump of clay is converted into a form resembling the finished vessel. Usually one part, either the upper section and rim or the base, is completed and allowed to dry to some extent, commonly to the leather-hard stage. The remaining part is completed when the drying is sufficient to support the additional weight. Techniques commonly used for primary forming are throwing, coiling, preparing and joining slabs, pinching, and molding.

During secondary forming, the shape of the vessel is defined and completed and the relative proportions of various parts are established. Techniques used in secondary forming include turning, scraping, beating, trimming, throwing, coiling, and joining.

During the third stage, surface modifications change the texture and enhance the esthetic character of the vessel. Techniques include scraping, smoothing, polishing, burnishing, applique, incising, impressing, and carving. These decorative techniques are part of the forming sequence because they are tied intimately to the varying properties of clay bodies as they dry and may be completed before secondary forming processes begin. For example, the rim of a vessel may be constructed during primary forming and a rouletted decoration applied to it before secondary forming begins. Surface modification does not involve materials other than the clay body from which the vessel is made. This differentiates it from decorative processes that employ different materials (such as pigments, slips, glazes, and organic coatings).

Support and Removal During Forming

A vessel at the plastic stage of forming will change shape when sufficient pressure is applied and must be supported in such a way as to eliminate unwanted deformation. The support technique is closely tied to the shape of the base. Flat, wide bases can rest on any flat area and, provided the lower walls are sufficiently thick, the vessel will be adequately supported. While the base is in a plastic condition, it will take impressions from the surface on which it rests. If a vessel is cut from its support, cut marks will be evident. This cutting is essential for wheelmade vessels, which must be removed from the wheelhead before the next vessel can be formed. Support impressions will be obliterated by finishing techniques such as smoothing and polishing, and by secondary forming techniques such as scraping to thin the base.

Round or pointed bases are an indication that special techniques were used; otherwise unacceptable deformation of the plastic clay would certainly occur. Three major types of support are commonly used:

Flat-surface Supports. Examples include a flat mat, a level part of the ground or house floor, a piece of wood or stone, or any other material suitable for handbuilding techniques; turntables made from stone, unfired clay, wood or other materials; and the flat surface of the wheelhead on a potter's wheel (Figs. 12 a, 42).

Mold Supports. These may be natural or man-made, concave or convex. Concave forms are more common because the clay shrinks away from the mold as it dries; with a convex mold, the clay shrinks onto the mold and may crack. Examples of molds include baskets, the half coconuts used by the Mailu of Papua, broken vessels (Fig. 42 b), and special molds, such as used by Pakistani potters to form round-based vessels on the wheel. In the latter case, the mold is supported in a ring of cloth placed on the wheelhead (Fig. 43).

Chuck Supports. These are associated with the potter's wheel. The chuck is usually a ring, inside which a vessel can be set, or a dome over which it can be placed upside down. The function of the chuck is to hold a partly finished vessel in position so that its shape can be modified and to insure that the vessel is re-centered axially on the wheelhead. If the chuck is newly made from soft clay (Fig. 44), the vessel will stick to it. To prevent this, the chuck is usually covered with a thin cloth or dusted with a parting agent, such as fine sand. Where it has not subsequently been

Fig. 42. Two kinds of supports for forming vessels. **a,** Flat-surface support in the form of a fragment of matting. Waiwai, Guyana. **b,** Mold support improvised from the top of a broken jar, which is rotated with the left hand while the rim is pinched and smoothed with the right hand. Boera Village, Papua New Guinea.

Fig. 43. Mold support used on a potter's wheel. It has been placed on a cloth pad on the wheelhead and centered, Pakistan.

Fig. 44. A chuck made from fresh clay, placed on the wheelhead to support a large vessel while forming is completed. Pakistan.

removed by smoothing, a "contact line" impression is left on the vessel where it made contact with the chuck. If significant pressure was applied, the walls may be distorted at the contact area.

Eccentricity in thickness of the wall is indirect evidence that a chuck was used. If a vessel is removed from a wheel, replaced upside down in a chuck, and not accurately recentered, operations such as turning will remove more clay from one side than the other (Fig. 74 f).

Vessels made without using the wheel are at times supported on chuck-like devices, such as a ring made from plant fiber or cloth. Since the principal function of the chuck used on the potter's wheel is accurate recentering, whereas similar devices employed with non-wheel techniques serve only to hold and support the vessel, the latter should be termed supporting rings rather than chucks.

Methods of Rotation

Establishing the presence or absence of rotation during vessel forming is critical to the reconstruction of forming techniques. Three categories can be distinguished: continuous rotation (wheel forming), interrupted rotation (using a turntable), and static forming.

Continuous and interrupted rotation can be differentiated using the following attributes:

(1) Continuity of surface markings around the circumference. Continuous lines indicate continuous rotation; interrupted, wavering lines indicate interrupted rotation. In assessing the continuity of lines, both horizontal and vertical movement of the tool must be considered. Spiral lines are the most common on thrown vessels, except where an intentionally horizontal line was formed by holding the hand or tool stationary against the revolving vessel. Markings relevant for assessing continuity are grit drag lines (from turning, scraping), fine parallel markings (from fingertips), grooves (from fingers), facets (from flat-edged smoothing tools), repetitive impressions (rouletted decoration), and rhythmic ridges, especially on the interior (from fingers).

Both continuous and interrupted markings may occur on the same vessel. For example, a vessel can be thrown, leaving continuous markings, and later decorated by incising a series of vertical lines. One stage of forming may involve continuous rotation and another stage discontinuous rotation.

(2) Variation in wall thickness. A uniform wall thickness around a vessel generally indicates it was revolving rapidly as pressure was applied during forming. Irregular variations in thickness around the circumference indicate partial rotation between each application of pressure or each removal and addition of clay. Regular variations in thickness can result from continuous or discontinuous rotation and must be in-

terpreted in conjunction with other kinds of evidence.

(3) Circularity. This is not necessarily a reliable indication of continuous rotation. A vessel completed by using a beater and anvil technique is often almost circular whereas, contrary to general opinion, wheel-thrown vessels are usually not. The best approach is to place the vessel on a wheel and rotate it at about 30–50 rpm. If a center of rotation can be established, then the vessel was almost certainly continuously rotated during forming. If not, it is unlikely that rotation was continuous unless the irregularity can be attributed to a later operation.

(4) Eccentricity of inner and outer walls. If the outer wall and inner wall are both circular in horizontal section but the circles have different centers, this is definite evidence of continuous rotation at two different stages of forming (Fig. 74 f).

Fig. 45. Vessels formed in batches at a potter's workshop in Pakistan. Some batches have been turned upside down to permit the bottoms of the vessels to dry.

Effects of Drying

Successive stages of the pottery-making process require different properties in the clay body. These changes are brought about by drying. As clay suspended in sufficient water to form a slip dries, it changes progressively from a fluid to a plastic state where it can be shaped by hand, to leather hard where it can be shaped only by cutting away material, to a dry state (Fig. 11). This progression is of special importance in the analysis of manufacturing techniques because the water **content** of a body cannot be increased after forming is underway. The sequence of events is thus governed by the one-way change in properties of the material.

Accompanying the change in working properties is a change in volume. In a homogeneous slip, the minerals are suspended uniformly in water. As the water is removed, the mineral particles move closer together and shrinkage of the overall mass results. Expressed in the simplest way, this means that a dry pot is smaller than when it was formed.

A reliable means of controlling and delaying drying is essential for mass producing pottery. A potter making large numbers of vessels will invariably work in batches, producing a batch of one shape at a time and dividing the process into stages, each of which involves giving all the vessels the same treatment (Fig. 45). Take, for example, a bowl with two handles. A batch of bowls, perhaps 30 or 40, will be thrown. They will then be allowed to dry until the rims have stiffened sufficiently for them to be inverted so the bases can dry; all the bowls will then be inverted. After the bases are leather hard, the potter will turn the whole batch, one at a time. He thus needs to form only one chuck on the wheelhead; the vessels being uniform, all will fit this chuck. He will then prepare the required number of handles (60 or 80). By the time he has completed the last one, the first will have dried sufficiently to be applied. After this operation is completed, the vessels will be ready.

Obviously, climate has an effect on drying and hence on the whole process of pottery production; this point is discussed at some length by Arnold (1975).

Most of the cracks on sherds or excavated vessels can be attributed to firing or post-firing damage for the simple reason that vessels developing serious cracks during drying will be discarded. A full discussion of drying (and other unwanted) cracks has been provided by Hamer (1975:77–85). Only those that may have been overlooked, considered minor or mended by the potter are summarized here (Fig. 46).

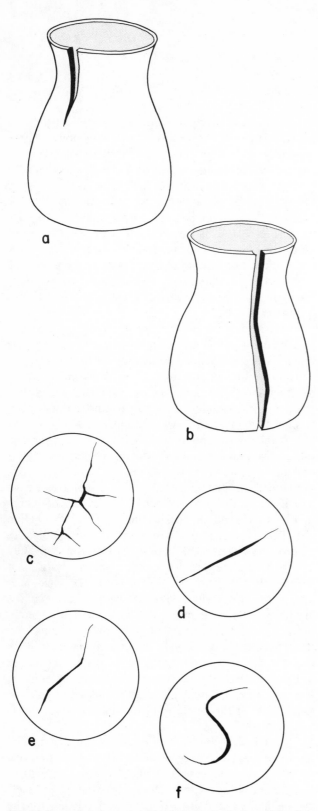

Fig. 46. Typical drying cracks (scale exaggerated). **a,** Extending down from the rim. **b,** Extending vertically from rim to base. **c,** Pattern common on bases of round-bottomed vessels. **d,** Straight crack indicating the base was formed using light pressure. **e–f,** S-shaped cracks, restricted to the bases of thrown vessels.

The principal distinctions between drying cracks and firing cracks are:

(1) The edges of cracks that form during drying tend to be irregular, frayed, and rough as a consequence of slow development. Firing cracks tend to be more regular, sharp-edged, and smooth-faced.

(2) If a crack results from drying, the edges tend to remain in alignment on the surface; if from firing, the edges are more likely to be displaced by warpage.

(3) Drying cracks usually occur on the base and where two pieces of clay have been joined (Fig. 68).

When drying cracks become a recurring problem, potters change materials, modify forming procedures to produce less stress, alter the drying environment, change firing methods, and even change the forms of vessels to those less susceptible to cracking. Prevalence of cracks on a particular form or assemblage in an archeological complex can be anticipated to be followed in time by one or more of the above changes.

Tool Usage

Although the effects of tools are observable, their specific nature cannot be inferred. An incised line can be said to have been produced with a sharp-pointed tool, but whether this tool was wood, bone or metal, or had a long or short handle, is indeterminable. Description is almost invariably restricted to the character of the working edge or surface. It is adequate to specify a general class, such as ''multiple-pointed tool,'' ''single-pointed tool,'' ''flat-surfaced tool'' or ''dentate-edged tool.'' All these kinds of edges and surfaces may be combined on a single tool or isolated on several different tools.

The effect of a tool depends on a number of variables, the most significant for forming analysis being the moisture content of the clay. A sharp-pointed tool used with constant pressure will cut a deep line with raised margins in plastic clay, a shallower sharp-edged line in leather-hard clay, and a very shallow line with irregular edges in dry clay (Fig. 47). Distinctions such as these indicate the stage in forming when specific operations were completed.

PRIMARY FORMING TECHNIQUES

The following outline describes some of the better known forming techniques and the physical attributes normally correlated with them.

Fig. 47. Effects of incising on surfaces at different stages of drying. **a,** Thrown-up edges indicating a plastic condition. **b,** Clean lines indicating a leather-hard condition. **c,** Chipped edges indicating a very dry condition.

Coiling

Rolls or "coils" of uniform thickness are produced by rolling clay horizontally on a flat surface or vertically between the hands. Diameters of coils range from 5 to 10 mm for thin-walled vessels (wall thickness less than about 5 mm) to 5 cm or more for large vessels with wall thicknesses of 2 to 3 cm. In general, coil diameter is about double the wall thickness. Length may range from about 10 cm to one meter. The longer the coil, the more skill is needed to produce it with a uniform diameter.

Building up a vessel with coils is accomplished by placing them around the circumference and gradually increasing the height (Figs. 42, 48). This produces a ridged and grooved surface, which is evened by scraping and smoothing. A variant of this technique is known as "ring building." Coiling involves a spiral, whereas ring building involves laying a series of circular coils on top of one another. Since essentially the same procedures are required and the possibility of distinguishing them in archeological ceramics is remote, I recommend that the term "ring building" be avoided or used as a synonym for coiling.

Coiling is essentially a primary forming technique, meaning that it is used to produce the overall shape of a vessel that is refined by other techniques. Coiling can be combined with other primary techniques. For example, the lower part of a vessel may be thrown on a wheel or pinched and the upper part completed by adding one or more coils (Figs. 12, 66).

The following attributes are associated with coiling (Fig. 49):

Surface Markings. Usually none, unless the coils have not been obliterated by subsequent finishing.

Surface Finish. See surface markings.

Surface Deposits and Segregation Effects. Usually none.

Variations in Wall Thickness. Invariably present. Walls may be twice as thick at some points as at

Fig. 48. Forming a vessel by coiling. The lowest coils are supported in a half coconut shell, which rests on a ring of coconut fiber. The potter is obliterating the joins between the coils on the interior. Mailu Island, Papua New Guinea (cf. Fig. 42 a).

others. Regular "corrugations" will be evident if the junctions were not obliterated. (Irregular or random variations in thickness usually result from later finishing operations, such as scraping and smoothing.)

Fracture. Sherd edges irregular, with meandering contour. Edge tends to break into more or less "cubic" facets if the clay body was very fine grained. Occasionally, a step-like fracture occurs. If joined

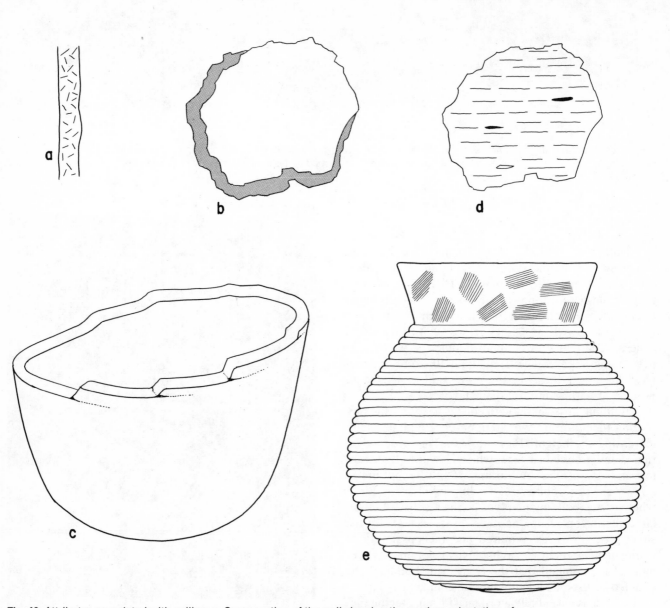

Fig. 49. Attributes associated with coiling. **a,** Cross section of the wall showing the random orientation of inclusions. **b,** Fracture of the edge irregular and meandering. **c,** Rare step-like fracture along junctions between coils. **d,** Perfect preferred orientation of inclusions in a radiograph taken normal to the surface. **e,** Random smoothing marks (here shown on the neck) and unobliterated junctions between coils (here shown on the body).

when too dry, separations along coil lines result. Laminar fracture absent.

Preferred Orientation of Inclusions. Random in a cross section cut vertically (perpendicular to direction of coiling, Fig. 50); parallel but rarely visible in cross sections cut along the coil lines. Preferred orientation is best observed in X-radiographs taken normal to the surface. Inclusions orient perfectly (all parallel) along the centers of coils (Fig. 49 d), the orientation

being produced when the coils were initially rolled. If the complete vessel was formed by coiling, the orientation will follow a spiral or concentric pattern on the base and be parallel on the walls (Fig. 51).

Particle Size Distribution. No general characteristics; likely to be correlated with wall thickness.

Vessel Shape. Round and pointed bases most common.

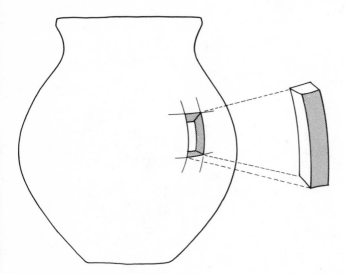

Fig. 50. Position of cuts for obtaining a vertical cross section of the wall of a complete vessel.

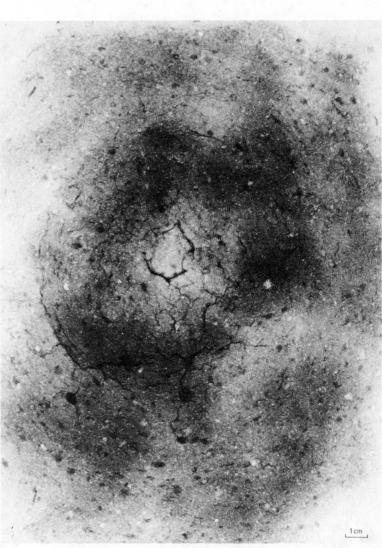

Fig. 51. Radiograph of the base of a coiled vessel showing the spiral orientation of the voids (dark spots). Note the internal fire cracking at the center. Mailu Island, Papua New Guinea.

1 cm

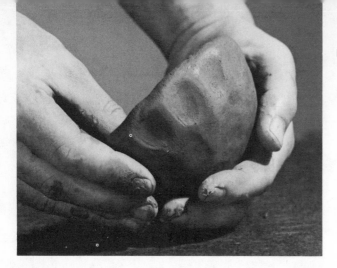

Fig. 52. Forming a small bowl by pinching.

Pinching

This is probably the simplest technique. It involves squeezing clay between fingers and thumb or between the fingers of opposing hands. The walls can be thinned and increased in height by repeating this action rhythmically at closely spaced intervals as the vessel is revolved. Small vessels can be revolved in the hand; larger forms are usually placed on a turntable. Although small vessels may be formed completely (Fig. 52), pinching is normally used to begin the base (especially rounded bases) or as a finishing technique for reducing gross variations in wall thickness, especially near the rim.

The following attributes are associated with pinching (Fig. 53):

Surface Markings. Usually none. The surface tends to be relatively smooth and regular, making finishing by scraping, trimming, etc. unnecessary. Refinement by burnishing or polishing likely.

Surface Finish. Smooth unless altered by later operations.

Surface Deposits and Segregation Effects. Normally none.

Variations in Wall Thickness. Regular, rhythmic, shallow indentations moving upward vertically, each line directly above the other. The size and shape of the indentations correspond to fingertips.

Fracture. No special characteristics.

Preferred Orientation of Inclusions. May be vertical in a cross section cut perpendicular to vessel stance, but orientation is not strong. In X-radiographs, all inclusions are parallel to the surface, but no horizontal or vertical orientation is obvious. Appearance is essentially the same as obtained using beater and anvil, but without evidence of compaction.

Particle Size Distribution. No distinctive relationships; a wider range can be tolerated than with most other techniques.

Vessel Shape. If used as a primary forming technique, round bases and small vessels are characteristic. If used as a secondary technique, any shape can be produced.

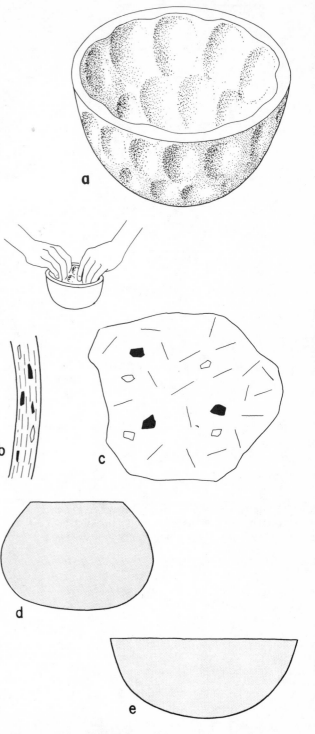

Fig. 53. Attributes associated with pinching. **a,** Rhythmic, closely spaced grooves, especially on the interior surface. **b,** Preferred orientation of inclusions in cross section. **c,** Random orientation of inclusions in a radiograph taken normal to the surface (black = voids, white = mineral grains). **d–e,** Typical vessel shapes; maximum diameter 20 cm.

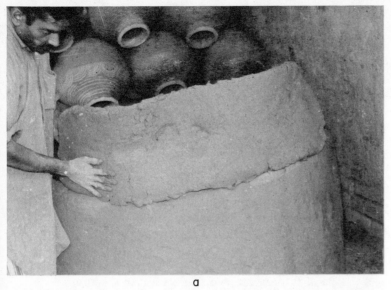

a

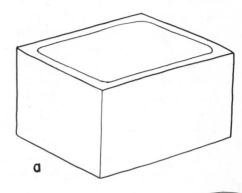

Fig. 54. Slab building. **a,** A large slab of clay has just been placed on the completed portion of a large vessel. **b,** The junction is smeared over to bond the slab to the lower wall. Pakistan.

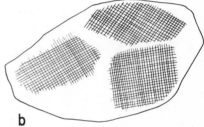

a

b

Slab Building

Flat slabs are formed by pressing the clay on a flat surface, by rolling it on a flat surface with a cylindrical tool or by flattening it between the hands. The edges are joined by pressing or smearing (Fig. 54). This technique is well suited for rectangular shapes and for producing large vessels rapidly. It is difficult to recognize from archeological specimens, but should be considered a possibility whenever very large vessels are encountered.

The following attributes are associated with slab building (Fig. 55):

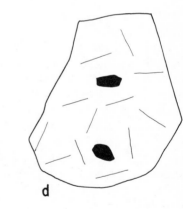

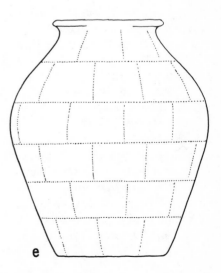

Fig. 55. Attributes associated with slab building. **a,** Typical box shape, with sharp corners where slabs join; note rounding of corners on the interior. **b,** Surface markings, either uniform texture or combing at different angles. **c,** Preferred orientation of inclusions parallel to the surface seen in cross section. **d,** Random preferred orientation in radiograph taken normal to the surface. **e,** Large size of vessels; dotted lines show the typical arrangement of slabs in a series of tiers.

Surface Markings. Dependent on later finishing operations for preservation. Original markings likely to be variable, depending on the method of producing the slabs. If slabs were rolled out on a flat surface, the surface texture will be smooth and "featureless."

Surface Finish. The vessel is often scraped or combed in several directions to even out differences between the slabs and joins. This distributes clay from the thick joins uniformly over the surface, producing a characteristic finish, but this may be altered by subsequent treatments such as smoothing and polishing.

Surface Deposits and Segregation Effects. None.

Variations in Wall Thickness. Variations at the joins are normally removed during finishing. No regular or rhythmic variations.

Fracture. None characteristic. Fracture may occur along junctions between slabs, but the join is normally thoroughly smeared over and compressed to prevent this. Laminar fracture can occur if strong pressure was used in forming the slabs.

Preferred Orientation of Inclusions. Aligned parallel to the surface, but otherwise random.

Particle Size Distribution. No general criteria.

Vessel Shape. Rectangular shapes are diagnostic; large vessels suggest this technique may have been used.

Drawing

A lump of clay is opened by forcing the fist into it. The walls are then refined by squeezing the clay between the hands while simultaneously pulling or stretching it upward (Fig. 57). The technique is also used in combination with coiling to produce large vessels. A coil is formed, laid in place and then drawn up a section at a time, working gradually around the circumference. The shape may be refined with a beater and anvil, obliterating evidence of drawing (Fig. 69).

The following attributes are associated with drawing (Fig. 56):

Surface Markings. Removed by later operations. At the time the technique is used, a series of vertical grooves is left by the fingertips.

Surface Finish. Obliterated by later finishing (smoothing, etc.).

Surface Deposits and Segregation Effects. Generally absent.

Variations in Wall Thickness. Rhythmic vertical variations following the original finger grooves may be discernible by feeling the horizontal plane of the wall.

Fracture. None characteristic.

Preferred Orientation of Inclusions. Unlikely to be observable in cross sections; vertical orientation in X-radiographs is diagnostic.

Particle Size Distribution. None characteristic.

Vessel Shape. None characteristic.

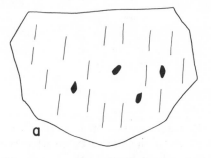

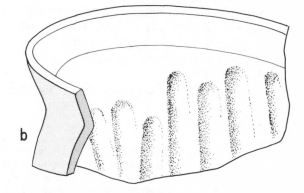

Fig. 56. Attributes associated with drawing. **b,** Vertical orientation of inclusions in a radiograph taken normal to the surface. **b,** Surface markings on the interior consisting of vertical grooves made by the fingers.

a

d

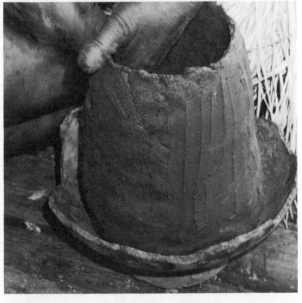

b

e

c

Fig. 57. Drawing. **a,** Opening a lump of clay. **b,** Drawing the walls upward. **c,** Rubbing over the drawing marks. **d,** Scraping with a shell to achieve uniform wall thickness. **e,** Forming the rim by pinching and rotating. The top of a broken jar serves as a mold support. Boera Village, Papua New Guinea.

Throwing

The hand and finger actions are the same as in pinching and drawing, but the vessel is formed on a rapidly revolving potter's wheel (Fig. 58). The rotation presents new working faces continuously to the potter's hand, greatly speeding the production of a vessel. The speed appropriate to throwing is between about 50 and 150 rpm, being inversely proportional to the diameter of the vessel at the point where pressure is applied. Thus, the neck of a bottle will be formed at high speed (about 150 rpm) and the upper walls of a large dish at minimum speed (50 rpm or less).

Throwing is a general term referring to the operations of forming vessels on the potter's wheel. Many specific techniques are used during the process, some of which leave characteristic attributes.

Specific Techniques (Fig. 59).

Wetting. When clay is placed on the wheelhead, both clay and wheelhead must be dry to prevent adhesion when pressure is applied. During all operations, sticking is a disadvantage so either the clay or the hands are frequently moistened with water, which acts as a lubricant and allows the clay to pass smoothly through the hands.

Centering. A ball of clay is placed on the wheelhead and pressure is exerted by both hands in such a way that the ball revolves concentrically with the axis of rotation of the wheel. A ring of clay may be substituted for the ball. If the clay is not properly centered, the lifting operation will produce a vessel with walls thicker on one side than the other.

Opening. Before the walls can be lifted and thinned, a hole must be made in the center of the ball. This is done by pushing the thumbs down the axis of the ball as it rotates or (with large vessels) forcing the fist into the clay.

Lifting. Lifting involves holding one hand inside and the other outside the vessel and exerting pressure while lifting upwards, so that the walls are thinned and raised simultaneously. This operation differs from the technique of drawing only in the presence of the revolving wheel.

Shaping. Although highly skilled potters can lift the clay and complete the form of the vessel in a single operation, additional application of pressure may be required to refine the shape. Shaping involves changing the diameter at any given level without increasing overall height.

Collaring. Narrowing the diameter at any point, usually near the top, by placing the hands opposite one

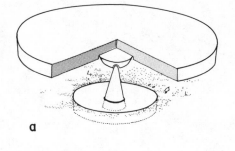

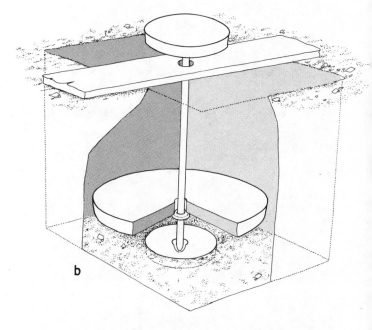

Fig. 58. Two basic types of potter's wheels. **a,** Single disk with one bearing (after Saraswati and Behura 1966:11). **b,** Double disk with two bearings.

another on the exterior and squeezing inwards. Unless the wheel is rotating at high speed, the clay will buckle and collapse during collaring.

Leveling. If the centering or lifting stages have not been executed perfectly, the rim may be uneven. Leveling is accomplished by holding a finger inside the rim to keep it steady and using a sharp-pointed tool, such as a needle, to cut off the uneven edge.

Folding. The top of a vessel is flared gradually outwards and then rolled completely back, parallel to and touching the wall below, to create a rim of double thickness. This can be shaped to any desired profile. If the clay is not fully bonded, the rim will be hollow.

Cutting. After it is completed, a vessel must be removed from the wheelhead before another can be made. It is usually detached by passing a wire or thread along the top of the wheelhead, which severs the bond.

Removal. This operation requires considerable skill to prevent the vessel from being deformed. The vessel and the potter's hands must be dry or the vessel may slip (Fig. 60).

Throwing from the Hump. Instead of forming each vessel from a separate lump of clay, a very large lump is placed on the wheelhead. Clay at the top sufficient for one vessel is centered; the vessel is thrown and cut off, usually by holding one end of a piece of string and touching the other end to the base of the vessel where the cut is desired. The revolving wheel carries the string around the vessel; the end held is then pulled, causing the string to cut through and free the vessel. The clay is again centered at the top and another vessel is thrown. The process is repeated until all the clay has been used (Fig. 61).

The following attributes are associated with throwing (Fig. 62):

Surface Markings. These vary with each stage of the throwing operation.

Centering. All obliterated by later operations.

Opening: When the thumb or hand is pushed down the center of the lump of clay, it is pushed sideways to widen the hole. This leaves a spiral groove across the interior of the base, which may be flat, recessed or have a slight cone-shaped prominence at the center; these variations will occur on vessels made by the same potter. The spiral groove is preserved on closed forms but is usually removed by later smoothing on open forms. Smoothing by holding a tool or the hand stationary against the base produces fine parallel lines that may be visible only under 5 or 10x magnification.

Lifting. The spiral groove left on the walls will be clearest on the interiors of closed vessels. The direction of rotation can be determined from lifting grooves. Hold the vessel vertical or place it on a flat surface and rotate it slowly. Follow visually one groove; if it moves upward, the direction of rotation is the same as the original. Alternatively, look down at the exterior; if the grooves slope upwards from left to right, the wheel originally rotated clockwise.

Both grooves and ridges are produced by lifting. Their specific shapes vary considerably, but a skilled potter can duplicate a particular marking by varying the position of the fingertips and the rate of lifting.

Shaping. If shaping is done with both hands,

grooves and ridges similar to lifting markings will be produced, but they will be shallower and less pronounced. Also, they may be horizontal rather than spiral. A series of fine lines may be left by the fingers.

If shaping is done with a tool, it will leave fine parallel lines. These may be associated with fine grit drag-marks if coarse inclusions are present. A straight-edged tool used on the exterior may leave non-lustrous spiral or horizontal "bands" or stripe-like facets.

Collaring. Compression ridges are produced on the interior that are unlikely to be confused with other kinds of surface markings. The usual position is beneath or inside the neck of narrow-necked vessels. The ridges are either vertical or slightly diagonal.

Cutting. If the vessel is stationary, cutting with a string or wire will leave straight, parallel grit drag-marks. If the vessel is revolving, a characteristic spiral marking or "shell pattern" occurs (Figs. 63, 64). These marks may be erased during subsequent operations.

Removal. Hand impressions will appear near the base, if not obliterated by later smoothing. The base may have impressions of the surface on which it was placed immediately after removal.

Surface Finish. If the surface was finished on the wheel, a tool held steady against it forms a series of continuous lines whose character depends on the edge and the angle at which the tool was held. These lines are flowing and continuous, whereas lines formed on a stationary vessel are irregular and discontinuous. A tool moved up and down against a revolving vessel forms a wavy line or lines, or a spiral.

Surface Deposits and Segregation Effects. Water added during forming produces a slurry, which is distributed over the inner and outer surfaces. In cross section, it resembles a slip of the same color as the body. The slurry will be distributed non-uniformly in spiral or horizontal bands of varying thickness.

Variations in Wall Thickness. A vessel thrown in one piece is usually thicker-walled near the base because the plastic clay has to support more weight. If not thinned by later operations, bases are more likely to be encountered intact than the more fragile upper walls (Fig. 38). No variations in thickness occur around the circumference (horizontally). If ridges formed during lifting were not obliterated, rhythmic variations corresponding to these ridges and their troughs can be felt.

Fracture. A spiral fracture is common. Fractures near the base reflect pressures imposed on this area by lifting. S-shaped cracks on the base reflect stress imposed during opening (Fig. 46 e–f).

a

b

c

d

g

f

i

e

h

Fig. 59. Stages in throwing a vessel. **a,** Initial ball of clay. **b,** Centering after wetting the ball. **c,** Opening. **d–e,** Lifting. **f–g,** Shaping the body of the vessel. **h,** Shaping and refining the rim. **i,** Trimming away excess clay at the base.

Fig. 60. Removing a vessel from a potter's wheel. Note the positions where marks may be left on the surface by the hand

Fig. 61. Throwing from the hump. **a,** Shaping the vessel. **b,** Removing the vessel after cutting underneath. The top of the hump will be recentered and the cycle repeated until the clay is used up. Hebron, Palestinian potter.

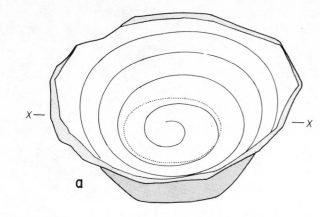
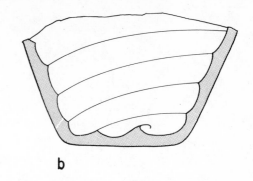
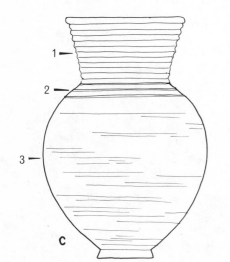
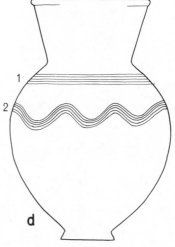
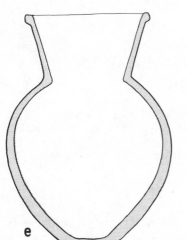

Fig. 62. Attributes associated with throwing. **a,** Spiral rhythmic grooves and ridges on the interior of the base. **b,** Cross section X–X showing the variations in wall thickness corresponding to the ridges and grooves. **c,** Rhythmic grooves associated with lifting, where not obliterated by later operations (1); continuous horizontal lines on the exterior (2); fine continuous grooves produced by smoothing with the wheel revolving (3). **d,** Variations in manipulation of tools: uniformly horizontal lines indicating the tool was held stationary (1); wavy continuous lines indicating it was moved up and down while the vessel revolved (2). **e,** Increasing thickness of the wall from rim to base. **f,** Diagonal preferred orientation of inclusions in a radiograph taken normal to the surface. **g,** Preferred orientation of inclusions parallel to the surface in cross section.

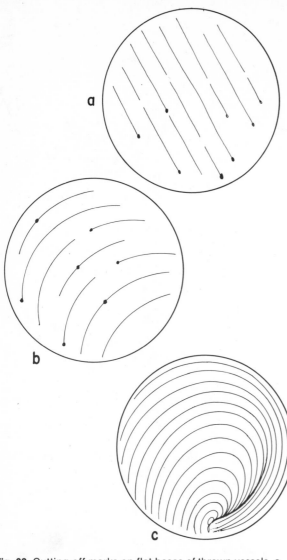

Fig. 63. Cutting-off marks on flat bases of thrown vessels. **a,** Straight parallel grit drag-marks indicating the vessel was stationary. **b,** Curved parallel grit drag-marks indicating the vessel was rotating slowly. **c,** Spiral pattern indicating the vessel was rotating rapidly.

Fig. 64. String-cut bases exhibiting the spiral pattern indicating cutting was done while the wheel was revolving rapidly. Note the variations in the markings, although both vessels were made by the same potter on the same day.

A tendency to laminar fracture may be observed on sherds. The nature of the fractured edge is correlated with particle size distribution and firing temperature; low firing produces an irregular edge; high firing, a glassy conchoidal edge.

Preferred Orientation of Inclusions. Alignment parallel to the surface, often best observed in a freshly broken edge rather than a cut cross section. Radiographs taken normal to the surface show diagonal alignment, reflecting application of pressure horizontally (during rotation) and vertically (during lifting). Horizontal orientation depends on the direction and speed of rotation (Rye 1977). Radiographs normal to the base show a spiral orientation resulting from opening the ball of clay.

Particle Size Distribution. More than with any other technique, particle size is directly proportional to wall thickness and vessel size. A vessel with walls

about 5 mm thick would normally have inclusions smaller than about 1 mm; a vessel with walls 2 cm thick would have inclusions finer than about 5 mm. Thrown vessels require more careful kneading of the clay, so voids are likely to be few and small.

Vessel Shape. Seldom perfectly circular. Imperfect centering is the rule and vessels rarely revolve uniformly. Further distortion occurs during removal and drying. Although thrown vessels can be modified to angular shapes, evidence of their initial roundness can usually be detected.

Molding

Molding generally involves pressing plastic body into or over a mold, which is made from clay and fired for durability (Fig. 66). It can be concave or convex, but must have at least a slight taper. A porous mold will remove moisture from plastic clay placed against it, allowing it to dry slightly. If the clay is too soft, the cast will stick and later crack; for this reason, a parting agent is used. Traditional parting agents are sand, dry powdered clay, ash or other finely divided and readily available materials. The clay must be pressed firmly into the mold. A variety of techniques can be used, such as pressing uniformly with the fingers; beating with a stone or anvil-like object; placing the mold on a wheel and pressing the clay into it as it revolves. Evidence of the method should be sought if molding is suspected.

Traditional potters may make molds, especially for complex vessels, or use pieces of broken vessels. Molds may be decorated with incised lines, impressions (Fig. 66 b) or relief; relief will be recessed on the cast. Whether details of the surface texture of the mold appear on the cast depends on the texture of the clay used for casting. A clay with very finely graded accessory minerals will preserve finer detail than one containing coarse grit. The neck and rim may be formed after the mold is removed (Fig. 67).

The following attributes are associated with molding (Fig. 65):

Surface Markings. These will invariably be different on the interior and exterior. The side against the mold reproduces that surface; the other side shows attributes derived from the method of pressing. Grit drag-marks are absent on the mold side, but may occur on the pressed side if it was later scraped to uniform thickness. The mold side has a uniform-textured surface, apart from raised or recessed areas. All raised or recessed areas will have tapered margins, without undercuts. Seams are highly characteristic, occurring where the parts of the mold joined or at the edge of the mold (Figs. 39, 66 c).

Surface Finish. Smoothing, burnishing, and similar treatments rarely appear on the mold side, especially if raised or recessed decoration is present. Seams may be cut away, leaving evidence of cutting.

Surface Deposits and Segregation Effects. Powdered clay, ash, sand, and other materials used as parting agents generally form a surface layer characteristic of molding. The deposit appears on the mold side only; it may be recognized by visual inspection of the surface or in thin section (Fig. 65 c).

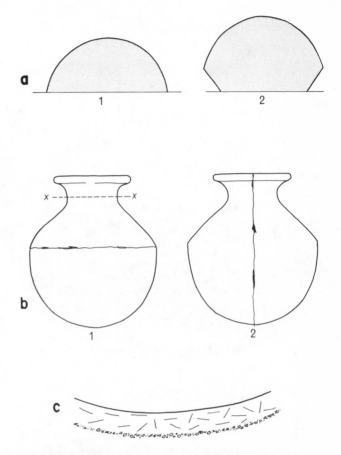

Fig. 65. Attributes associated with molding. **a,** Shape of the bottom: (1) suitable shape, without undercuts; (2) unsuitable shape, with undercuts that prevent the molded vessel from being removed. **b,** Evidence of a seam on the surface: (1) horizontal seam (note that the upper and lower halves could be molded, but above line X–X the neck and rim must be formed separately); (2) vertical seam allowing the whole vessel to be formed using a two-piece mold. **c,** Deposits caused by adherence of a parting agent to the surface adjacent to the mold (here, the exterior).

Variations in Wall Thickness. If the mold surface was regular, all variations will appear on the opposite side.

Fracture. None characteristic, except along joins between parts molded separately (Fig. 68).

Preferred Orientation of Inclusions. Parallel to the surface, but otherwise random if pressure was light. Combining molding with other techniques, such as revolving the mold on a wheel while applying pressure, may produce characteristic orientations.

Particle Size Distribution. None characteristic.

Vessel Shape. Molded portions will have a surface contour compatible with removal from the mold, free of undercuts. A great variety of shapes is possible.

Fig. 66. Molding. **a,** Two-piece mold in which round-bottomed jars are formed. **b,** Impressed decoration on the interior of the upper half. **c,** Vessel with a molded base and thrown walls. Northwest Frontier, Pakistan.

a

b

Fig. 67. Adding the neck and rim to a vessel formed in the two-piece mold shown in Figure 66. **a,** The vessel, with the lower half of the mold in place, rests on a wheelhead while a coil of clay is bonded to the top. **b,** The coil is trhown to form the neck and rim. Northwest Frontier, Pakistan.

Fig. 68. A vertical crack confirming that this vessel was made in a two-piece mold. Chimu culture, Peru.

SECONDARY FORMING TECHNIQUES

Beating

Tools may be used to apply pressure to clay. Operations fall into two groups: using a tool with no opposing pressure and using a tool with opposing pressure. They are usually conducted when the clay is leather hard.

Beating operations without opposing pressure include using a tool on the outside to make minor refinements in shape, to produce facets on a vessel formed by another technique (such as throwing or coiling), to flare out the rim and produce a regular orifice, or to close the rounded base of a vessel formed rim first, upside down.

Beating operations with opposing force include using a tool to pack clay into or over a mold; using a tool on the exterior opposed by the hand on the interior to refine overall shape, and using a paddle and anvil or beater and anvil (Fig. 69). In the latter technique, a rounded stone or special tool made from clay and fired is held inside the vessel, opposite the point where it is hit firmly with a paddle. The paddle is usually wood and may have a plain or decorated surface. The blows thin and compact the wall and their rhythmic repetition around the vessel increases its size.

The following attributes are associated with beating, including anvil use (Fig. 70):

Surface Markings. Any marks on the beater will leave casts on the clay. The final result is a series of repeated casts. Depending on the spacing of the blows and the shape of the beater, a series of facets (flat beater, large spacing) or a uniformly rounded surface (concave-faced beater, close spacing) may be produced. Anvil markings appear on the interior (Fig. 116). Their shape depends on the relationship between the curvatures of the anvil and wall. If both are identical, the anvil impressions will be very shallow and cover a large area; if the anvil has a smaller curvature than the vessel, it will produce a series of circular or nearly circular concavities that often overlap. The anvil surface never has a greater radius of curvature than the interior of the vessel.

Surface Finish. Dependent on the texture of the beater; if smooth, the surface will be smooth; if textured, the surface will be textured. Wooden beaters bound with cord, with carved designs, or irregular grain produce textures that may be more easily identifiable from plasticine impressions.

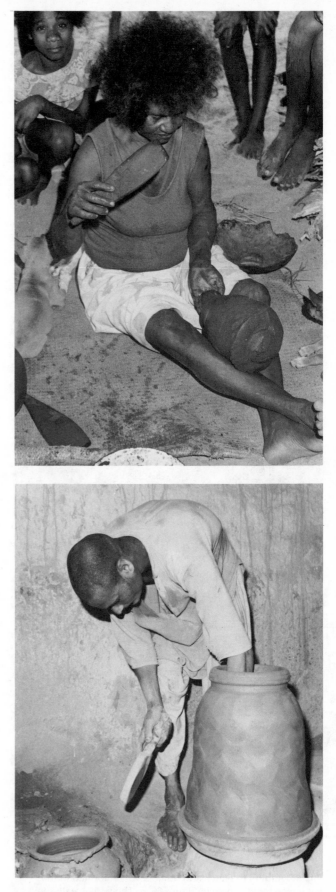

Fig. 69. Beater and anvil. **a,** Refining the shape of a vessel formed by drawing (see Fig. 56). Boera Village, Papua New Guinea. **b,** Shaping the walls of a large vessel. Northwest Frontier, Pakistan.

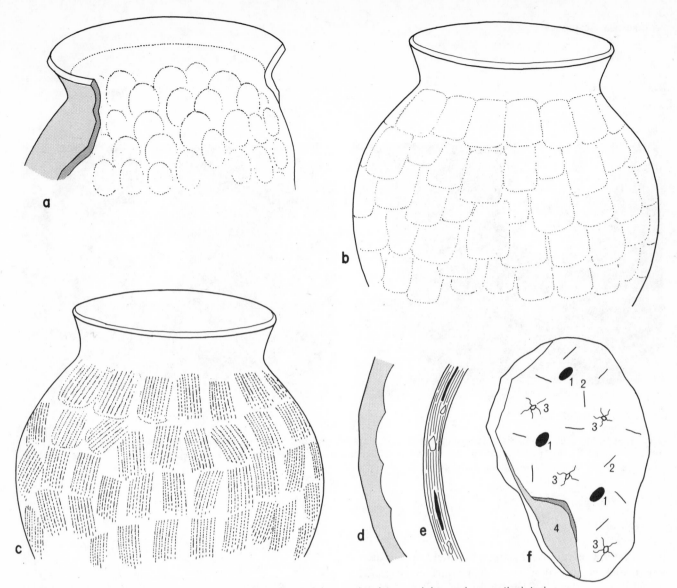

Fig. 70. Attributes associated with beater and anvil. **a,** Overlapping or closely spaced depressions on the interior, left by the anvil. **b,** Facets on the exterior left by the flat beater. **c,** Facets with cord impressions produced by a cord-wrapped beater. **d,** Variations in wall thickness corresponding to the exterior facets and interior grooves (exaggerated): **e,** Perfect preferred orientation of inclusions parallel to the surface, associated with strong lamination and elongated voids. **f,** Random orientation of voids (1) and solid inclusions (2) in a radiograph taken normal to the surface; star-shaped cracks around large minerals (3); laminar sherd-edge fracture (4).

Surface Deposits and Segregation Effects. If water was used to wet the beater, a very thin slip-like coating may form on the exterior. This coating will have the same color as the body.

Variations in Wall Thickness. Use of a beater without support produces thinning of sections corresponding to the center of each blow. Vessels formed with beater and anvil characteristically have a rhythmic variation in thickness, with the thinner zones corresponding to the points of application of the blows.

Fracture. Beating creates very distinct stresses parallel to the walls and laminar fracture is characteristic. Occasionally, complete lens-shaped areas break away from the surface. Compaction causes a pattern of star-shaped cracks to form around large mineral inclu-sions, especially during firing. They may be observable on the surface but are more readily seen in X-radiographs.

Preferred Orientation of Inclusions. The high degree of orientation parallel to surfaces is the main attribute for recognizing this technique. A cut or broken cross section shows very strong orientation parallel to the surfaces and a characteristic laminar appearance.

Particle Size Distribution. No general attributes.

Vessel Shape. Vessels generally have a rounded base and narrow neck because this shape is easy to rotate when one hand is inside, using simple wrist con-tact. Relatively large vessels are characteristic, a diameter less than 20 cm being difficult to handle.

Fig. 71. Scraping a leather-hard surface using a shell. **a,** Grit drag-marks and "torn" appearance of the grooves produced when the angle of the cutting edge is almost 90 degrees. **b,** Smoother appearance of the grooves produced when the tool is held at an acute angle.

Scraping

Material is removed using a tool held perpendicular or almost at a right angle to the surface (Fig. 71), usually when the clay has slight plasticity, at a soft leather-hard stage. Some clay is removed and some displaced, eliminating gross irregularities. Removal is facilitated if the tool has a hard, sharp edge; redistribution is facilitated if the tool has a serrated, crenated or toothed edge, especially if a second scraping is conducted in the opposite direction to the first.

The following attributes are associated with scraping (Fig. 72):

Surface Markings. Grit drag-marks common; coarse inclusions produce deep lines that generally cannot be obliterated by later finishing. Other markings vary with the tool: a comb-like tool leaves a series of "incised" lines, a straight-edged tool may leave a ridge where the movement ceased. In most cases, a series of shallow facets are left.

Surface Finish. Depending on the size of the inclusions, varies from rough (coarse inclusions) to irregular (fine inclusions).

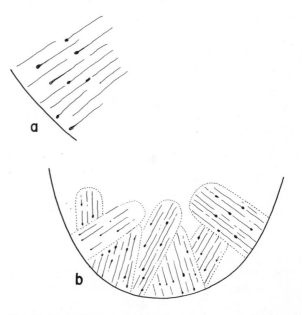

Fig. 72. Attributes associated with scraping. **a,** Grit drag-marks. **b,** Grooves or facets with varying orientations, rough texture, and grit drag-marks.

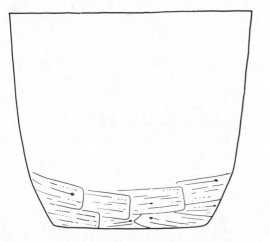

Fig. 73. Attributes associated with trimming. Sharp-edged facets of unequal size and shape, some with grit drag-marks, are characteristic.

Trimming

Material is cut away when the clay is leather-hard using a tool, such as a knife, with the blade held at an acute angle to the work surface. If the clay is slightly soft, an edge will be thrown up along the margin of the cut; at the correct consistency, a sharp edge will result. A wire or string cuts very effectively, but is more likely to be used to produce facets than to trim away excess material.

The following attributes are associated with trimming (Fig. 73):

Surface Markings. Grit drag-marks occasionally occur; sharp-edged facets invariably are produced, but may be removed by later finishing. If the clay was soft leather-hard when trimmed, the end of the cut usually has a narrow zone showing tearing where the piece removed was lifted or fell away. Facets tend to be irregular in shape, size, and location.

Surface Finish. The surfaces of facets are generally smooth when cut with a knife. If a wire was used, the surface is not smooth and has a distinctive texture, especially if there are coarse inclusions.

Variations in Wall Thickness. Some variation because of the formation of facets.

Shaving

This is a specialized kind of trimming, in which the tool is a clay plane, similar to the plane used in woodworking. It is used for faceting the surface.

The attributes associated with shaving are the same as those for trimming, but the facets are usually very pronounced and contribute to the esthetic effect.

Turning

Essentially the same operation as trimming, except that the vessel revolves very rapidly (about 150 rpm) on the potter's wheel. The tool is held at an acute angle to the work surface. The operation is analogous to turning wood or metal on a lathe. In modern industries, the vessel is held horizontally on a specially designed lathe, but in traditional industries it is usually placed upside down on the wheelhead. Larger vessels will be kept on the wheelhead by their weight, but smaller ones must be supported. A chuck can be used. For a bowl, the chuck is a solid dome over which the vessel is placed; for a tall closed shape, the chuck is a ring inside which the vessel rests. Alternatively, the potter may hold the vessel with the free hand. Turning is wasteful and the clay removed is usually added to the material for the next batch of body.

The following attributes are associated with turning (Fig. 74):

Surface Markings. The turning tool leaves a facet; because the tool is held continuously against the rotating vessel, the facet or facets tend to follow a spiral path from the center of the base downward. If, as is normally the case, the vessel is thrown on a wheel, the direction of the turning spiral contrasts with that of the spiral throwing ridges on the upper part of the vessel. Grit drag-marks are common when inclusions are coarser than about 0.5 mm; their direction is the same as the turning spiral (Fig. 75).

Surface Finish. Dependent on the size of inclusions. When inclusions are coarse, turning produces a rough texture; when fine, the turned surface is smooth. The spiral path of the facets is evident unless obliterated by later operations. Burnishing over the turning markings, with the wheel revolving, is common. Burnishing markings will tend to have the same spiral orientation as the turning markings.

Variations in Wall Thickness. The most common is eccentricity, caused by forming the vessel with a fixed axis of rotation, removing it from the wheel to dry to leather hard, and then replacing it using a slightly different axis of rotation. The base can be thinner or thicker than the walls. Other variations derive from modifications from initial shapes. For example, a carination can be formed easily during turning. A variety of grooves can be cut. If the base is thick, a footring can be produced by turning; if so, the thickness of the wall may be different inside and outside the ring.

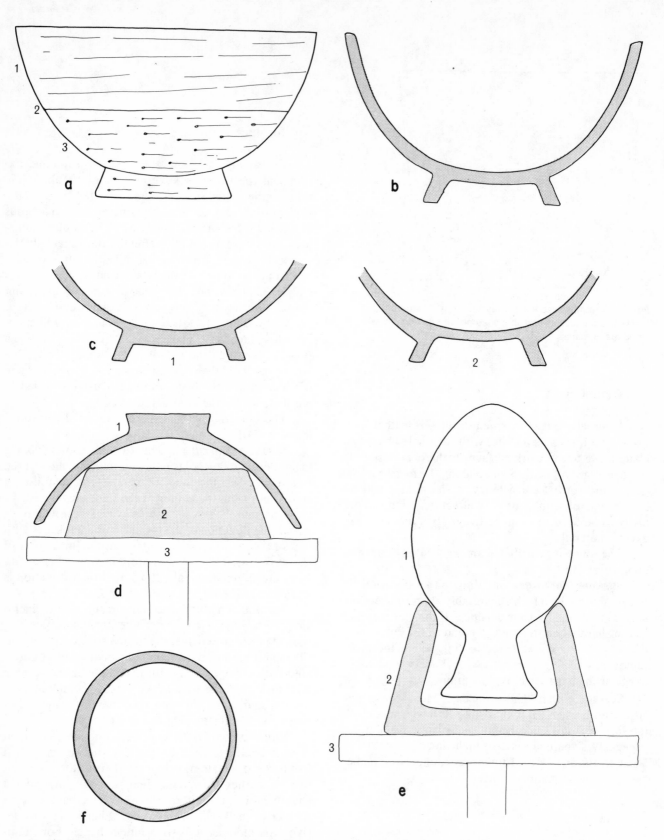

Fig. 74. Attributes associated with turning. **a,** Throwing markings remain on the upper wall (1); dividing line (2); turning markings on the lower wall consisting of spiral faceting with grit drag-marks (3). **b,** Typical profile of a turned bowl. **c,** Thickness variations resulting from forming a footring by turning: wall becomes thinner toward the exterior of the ring but is thicker inside it (1); wall becomes thicker towards the exterior of the ring but is thinner inside it (2). **d–e,** Vessels supported by chucks: vessel (1), chuck (2), wheelhead (3). Note the contact line between chuck and vessel, which will be apparent on the surface. **f,** Eccentricity of wall thickness indicating the axis of rotation was slightly different during turning than during throwing; the exterior circumference corresponds to the turning center and the interior one to the throwing center.

Fig. 75. Turned vessels. **a,** Few grit drag-marks, but pronounced facets. **b,** No facets but pronounced grit drag-marks. Both vessels have rouletted decoration. Baluchistan.

DECORATIVE FORMING TECHNIQUES

An artificial division has been made in much archeological literature between "forming" and "decorating" vessels. From this viewpoint, the techniques discussed above are associated with producing a vessel and those described below establish its esthetic character. To the potter, form is not clearly separable from decoration; each influences the other.

Potters sense form and decoration as much by tactile as by visual qualities, three dimensionally rather than two dimensionally. All textural qualities contribute to the tactile sensing, making all textural attributes part of the esthetic quality of a vessel. In this sense, all forming operations contribute to the "decorative" qualities of the product.

Forming and decorating are part of the total sequence of events. The "decorative" techniques discussed below are part of this continuum. They can be grouped into four general categories: (1) surface finishing, (2) cutting, (3) displacing, and (4) joining.

Surface Finishing Techniques

Smoothing, burnishing, and polishing constitute three grades of surface texture produced by closely related techniques. All involve rubbing a tool against leather-hard clay to modify the texture and light-reflecting qualities of the surface. When burnishing and polishing are performed on a slip, their effectiveness depends on the evenness and smoothness of the underlying surface, unless the slip is thick enough to obliterate irregularities.

Although the three grades of surface modification form a continuum, they can be differentiated by the following attributes (Fig. 76):

Smoothing. The surface has a regular overall texture and a matte rather than glossy appearance.

Fig. 76. Burnished and polished surfaces. **a,** Incompletely burnished. **b–c,** Burnished leaving striations. **d,** Polished with uniform luster.

Smoothing can be done when the vessel is dry.

Burnishing. The surface may be regular, but the tool is used directionally so a pattern may be produced. Because the burnished lines have a consistent luster, the overall effect is a combination of luster and matte or a non-uniform luster.

Polishing. The surface is regular and has a uniform luster.

Cutting Techniques

A series of effects can be produced by various cutting operations. The most common are:

Carving. Decorative lines or areas of varying depth, width, and inclination to the surface are commonly produced by two or more cuts inclined toward one another so that the waste material is cleanly removed (Fig. 77). Carving should be done when the clay is leather hard. If it is too soft, the cuts cannot be executed cleanly and the waste is difficult to remove because it sticks both to the wall and the tool. If the clay is too hard, deep cuts cannot be made. Carving is most successful on bodies having fine inclusions; coarse inclusions tear and disfigure the carved lines.

The presence of two or more separate cuts forming each line distinguishes carving from incising. In contrast to incising, carving produces a distinctly three-dimensional effect, which has also been termed "excision" and "champ-levé."

Combing. This is a special form of incising in which a multiple-pronged tool is used (Fig. 62 d, 78). The attributes are the same as those associated with incising.

Drilling. Drilled holes are more often produced for functional than decorative reasons, either when the clay is bone dry or after firing. The hole takes the shape of the drill profile. It is always circular in the plane of the vessel wall and may be conical or biconical (if drilled from both surfaces).

Drilling produces a relatively clean cut, without jagged margins. The raised edges on the exit normally associated with piercing are absent.

Incising. A narrow-ended tool is applied to the surface with sufficient pressure to cut it. Variations in the size and shape of the tip (pointed, square, beveled, etc.), the amount of pressure, the stage of application (before or after polishing or slipping), the dryness of the clay (soft, leather hard, hard), and the skill of the potter permit a vast range of esthetic effects. Depth and width of lines made by the same tool may be uniform or irregular, depending on the pressure and angle of the tool. Smoothing after incising may obliterate parts of lines if the clay is plastic. Incisions applied after slipping cut through the slip, revealing the color of the body; those executed prior to slipping are colored or filled with slip. The sequence of execution should be recorded. Incisions have elevated margins when made on soft clay; even margins when made on leather-hard clay, and chipped margins when made on very dry clay (Fig. 47).

Perforating. This technique is closely related to carving, but differs in that the tool is held almost perpendicular to the surface and the cut extends through the wall (Fig. 79). It is easiest to accomplish when the clay is leather hard.

Piercing. A tool with a pointed, cylindrical or U-shaped end is applied to leather-hard clay, producing a circular hole. Clay may be removed or pushed through to the opposite surface. In the latter case, the exit will have a raised, sharp, ragged margin.

Sgraffito. This specialized form of incising is used on glazed ware. A slip is applied and a design incised through the slip. When a glaze is applied and fired, the color of the incised line contrasts with the slip.

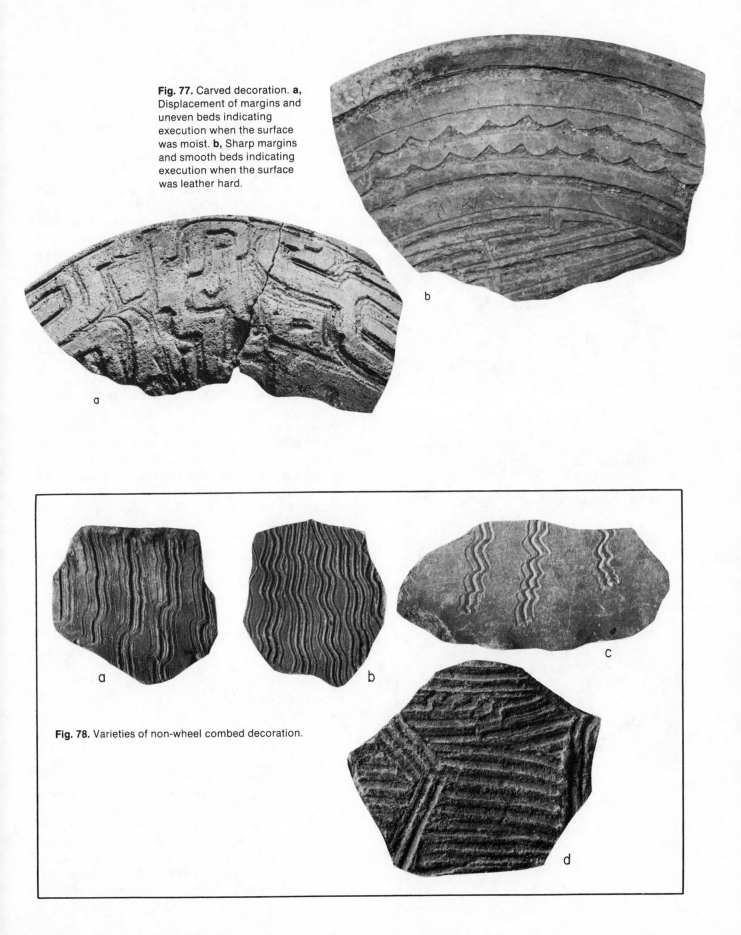

Fig. 77. Carved decoration. **a,** Displacement of margins and uneven beds indicating execution when the surface was moist. **b,** Sharp margins and smooth beds indicating execution when the surface was leather hard.

Fig. 78. Varieties of non-wheel combed decoration.

a

b

Fig. 79. Perforated decoration. **a,** Using a knife with a sharp point to cut the clay; this vessel has a separate inner wall to contain fluids. **b,** Pedestal bowl with perforated and painted decoration.

Displacement Techniques

A range of decorative techniques involves displacing clay or bonding plastic to leather-hard clay by applying pressure. The most common are:

Impressing. A tool is pressed into plastic or, more commonly, leather-hard clay, leaving a negative of its motif. A large variety of tools can be used (Fig. 80). At one extreme are "natural" objects, such as fingernails, shells, bamboo stems, and hollow canes, which produce effects subsumed under the general term "punctation." At the other extreme are instruments specially made for impressing, such as seals and cord-wrapped sticks, which produce effects often labeled "stamping." Markings left by carved or cord-wrapped paddles used in beater-and-anvil forming also fall into this category, as does rocker stamping.

The attributes associated with impressing vary according to the tool. Because clay is not removed, displacement is often noticeable. If the area of impression is larger than about one square centimeter, the force exerted will deform the wall unless opposing pressure is applied on the opposite side. Evidence of opposing pressure can often be detected, usually in the form of fingertip impressions.

Seals or stamps may have designs carved into them that create raised decoration when pressed against the surface, whereas seals with relief patterns produce a depressed imprint. Attributes correlated with seal impressions are similar to those for molding; the absence of undercuts is the most significant clue.

Rouletting. This is a special form of impressing that involves a wheel or cylinder. The motif encircles the tool, which often has an axial hole through which a shaft can be inserted to facilitate rotation. A similar effect is produced by wrapping a cord around a stick or group of sticks (Hurley 1979). When rolled over the surface of a vessel, the roulette leaves a band containing repetitions of the motif (Fig. 81). Rouletted decoration is best applied to leather-hard clay; plastic clay tears free and clogs the tool very quickly; dry clay resists the impression.

Each revolution of the roulette can be traced if the pattern on the tool is slightly irregular. Repetitions of irregularities may be most readily observed from a cast of the surface made with plasticine.

Sprigging. This term applies to the combination of impressing and applique techniques. Generally, mold-made medallions or relief are stuck onto the surface of a leather-hard vessel. Another version involves

Fig. 81. Rouletted decoration. This tool is a metal gear, held stationary against a revolving vessel.

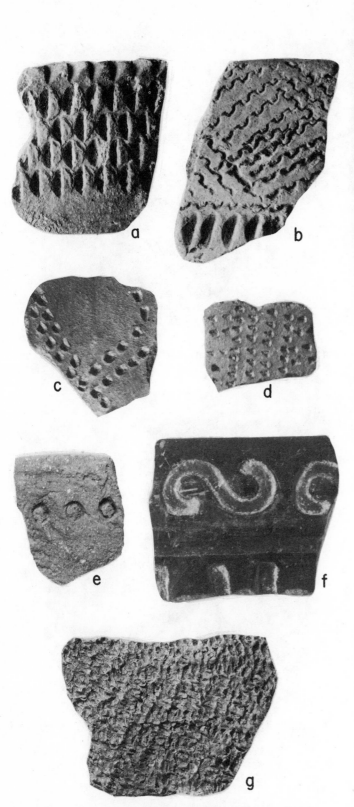

Fig. 80. Varieties of impressed decoration. **a,** Fingernail and fingertip marks. **b,** Stamping with the edge of a fluted shell. **c–d,** Punctation. **e,** Stamping with a hollow cane. **f,** Stamping with an S-shaped tool. **g,** Marks produced by a cord-wrapped paddle.

pressing a seal into soft clay to form a medallion, which is affixed to the surface of a vessel using pressure around the edges.

In contrast to impressing, sprigged decoration is raised. If the application is deferred until either the decoration or the vessel is too dry, a crack may develop at the contact line; in extreme cases, the separation may be complete.

Joining Techniques

Plastic clay can be applied to the surface of a vessel for decorative effect. Two general categories can be distinguished:

Application (Applique). Shaped pieces of clay are bonded to the surface by pressure. Common shapes are coils and spheres. Handles, spouts, and other functional parts are also applied, usually with the aim that they be esthetically pleasing as well as functional (Figs. 82, 83).

Applied decoration can be produced by a wide range of sub-techniques, but all require that the vessel be leather hard and the piece applied have a plastic consistency. Evidence of deformation will appear around the margins of the applied piece, along with marks produced by smearing clay from its margins over the adjacent surface of the vessel to effect a smooth strong join. If the applied piece is small, bonding may be accomplished by pressure alone; in such cases, no smearing will be observed.

Evidence that relief was applied rather than

Fig. 82. Applied decoration. Varieties of applied nubbins and fillets.

formed as a unit with the vessel is best seen in cross section. If attachment and vessel were not at suitable stages of dryness, cracks may develop around the margins of the attachment during drying.

Modeling. Although sometimes used as a synonym for forming, modeling is defined here as adding pieces of clay to an existing form and shaping them to produce three-dimensional decoration. It is an elaboration of application. Application involves relatively simple geometric shapes, whereas modeling employs human and animal figures, flowers, mythical representations, complex abstractions, and other forms to create the effect of sculpture. The clay is added to a leather-hard base and shaped with fingers and tools (Fig. 84). Some vessels may be produced entirely by modeling. Complex modeling is achieved using a variety of tools and analysis of the patterns of tool use may aid in differentiating modeling techniques.

If modeling is used as a major forming technique, it is likely to be combined with coiling, beating, smoothing, burnishing, incising, impressing, and other operations. Analysis of modeled forms should include analysis of any other associated techniques.

Fig. 83. Applied decoration. Coils added to the exterior, smoothed over, and ornamented by painting. Nigeria (Courtesy Trustees of the British Museum).

Fig. 84. Modeled decoration. **a,** Nigeria (Courtesy Trustees of the British Museum). **b,** Panama (Courtesy Smithsonian Institution).

6   Firing

The purpose of firing is to subject pottery to sufficient heat for a sufficient time to insure complete destruction of the clay-mineral crystals. The minimum temperature varies for different clay minerals, the lowest being about 500° and the highest about 800°C. When heated above these temperatures, clays take on the characteristic properties of ceramics: hardness, porosity, and stability under a wide range of chemical and physical conditions.

The technology of firing involves producing ceramics with predetermined properties by altering the physical state of the materials. Three phases are distinguishable: (1) a solid phase (crystalline substances), (2) a vitreous phase (glassy substances), and (3) a gaseous phase (pores). The three primary categories of utilitarian pottery can be characterized in terms of these phases as follows:

Earthenware: Crystalline phase predominant; vitreous phase minor or absent; many open and interconnected pores.

Stoneware: Crystalline and vitreous phases both present; some interconnected pores, some closed pores (sealed during the vitreous phase).

Porcelain: Vitreous phase predominant (up to 80 percent vitreous matter); crystalline phase minor; open or interconnected pores absent or very rare, closed pores present.

The predominance of glass or vitreous material in porcelains accounts for their characteristic translucence. Earthenwares and stonewares do not have this property.

The principal variables controlled by the potter are the rate of heating, the maximum temperature, and the atmosphere surrounding the objects. The rate of heating is important because sufficient time must be allowed for completion of desirable chemical reactions. It is undesirable to fire too slowly, however, because fuel is wasted. Reactions take place at specific temperatures and the appropriate temperature must be reached, but exceeding optimum temperature produces various kinds of damage, such as warping. The atmosphere during firing affects all types of ware at all temperatures because its constituents react with the constituents of the vessels. The terms oxidizing, reducing, and neutral describe whether there is an excess of oxygen, carbon monoxide, or carbon dioxide. The character of the atmosphere is governed primarily by the amount of air provided to burn the amount of fuel available. An excess of air creates oxidizing conditions; insufficient air allows carbon monoxide to form, creating reducing conditions; a ratio of air to fuel that allows complete combustion provides neutral conditions.

Most traditional firing techniques can be grouped into two categories: (1) vessels and fuels are set together, and (2) vessels and fuels are segregated. The former is "open" or "mixed" firing and the latter is "kiln" firing. Although emphasis will be placed on these, intermediate forms in which vessels and fuel are set together in a kiln-like structure are also known from various parts of the world (Fig. 87).

TECHNIQUES

Open Firing

Although open firing involves no building or maintenance of structures, it requires a high degree of

Fig. 85. Open firing on Mailu Island, Papua New Guinea **(a–b)** and the Northwest Frontier, Pakistan **(c–d). a,c,**
Starting the fire. **b,** Firing in process. **d,** Vessels after the fuel has burned; note the fire clouds.

skill and observational ability to be successful (Fig. 85). No doubt the earliest pottery was fired in open fires or cooking hearths. A variety of open-firing methods is still used in many parts of the world, including India (Saraswati and Behura 1966), Pakistan (Rye and Evans 1976), South America (Litto 1976), Papua New Guinea (Lauer 1974) and North America (Shepard 1968). Despite the volume of ethnographic descriptions, few measurements of temperatures have been made. Data from several firings are compared in Table 3.

Temperature. During positioning, some fuel must be placed beneath the vessels because heat rises and most of that generated by fuel above them is dissipated into the air. Potters can take advantage of prevailing winds to achieve more complete combustion by leaving gaps between pieces of fuel that facilitate flow of air.

All methods of open firing have restricted maximum temperatures and even localized "hotspots," where a draft allows a strong airflow, are unlikely to exceed about 1000°C. Limiting temperature may be desirable. For example, pottery tempered with shell or calcite or containing limestone inclusions is weakened by firing above 800°C.

Rate. Some control over firing rate can be exercised through choice of fuel. For example, animal dung burns slowly and uniformly, raising the temperature gradually, whereas grass, straw, and twigs burn very quickly, raising the temperature rapidly. Potters using quick-burning fuels commonly preheat vessels to remove all vestiges of free moisture and lower the risk of shattering.

Atmosphere. Controlling the atmosphere is virtually impossible once firing has begun. The positioning of fuel and vessels before firing can affect the flow of air, but it is very difficult to maintain a true oxidizing atmosphere throughout the firing.

Some potters add fuel as the firing progresses, but many do not. Temperature measurements show that adding fuel to the outside lowers the temperature at the center by decreasing the available air. Furthermore, flames from the margins travel upwards and this heat is wasted. In order for additions to be effective, specialized stoking methods and suitable fuels are essential.

As the fuel burns away, the vessels are exposed to air. Too rapid cooling can cause wide-mouthed forms to crack at the rim, so they are usually placed upside down. In this position, the rim heats more slowly and is insulated by ash and embers during cooling. Thin-walled vessels, which suffer less thermal stress because of lower thermal gradients through the walls, may be removed and allowed to cool rapidly.

Variations. A simple modification of the basic procedure is improving circulation by placing the fuel and vessels on stones set far enough apart that air can flow between them and up into the setting. A further modification is to cover the fuel and vessels with a layer of non-combustible insulating material, such as sherds, stones, wet grass, dung or mud. If holes are left in this covering, air can flow in underneath, up through the setting, and out of these "flues," and more heat is captured. If the fuel falls away as it burns and allows air to flow around the vessels, oxidizing conditions can be maintained near maximum temperature and during cooling.

Pit firing involves creating a similar setting in a depression (Fig. 86). This technique is well suited to producing black pottery because of the ease of excluding air. Oxidized surfaces can be obtained by exposing the vessels while their temperature is high. Black pottery can also be produced by placing fuel and vessels inside larger vessels, which are sealed. This method has been observed in India (Saraswati and Behura 1966:129) and Colombia (Litto 1976:153).

Further sophistication leads to permanent structures, such as a circular wall or a three or four-sided enclosure. The fuel and vessels are often placed in alternating layers (Fig. 87) and air access may be provided by holes in the walls at or near ground level and passages left through the setting. Such structures allow the pile of vessels and fuel to rest against the walls, but do not appear to offer any other significant advantages. They represent an intermediate stage between open firing and true kilns.

Kilns

Kilns consist of a firebox and a chamber. The fuel is broken down, producing gases that travel through flues into a chamber, where they react with the vessels as well as heat them. Air can be admitted through openings in the firebox to produce an oxidizing atmosphere or excluded to produce a reducing atmosphere. The principal advantages of kilns are: (1) temperatures in the range of 1000° to 1300°C can be achieved, (2) atmosphere can be controlled, and (3) rate of temperature rise can be controlled.

The transition to producing wares at higher temperatures involves more than substituting kilns for open fires. Forming techniques suitable for low-fired

Fig. 86. Pit firing. **a,** Digging the pit. **b,** Lining the sides with stones. **c,** Vessels resting on a layer of bark. **d,** Vessels covered with an 8 cm thick layer of bark, then flat stones. **e,** Feeding kindling into an access hole. **f,** Access holes closed, firing in progress. Pakistan.

pottery cause stresses that damage vessels when the firing temperature is raised. For example, the base of a thrown bowl is stressed when the clay is opened out rapidly (leaving a characteristic spiral on the interior). This stress is not significant in low-fired wares, but is accentuated at temperatures above about 900°C, causing S-shaped cracks. These can be avoided by relieving the stresses during forming, but unless the potter understands the need to modify his technique, many vessels will be damaged. Similar adjustments must be made in materials, because many clays that fire well at low temperatures will fuse and collapse if the temperature is raised. Significant increases in firing temperature thus require changes in all other aspects of ceramic technology.

General Considerations. In traditional societies, kilns are usually constructed from unfired brick or freeform adobe. Stone can be used provided the interior receives a thick plastering with clay and firing temperatures are below about 1000°C. Even at this temperature, most stone is fractured and weakened; at higher temperatures, it either melts or fractures so severely that its strength is lost.

The unfired bricks are fired when the kiln is first used. Because the inner face becomes hotter than the outer one, a cross section of a brick from a kiln shows a distinct variation in hardness and usually also in color. Areas subjected to direct flame and greatest heat, particularly the firebox and flues, show buildup of slag, a glassy material resulting from the reaction between ash from the fuel and the surface of the brick. The deposit can reach a thickness of 5 cm, although less than 1 cm is more normal. Where it is thick, it may flow at high temperatures leaving flow markings on vertical faces. When ancient kilns are excavated, these slag deposits allow identification of various parts, being greater in the firebox and less or absent in the chamber where the vessels were placed.

Updraft Kilns. The simplest kiln to build and fire is the updraft kiln (Fig. 88). The chamber is more or less directly above the firebox, creating the effect of a chimney. In the simplest design, fuel is placed in the firebox through a stokehole, through which air is also admitted. The flames and combustion products rise through flues in the top of the firebox, which is also the floor of the chamber, and exit through flues or openings at the top of the kiln.

Greek, Roman, and other Mediterranean pottery, and Islamic glazed ware were fired in updraft kilns below about 1100°C. Temperatures recorded in some modern firings are given in Table 3.

A reducing atmosphere is difficult to produce (Mayes 1962). Blackening by carbon staining is usually achieved by sealing the kiln during cooling, after filling the firebox with fuel (Rye and Evans 1976).

A disadvantage of updraft kilns is the uneven distribution of temperature. Not only is there a tendency to fire hotter at the bottom; continuous vertical passages in the setting tend to draw more strongly and produce local overheating, which results in overfiring of adjacent vessels (Cardew 1969:180). The waster dump associated with such a kiln will contain many vessels damaged by overfiring, usually on one side only (Fig. 2).

These kilns were widely used around the Mediterranean in antiquity. The present distribution extends from the Mediterranean to India. Updraft kilns are also used in many parts of South America (Litto 1976). Modern examples are discussed by Hampe and Winter (1962), Matson (1972), Wulff (1966), Rye and Evans (1976), and Saraswati and Behura (1966). Experiments in reconstructing and firing Romano-British updraft kilns are reported by Mayes (1961, 1962).

Downdraft Kilns. In order to achieve temperatures up to about 1300°C, downdraft kilns are required. These also have a firebox, but the flues direct the hot gases upward over a "bagwall," where they are deflected downwards from the top of the kiln through the pottery to exit flues near the bottom of the chamber, and into a chimney (Fig. 89). The chimney is required because the path is much longer than in an updraft kiln and the flame must be pulled through the chamber.

The atmosphere can be controlled in a well constructed downdraft kiln, and reduced stoneware and porcelain are commonly produced.

Many variants have been developed in China and Japan, the most notable being construction on a slope of a type with interconnected downdraft chambers that make maximum use of heat produced by the fuel (Sanders 1972, Rhodes 1968, Olsen 1973).

Uses. Kilns are used for firing various accessories and equipment used by potters, such as molds and anvils for beater-and-anvil forming, in addition to vessels. They may also be used in preparing glaze (Rye and Evans 1976:95); for calcining or heating materials such as flint and other rocks that are difficult to crush, in order to fracture them and make crushing easier. Pigments may require heating to decompose materials such as sulphides, which would adversely affect glazes.

a

b

Fig. 87. Incipient form of updraft kiln, with fuel and vessels intermixed. **a,** Interior of the empty kiln; air inlet at the right. **b,** Placing flat cakes of dung over a thin layer of straw, which covers a layer of flat sherds. **c,** Placing a second layer of vessels on a layer of dung covering a lower layer of vessels; note the flat sherds at the left, which line the entire interior. **d,** The setting has been covered with a layer of broken fired vessels, which is now being covered with straw. **e,** The kiln after the covering is complete and firing has begun (smoke is emerging at the front left of the top), showing the exterior walls and the air inlet. Pakistan.

c

d

e

Table 3. Conditions and temperatures in open firings and updraft kilns.

| Place | Mailu Is. (Irwin 1977) New Guinea | | | Goodenough Is. (Lauer 1974) New Guinea | | | |
	Firing 1	Firing 2	Firing 3	Firing 1	Firing 2	Firing 3	Firing 4
Type of firing	open	open	open	open	open	open	open
Fuel	dried midribs of coconut fronds, and coconut husks			sago fronds			
Glazed/un-glazed	unglazed	unglazed	unglazed	unglazed	unglazed	unglazed	unglazed
Types of pots	(1) cooking pot	(1) cooking pot	(1) cooking pot	(4) cooking pots	cooking pots	cooking pots	cooking pots
Preheating	yes (flaming coconut leaves swirled around inside pot)	yes	yes	no	no	no	no
No. thermo-couples	3	3	3	3	3	3	3
Max. temperature reached	920°C	840°C	875°C	880°C	700°C	680°C	870°C
Location of thermocouple which recorded max. temperature	top of firing (base of inverted pot)			top of firing (base of inverted pot	bottom of firing (rim of inverted pot)		middle of firing (exterior of inverted pot)
Lowest temp. reading in the firing when max. temp. was reached	570°C	620°C	620°C	660°C	370°C	210°C	760°C
Location of thermocouple recording as above (lowest temperature)	bottom of the firing (rim of inverted pot)			bottom of firing (rim of inverted vessel)	top of firing (base of invert-ed pot)	middle (exterior vessel wall)	bottom of firing (inside rim of inverted pot)
Time from start to max. temp.	8.3 mins	10 mins	7.8 mins	4 mins	11 mins	6 mins	11½ mins
Time from max. temp. to when the pots are removed	4 mins	3 mins	5.8 mins	6 mins	2 mins	7 mins	29½ mins

Amphlett Is. (Lauer 1974) New Guinea		Ya'bad (Rye, unpub) Palestine	Azakhel Bala (Rye, unpublished) N.W.F.P. Pakistan	Hebron (Rye, unpublished) Palestine	Jaba'a (Rye, unpublished) Palestine
Firing 1	Firing 2				
open	open	open	updraft kiln	undraft kiln	updraft kiln
	wood	twigs & dung	pine and other scrap wood	rubber tires	rubber, dung dampened with diesel fuel
unglazed	unglazed	unglazed	lead glazed	unglazed	unglazed
cooking pots	cooking pots	calcite tempered cooking pots	casserole dishes and bowls	large water jars, flower pots	various
no	no	yes (previous day)	no	yes (12 hours water smoking)	yes (6 days water smoking)
3	3	3	2	3	3 (all 3 near top of kiln)
730°C	918°C	755°C	1030°C	1075°C	715°C
bottom of firing (outside rim of inverted pot)		top of firing	top of the kiln	bottom of the kiln	top of the kiln
560°C	860°C	500°C	850°C	750°C	590°C
bottom of firing (outside rim of inverted pot)	bottom of firing (outside rim of inverted pot)	center of setting	base of kiln chamber	top of the kiln	top of the kiln
49 mins	26 mins	18 mins	8 hours 20 minutes	3 hours 31 minutes	11 hours 30 minutes
8½ mins	4 mins	some removed 15 mins after. Others after 1 hour 5 mins	2-4 days	1 day	3 days

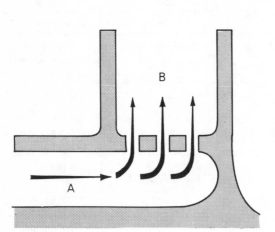

Fig. 88. Schematic cross section of an updraft kiln. **a,** Firebox. **b,** Chamber.

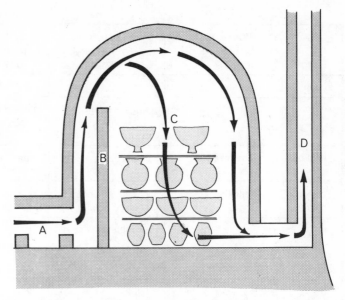

Fig. 89. Schematic cross section of a downdraft kiln. **a,** Firebox. **b,** Bagwall. **c,** Chamber. **d,** Chimney.

FUELS

Fuels are of speculative interest to the archeologist because they cannot be identified from sherds. The only means of determining fuels used in antiquity is to excavate a kiln or open-firing site. Unburned fuel, ash, and slag deposits might be found, but reconstructing the specific fuel from ash or slag would require sophisticated detective work by specialists.

In ethnographic studies, it is very important to establish the potter's reasons for using specific fuels. Fuel is one of the two major materials in terms of weight (the other being clay), so obtaining it may represent considerable time and labor.

Availability

In the ancient Near East, the principal sources are agricultural and industrial wastes: straw, dung cakes, grape-vine cuttings, grain stalks, cotton branches, flax straw, bean husks, sugar-cane pulp, oilseed pulp, olive-pressing pulp, and sawdust (Matson 1966). Bones of birds, fishes, and animals have also been reported (Forbes 1958:13–28). One of the advantages of waste fuels, especially those from agriculture, is that they are replenished annually, whereas wood can be depleted or even exhausted where extensive production of pottery occurs.

Criteria of Selection

Wood is the fuel most suitable for high-temperature kilns, but firing below about 1100°C can employ a wide variety of waste materials. A specific fuel is selected from the range available on the basis of technological considerations. A fast-burning fuel, such as straw, may liberate too much localized heat too quickly for the clay being used, making a slow-burning fuel such as dung more suitable. Women potters in Palestine vary fuels according to tempering materials. Cooking ware tempered with calcite is fired with slow-burning dung to a maximum temperature below 800°C, whereas storage vessels tempered with grog (crushed pottery) or straw are fired with dried bushes to about 800° or 900°C.

Some fuels are better for producing non-oxidizing conditions in open firings and simple kilns. Another factor may be pollution. If potters are working in a residential area, this may be an important consideration. Where open firing is practiced, a firing site distant from dwellings is usually chosen to minimize smoke and pollution nuisance. If this is impossible, fuels that burn without objectionable smoke and smell may be selected.

CONTROL

The techniques used by ancient potters to control firing cannot be inferred from their pottery, but insights can be obtained from ethnographic studies. How, for example, does a potter decide when the desired maximum temperature has been reached? How does a potter decide if the firing is proceeding too quickly or too slowly?

Open Firing

Although open firing may appear to be a relatively uncontrolled procedure, investigations among Mailu potters in Papua New Guinea show that a high degree of control may be achieved. The Mailu women fire one vessel at a time (Fig. 85 a–b), and often use the embers from the preceding firing as the basis for the next. Using two or three thermocouples to measure temperatures at short intervals throughout several firings, Irwin (1977:242–262) found that the variation in duration and maximum temperature by one potter was within the range of variation between potters.

Control was achieved by adding or rearranging fuel as the temperature rose and removing the vessel when the maximum temperature was reached. The potters said they monitored temperature by color. They removed vessels from the fire when the surface was a uniform color indicating a uniform temperature, an inference that was confirmed by the thermocouple readings.

Kilns

Potters using kilns supplement sensory cues with controls, such as draw trials. These are small vessels or specially made rings or blocks that can be withdrawn and examined for degree of firing. If glazes are being used, draw trials can indicate the extent of fusion and thus the stage for ending the firing. Another indicator of glaze fusion is inserting an iron rod in the kiln through a ''spyhole'' and observing its reflection on the glowing glazed surfaces.

Draw trials can also be used to check whether the atmosphere is oxidizing or reducing and to verify that the carbon has been fully burned from the core of wares fired at high temperatures. The progress of vitrification can be monitored by placing the piece, when cool, against the tongue; a porous surface will stick and a fully vitrified one will not. Experience is necessary to interpret correctly observations of behavior and responses made by potters to questions.

STAGES

When unfired vessels are heated in an open fire or kiln, a sequence of changes occurs in the fabric. The changes depend on the substances present, their relative amounts, and their state of division (particle size or surface area), as well as the rate of heating, maximum temperature, and firing atmosphere. The general changes can be summarized in six stages. A range of temperature is given for each stage because there is a significant overlap, one not necessarily being complete before the next begins. The stages are: (1) water smoking, (2) low-temperature decomposition, (3) clay-mineral decomposition and sintering, (4) organic combustion, (5) vitrification, and (6) cooling.

Water Smoking

Temperature ranges up to about 120°C. Vessels dried before firing have reached an equilibrium with the surrounding atmosphere, but have not lost all free water. At the beginning of firing, this water is released as the temperature increases up to 100°C (the boiling point). If the rate is very rapid, the water will instantaneously covert to steam and the resulting pressure can fracture the vessel. The term ''water smoking'' derives from the smoke-like appearance of the water vapor as it emerges from the chimney of a kiln.

The rate at which vessels can be heated depends on numerous variables. The packing of the body constituents and the predominant clay minerals are significant. Forming technique is relevant because it affects the compactness of the body. The presence of fine slips reduces the size of the pores through which water escapes, necessitating slower heating. Thick-walled vessels must be heated more slowly than thin-walled ones. In general, about two hours is usually a safe period during which the temperature can be raised to 100°C. For open firing, where it is relatively difficult to insure that parts of the setting are not heated very quickly by flames contacting the pots directly, preheating may be done by placing them near a fire (Fig. 90).

Attributes. Several types of breakage occur when vessels are heated too quickly in the water-smoking stage. Spalling is likely if large grains of temper are

Fig. 90. Preheating vessels in a blacksmith's forge. Pakistan.

Fig. 91. Damage by spalling. Waiwai, Guyana.

present, especially when the fabric has been tightly compacted during forming (Figs. 91, 115). Large lens-like portions of the outer wall flake off, leaving large craters that may weaken the vessel sufficiently to make it unusable. A series of spalls can completely shatter it.

Cracks will extend completely through the wall if the thickness is uneven. On flat-bottomed vessels, these cracks are most likely to occur at the base, starting near the center and running across and part way up the wall. Cracks may also propagate at the rim, but are less likely here.

Low-temperature Decomposition.

Temperature ranges up to about 350° C. Any organic material present naturally or added by the potter begins to decompose around 200° C. Some clay minerals begin to lose loosely bonded water, especially montmorillonite and illite.

Attributes. Too rapid heating will produce the same fractures and spalling as occur during the water-smoking stage.

Clay-mineral Decomposition and Sintering

Temperature range is generally between about 400° and 850° C, but varies upwards or downwards depending on the specific minerals present. For unglazed pottery, this is the main stage of firing. The clay

minerals decompose and the edges of the grains bond together by ion diffusion, a process known as "sintering." Kaolinite decomposition begins at 415° C, but at that temperature would take several weeks to complete; at 550° C, the reaction is complete in half an hour (Searle and Grimshaw 1959:657). As temperatures increase, reaction times decrease further. Temperatures of rapid decomposition for some of the common clay minerals are: kaolinite 585° C, halloysite 558° C, montmorillonite 678° C. Details of the decomposition of clay minerals have been provided by Grim (1962:98–125). Unless the clay minerals decompose completely, rehydration can occur, restoring the original properties. Thus, either the temperature must exceed that required for sintering or the time must be adequate for sintering to be completed at the temperature achieved.

Other minerals that decompose in this temperature range include carbonates and sulphates. Of these, calcium carbonate is the most likely to be present in traditional pottery in the form of fragments of shell, limestone or calcite.

Attributes. Pottery damaged by too rapid heating during the clay-mineral decomposition stage may be encountered at manufacturing sites. The diagnostic fault is "firecracking," which is characterized by a network of fine cracks over the surface, often exhibiting a hexagonal structure (Figs. 92, 98). In extreme cases, the vessel may fracture completely into pieces resembling those from a broken automobile windshield.

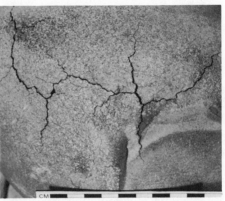

Fig. 92. Firecracking. **a,** A network of fine firecracks covering the surface of an unused cooking vessel. **b,** A fine network of surface cracks and a larger network of cracks extending through the walls of a round-bottomed vessel. Papua New Guinea.

The decomposition of calcium carbonate is significant because it can destroy pottery. When $CaCO_3$ decomposes, it forms calcium oxide (CaO). After the vessel has cooled, and even weeks or months after firing, the CaO can combine with water vapor in the air to form calcium hydroxide. Since the volume of calcium hydroxide is greater than CaO or $CaCO_3$, this expansion can exert enough pressure to rupture the walls and reduce a vessel to a loose pile of grains. In minor cases, a large grain in the wall causes a cone-shaped piece to spall off, leaving a cone-shaped crater with a whitish grain at its apex (Fig. 93). This destructive process can be prevented by keeping the firing temperature below that where calcium carbonate decomposes (i.e., 750–800° C). Another alternative is to introduce soluble salts, especially sodium chloride, into the body by using clays or temper that naturally contain them, using saltwater or seawater to wet the clay, or mixing ground salt with the plastic clay (Rye 1976).

Quartz changes its crystalline form at 573° C. Alpha quartz (the low temperature form) occupies a smaller volume than Beta quartz, so the inversion can create stresses in the fabric. If quartz grains are large, a series of fine radiating cracks will usually be formed. All other minerals expand when heated and if the expansion is appreciably greater than the surrounding fabric, a similar pattern of radiating cracks will be produced (Fig. 100).

Fig. 93. Lime spalling on an unglazed vessel. Pieces of fabric are being dislodged by the white grains; others have already been removed (bottom center).

Grog (crushed potsherds) expands up to the temperature of its previous firing, during which time the clay matrix contracts. The grog shrinks if the original temperature is exceeded, causing a characteristic cracking of the clay around large grains. This may not be evident except under a microscope or in thin sections.

Organic Combustion

Temperature ranges from 500° C upward. Traditional pottery almost invariably contains organic (carbon-based) matter, which begins to decompose at around 200° C. When the temperature reaches 500° C, carbon at the surface burns; if it increases further or is held constant for some time, carbon combustion extends into the walls. Under suitable oxidizing conditions, all carbon will be removed by about 900°C except graphite, which can resist oxidation up to about 1200°C.

Black pottery produced in many areas of the world obtains its color from the presence of carbon. Much unglazed traditional pottery has a black or gray "core" of unburned organic materal. An understanding of the processes involved in either removing or increasing the amount of carbon aids in interpreting the firing of unglazed pottery. An important paper by Duma and Lengyel (1970) summarizes the variables in more detail than is given here.

The most important constituents of firing atmosphere in the present discussion are oxygen and carbon monoxide. An oxidizing atmosphere exists when the amount of oxygen is greater than required for combustion of the fuel. In practice, this represents an excess of air because the oxygen is not supplied as a pure gas. Reducing conditions exist when there is not enough oxygen to combust the available fuel and carbon monoxide (CO) forms in the atmosphere surrounding the vessels. A reducing atmosphere may also contain hydrogen and carbon.

Under conditions of complete combustion, all carbon in the fuel is oxidized, producing carbon dioxide (CO_2). The essential constituents of an oxidizing atmosphere are therefore CO_2 and O_2. When the amount of oxygen is insufficient to form CO_2, CO is formed. In traditional pottery firing, a reducing atmosphere never consists of CO alone, but is a mixture of CO, CO_2, and nitrogen. If the proportion of CO is low (less than about two percent) and some oxygen is present, the atmosphere is described as "neutral."

When organic materials are present in the pottery, the effect of an oxidizing atmosphere is to remove them. Oxygen from the atmosphere combines with carbon released by decomposition of the organics and the resulting carbon dioxide (CO_2) dissipates as a gas. The oxidation of carbon proceeds more quickly if the pottery is very porous and more slowly if porosity is low. The size of the pores is also important, large pores allowing more rapid removal than fine pores. Although some free oxygen may be present in a reducing atmosphere or in some parts of a kiln where the reducing atmosphere has not been established, free carbon will usually remain in the pores of vessels. If the firing proceeds to a high enough temperature for vitrification, this carbon can decompose and cause severe bloating.

Iron not incorporated in the crystal structures of other minerals will be present above about 600°C as Fe_2O_3, which is reddish. On reduction, gray or black oxides are formed (FeO, Fe_3O_4). Reduction of iron oxides does not start below about 900°C. Pottery fired below this temperature cannot be said to be "reduced."

Vitrification

Vitrification is the process by which glass is formed in pottery bodies. When silicate minerals and oxides are heated sufficiently, they melt or fuse and form a viscous liquid. If this liquid were cooled very slowly, the minerals would recrystallize but pottery is generally cooled too quickly for this to occur.

The melting point of a mixture of constituents is lower than that of an individual constituent; for any given set of constituents, one specific mixture or composition will have the lowest melting point. This is termed the "eutectic" composition. The specific mixture of minerals in a pottery body determines the initial melting point or beginning of vitrification. Vitrification can begin at about 700°C, but generally does not become extensive below 900 to 950°C.

As the surface tension of the glass increases, it seals pores in the fabric, which becomes more densely packed and shrinks. This firing shrinkage can be as much as 10 percent linear shrinkage from the size of the dried vessel. If the temperature continues to rise, the volume of open and interconnected pores decreases further and the volume of closed pores proportionately increases. These closed pores contain gases such as CO_2, CO, SO_3, O_2, water vapor, unburned hydrocarbons, and nitrogen. As the temperature rises higher, the pressure of the gas in the sealed pores grows, but the viscosity of the surrounding glass de-

Fig. 94. Damage from overfiring. **a,** Squatting; note the firing cracks on the shoulder. **b,** Bloating on the shoulder and squatting at the rim.

clines. Eventually, this leads to an expansion or "bloating" of the pores, a process that can be visualized as analogous to glassblowing.

Many constituents of the firing atmosphere are capable of reacting with the pottery body at high temperatures. For example, ash from wood fuel can form a glaze above about 1200°C. Volatile constituents can be added purposefully. When common salt is thrown into the firebox above about 1200°C, it breaks down into sodium and chlorine. The sodium reacts with silica and alumina in the body to form a glassy layer, commonly known as "salt glaze."

Attributes. Bloating is characteristic of traditional ceramics overfired sufficiently to induce vitrification. It can be recognized from the spongy texture and blister-like areas on the surface, caused by the expansion of large air bubbles incorporated when kneading of the clay was incomplete.

As viscosity decreases, the body increasingly tends to behave like molten glass and vessels begin to warp, "squat," and "flow" as they are overfired (Fig. 94). In extreme cases, they completely collapse and become unrecognizable. Such overfiring is common in Middle Eastern kilns, where temperatures can be very uneven. It can also occur in open firings, especially when soluble salts are present in the body. Bloated or warped sherds found on waster dumps near traditional kilns are often dark colored as a consequence of reduction of the iron and retention of carbon.

Cooling

When the maximum temperature has been achieved in a kiln, it may be maintained for some time ("soaking") to allow equalization throughout the interior and continuation of the reactions. Alternatively in a kiln and invariably in open firing, cooling begins as soon as the maximum temperature is reached. The firing is terminated by not adding more fuel and/or allowing the remaining fuel to burn away. In some open-firing techniques, the end of firing is accomplished by removing the vessel using long sticks as tongs.

Cooling is not simply the process of getting pottery to a stage where it can be handled; it contributes markedly to the finished character of the ware. Both the rate and the atmosphere during cooling influence the final quality.

Most pottery is cooled in an oxidizing atmosphere. In kilns, this is achieved by allowing all the fuel to burn so the atmosphere is essentially the same as air. Access of fresh air is prevented because cool drafts will cause the vessels to crack.

When black pottery or certain specialized glaze effects are desired, a reducing atmosphere may be produced during cooling by introducing a fuel (which may or may not be the same as that used during firing) into the firebox (or among the vessels in the case of unglazed ware) and preventing access of air. The fuel smoulders slowly and produces the carbon monoxide necessary for blackening. Maximum deposition of carbon occurs between 650° and 400°C, so the kiln can be cooled to about 700°C before the fuel is introduced and the air access closed (Duma and Lengyel 1970:73; Lucas 1962:373; Rye and Evans 1976).

In open fires, oxidized cooling is accomplished either by removing the vessel from the fire or by insuring that it is not covered by ash or embers. Wherever access of air to the surface is prevented, oxidation cannot occur. If blackening is desired over all or part of the vessel, it can be produced by protecting that portion of the surface from contact with air. Using organic materials that smoulder will cause blackening in the temperature range between 650° and 400°C. Further discussion of these methods is provided by Lucas (1962:373).

The rate of cooling is difficult to control in an open fire unless the vessel is insulated, and with insulation an oxidizing atmosphere cannot be maintained. To prevent damage during cooling, potters rely more on vessel shape than control of rate. Round-bottomed vessels of uniform wall thickness, without sharp carinations or other angles, cool uniformly and are most resistent to cracking.

The rate of cooling in a kiln is determined mainly by the structure of the kiln. A vessel can be removed and allowed to cool in five or ten minutes. If the kiln structure is cooled very quickly by allowing cool air to flow through, it will crack or spall. The rate of cooling can be varied slightly by eliminating or minimizing entry of fresh air. In some kilns, openings at the top allow heat to escape. Even so, the time required for cooling kilns varies from about 24 hours to a week, depending mainly on the mass of the structure. Kilns constructed so the potter has to go inside to remove the ware must be allowed to cool to about 40°C.

CRITERIA FOR RECONSTRUCTING FIRING TECHNIQUES

In a traditional firing, temperatures, atmospheres, and rates of temperature rise all vary. Vessels in different parts of a setting will be subjected to different conditions. A single vessel may be exposed to variable conditions, especially if it is large. These circumstances make reconstructions of firing techniques based on one or two vessels or sherds meaningless.

The most valuable data for studying ancient firing

Fig. 95. Firing wasters resulting from open firings in the depression shown in the left half of the picture. Pakistan.

techniques would derive from excavation of a firing area (for open firing) or kiln, complete with wasters. Study of the material from excavations can be supplemented by experiments such as those of Mayes (1961, 1962), who reconstructed and fired replicas of Roman kilns excavated in Britain.

The following discussion is concerned mainly with reconstructing firing techniques from sherds or vessels from excavations, but some characteristics of wasters from manufacturing sites are also described.

Wasters and Firing Faults

Vessels damaged during firing are known as "wasters" (Figs. 2, 95). The percentage of wasters is the firing loss. This can be expressed quantitatively by the number of damaged vessels as a percentage of the number of vessels fired. In ethnographic studies, firing losses can be calculated and can provide a basis for comparing the efficiency of firing techniques. In my experience, traditional potters are aware of their normal rate of firing loss and can compare any specific firing with the norm.

Wasters cannot be used to calculate firing losses at ancient manufacturing sites because the number of firings and successfully fired vessels are indeterminable. It is possible, however, to calculate relative losses for various categories by sorting sherds and damaged vessels according to shape and/or function, such as bowls, cookpots, etc. A high frequency of a particular form, especially if it exhibits a consistent type of damage, may imply problems in its manufacture. Examining the duration of production of this form may help to explain a later modification offering less manufacturing difficulties.

When the range of maximum temperatures is highly variable throughout a setting, the most common causes of firing loss are likely to be underfiring and overfiring. These produce several diagnostic types of damage.

Underfiring. For unglazed ware, the softness and friability of sherds is an indication of underfiring. If the clay minerals have not decomposed, an underfired vessel or sherd is unlikely to be preserved except in very dry conditions because contact with moisture will cause it to slake and lose its shape. If sherds from dry sites are suspected to have been heated below the temperature of decomposition, this can be checked by breaking off a small piece and placing it in water. The suspicion is confirmed if the piece breaks down or slakes and falls apart. The time necessary for this to occur varies between one hour and one day. This test should be made whenever very soft friable pottery is encountered.

Extreme underfiring can be confirmed using X-ray diffraction, which will reveal whether the crystalline structure of the clay minerals is preserved. However, some clay minerals, especially montmorillonite, show up in X-ray diffraction scans because they can rehydrate in normally fired ware that has been exposed to moisture over a long period (Searle and Grimshaw 1959:264, 527, 650; Grim 1962:95).

Underfiring is detected on glazed ware by observing the glaze rather than the body. Underfired glazes have a dull, "earthy" or non-vitreous luster, which is especially evident when compared with a normally fired example. Underfired vessels are much less likely to be found in waster dumps than overfired ones because they can be salvaged by refiring.

Overfiring. Overfiring usually causes bloating or warping sufficient to damage the vessel. Extreme bloating is expressed by extensive thickening of the wall, with large pores extensively developed. Bloating produces spherical or rounded voids, whereas those attributable to organic material in the clay (apart from some seeds) generally retain the shape of the former inclusion. Extensive bloating is invariably associated with fusion or excessive vitrification of the body, either locally or over the whole vessel. The affected portion becomes pyroplastic and warps or squats, distorting the intended shape.

The usual form of distortion caused by mild overfiring is warping. The rim sags or warps into a characteristic shape when viewed from the side (Fig. 94). With glazed ware, this is associated with evidence of overfiring of the glaze. With unglazed ware, care must be taken not to confuse warping from overfiring with other causes of distortion. Warping is more likely to occur with high-fired wares (firing temperature above about 1100°C) and may result from localized pressure. Examples include vessels set on a flat surface containing a grain of grit, flat-bottomed vessels set on an uneven surface, and vessels placed on top of one another so that only point contact exists. In the first two situations, the rim would be expected to show warping from the horizontal plane; in the third, the wall would have a concave "dent" and the general shape might be distorted (Fig. 96).

With increasing overfiring, more glass forms and vessels begin to squat; if heating continues, they will collapse. The ultimate stage of overfiring is complete fusion, in which vessels fuse to one another and to the floor or shelves of the kiln. If found in a waster dump, this mass is easy to identify.

There is little point in attempting to determine the exact time, temperature, and atmosphere conditions of overfiring because so many other variables are involved and because extreme overfiring is a localized phenomenon, not only within a kiln but also within a single vessel (Fig. 97).

Rate of Heating and Cooling. Wasters can be produced by variations in the rate of heating or cooling during firing. Slower rates than normal waste fuel and labor, and with glazed ware may produce unusual effects, but this does not necessarily make the vessels unusable. Heating or cooling too quickly produces characteristic types of cracking and fracture. The four principal kinds are: firecracks, star-shaped cracks, spalling, and dunting cracks.

Firecracks. A network of fine cracks is formed on the surface, sometimes with a hexagonal structure (Fig. 98). In extreme cases, the cracks link and extend over large areas; they may even penetrate the wall, particularly if it has been weakened before firing by deeply incised decoration (Fig. 99). Firecracks form when heating is too rapid prior to decomposition of the clay minerals, mainly between about 300 and 500°C.

Star-shaped cracks. A series of crack lines radiates from a common center. The diameter of a "star" seldom exceeds one centimeter. They occur mainly on the exterior surface. A large mineral grain, commonly quartz, may protrude slightly at the center

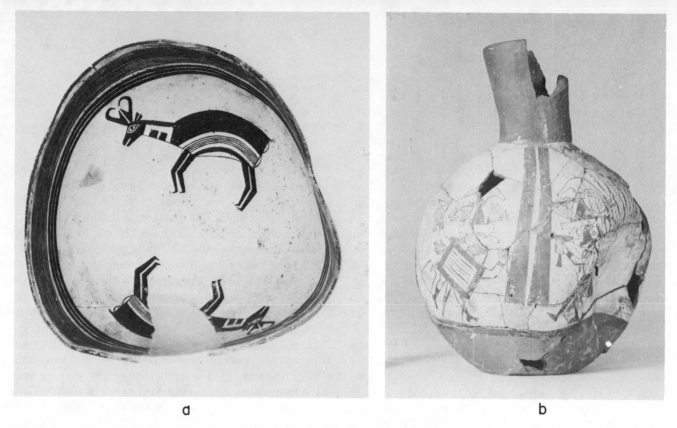

Fig. 96. Distortions of the wall contour during firing. **a,** Mimbres bowl. **b,** Mochica jar.

Fig. 97. Localized overfiring. **a,** Only the top of the vessel, which was resting on its side during firing, has been distorted. **b,** One whole side of a drum has completely fused and flowed, whereas the opposite side has fired normally.

Fig. 98. Firecracking and dunting cracks. **a,** Bowl with a network of superficial cracks especially prominent at the right and a vertical dunting crack at the left. **b,** Fine cracks on the center of the interior and dunting cracks on the rim.

Fig. 99. Firecracking extending through the wall. Note that most begin where the wall has been weakened by deep incisions. Papua New Guinea.

Fig. 100. Star-shaped cracks radiating from large inclusions. **a,** Plain surface. **b,** White-slipped surface.

(Fig. 100). The cracks are caused by expansion of the mineral grain within a densely packed fabric during rapid heating. If the grain is quartz, the cracking probably occurs at the quartz inversion temperature (573°C). This type of crack should not be confused with the defect in glazed ware known as "crow's feet" (Hamer 1975:84).

Spalling. When a vessel is heated too quickly, moisture in the center of the wall expands and causes large lens-shaped pieces about half the thickness of the wall to separate away (Fig. 91). Occasionally, a circular segment will penetrate through the wall. This phenomenon occurs at temperatures up to about 300°C and is especially likely if the walls are thick and not dried completely before firing.

Dunting Cracks. When a vessel is cooled very rapidly, heat is lost most quickly from the rim; this cooling places the rim in tension and a dunting crack may form. The crack is wider at the rim than at its lower end (Figs. 98 a, 101). Another common dunting crack consists of a series of concentric cracks around the vessel, joined by vertical fractures (Fig. 102). Dunting cracks can also form during heating. A fuller discussion is provided by Hamer (1975:107).

Lime Spalling. This fault is caused by the presence of grains of calcium carbonate (shell, coral, crystalline calcite or limestone) and can develop when the temperature is high enough to decompose the calcium carbonate, forming calcium oxide. Weeks or months after firing, the calcium oxide can combine with water vapor to form calcium hydroxide, which has a larger volume. The formation of calcium hydroxide thus exerts pressure on the fabric, which commonly causes a cone-shaped piece to flake or spall from the wall leaving a white powdery grain at the apex (Fig. 93). A drop of dilute hydrochloric acid placed on this white powder will cause vigorous effervescence.

In ancient sherds, the original spalling has been completed, but the process can be restarted by heating samples to about 850°C. This serves as an additional check that calcium carbonate is responsible for pitting and spalling of the surface. If the grains are larger than about 1 mm, reheating experiments should not be done with valuable specimens or should be confined to temperatures below about 750°C to prevent loss of the specimen from hydration of the CaO.

Accidents. In the firing of glazed ware, some wasters result from accidents. Props or shelves can break, causing part of the setting to collapse and molten glaze to fuse to shelves, the wall of the kiln, and other vessels. In mild cases, the vessels may be broken away by tapping with a stick, leaving signs of the fusing in the form of missing areas of glaze and sharp-edged fracture, which may or may not be ground smooth.

Another frequent form of damage in glaze kilns results from fragments of the roof falling onto and fusing to the vessels. These are normally deposited on the top of the vessel and on the interior of bowls. Old kilns can accumulate a layer of glaze, especially when lead or salt glazes are used, and this can also fuse and drip during firing producing a splash of glaze that contrasts with the general appearance of the surface of the vessel.

Very fusible glazes can flow down the sides of a vessel during firing and, in extremes, flow completely from the vessel, firmly fusing it to its support. If the glaze does not flow off completely, it can accumulate in a thick roll at its lower margin. This is observed on many Chinese stoneware bowls of the Sung Dynasty. The direction of flow can be used to reconstruct the position of the vessel during firing.

Firing Cores

When a sherd is freshly broken, the cross section can show a "core" distinct in color from the surface

_____ 10 CM

10 CM.
4 IN.

Fig. 101. Dunting cracks. **a,** Plain vessel. **b,** Painted bowl.

Fig. 102. Dunting cracks extending down from the rim and
horizontally around the circumference.

and subsurface zones. In pottery fired below about
1000°C, core effects are due primarily to removal of
carbon by oxidation or deposition of carbon from a
reducing atmosphere. Because these reactions are related to temperature, core effects are indicators of the
atmosphere and temperature of firing.

In the four cases examined below, the occurrence
of organic material is one variable and the firing atmosphere is the other.

**Atmosphere Oxidizing, Organic Material Ab-
sent.** Vessels fired under fully oxidizing conditions and
made from materials containing no organic matter will
have a cross section of uniform color (Figs. 103, 104-
1). The color of the surface may vary if one part of the
vessel was in direct contact with the flame and other
parts were sheltered. In this case, temperature differences rather than atmosphere variation produce the
differences in color.

**Atmosphere Oxidizing, Organic Material
Present.** Clays may contain up to 20 percent organic

materials, although less than 10 percent is typical. Pottery fired in oxidizing conditions with incomplete oxidation of the carbon will have a gray or black core,
distinct from the color of the surface or immediate
subsurface. The margins of the core will be diffuse and
grade into the surface color (Fig. 104-3, 4). This core
structure is probably typical of most unglazed pottery,
whether fired in the open or in a kiln. The relative
proportions of core and surface layers can vary within
one vessel, so interpretations of firing conditions
should not be made from this ratio alone.

**Atmosphere Reducing or Neutral, Organic Ma-
terial Absent.** Black pottery has been and still is
produced in many parts of the world by carbon deposition. In open firings, access of air must be completely
prevented by covering the parts of the ware to be blackened with ash, sawdust, grass or other similar material. This is done after the vessels have reached
maximum temperature and are beginning to cool. In
kilns, intentional blackening is also done during cooling. Most carbon deposition occurs during the first few
minutes after air is closed off. The reason for continu-
ing to exclude air is to prevent the carbon from being
reoxidized.

If organics were not present in the clay, the carbon deposition will not extend to the center of the
cross section if the pores are very fine, although it may
if they are coarse. Fine clays may show a "reverse
core" effect, the center being reddish and the surface

Fig. 103. Cross section of a sherd with a fine-textured fabric and completely oxidized firing.

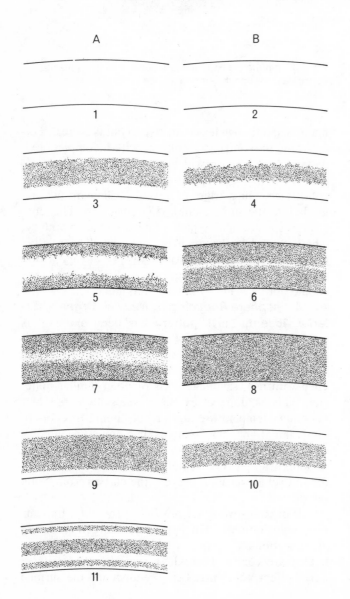

A   B

1   2
3   4
5   6
7   8
9   10
11

Fig. 104. Stylized cross sections comparing variations in the appearance of firing cores in fine-textured clays (Column **A**) and coarse-textured clays (Column **B**). **1,** Oxidized, organics not originally present; no core. **2,** Oxidized, organics may or may not have been originally present; no core. **3–4,** Oxidized, organics originally present; diffuse core margins. **5,** Reduced, organics not originally present; diffuse core margin. **6,** Reduced, organics not originally present; black or gray may extend completely through the wall leaving no "core." **7,** Reduced, organics originally present; diffuse core margin. **8,** Reduced, organics may or may not have been originally present; no core. **9–10,** Reduced, cooled rapidly in air; sharp core margin. **11,** Reduced, cooled rapidly in air, reduced again, cooled rapidly in air again; sharp core margins, "double core."

layer black. A diffuse margin separates the core from the outer layer (Fig. 104-5, 6). This effect can also be produced if completely oxidized vessels are used for cooking and the outer surface is blackened by reducing gases from the cooking fire. Consequently, sherds from such vessels should not be used in studies aimed at reconstructing firing conditions.

Atmosphere Reducing, Organic Material Present. If a body originally contained organic material and was exposed to a reducing atmosphere throughout firing, the freshly broken cross section will be gray or black throughout regardless of whether the texture is coarse or fine (Fig. 104-7, 8). There may be a core effect, generally with the center being lighter gray than the exterior surface; alternatively, the center may be black and the exterior gray.

Effects of Cooling Methods. In the four cases considered above, it was assumed that the same atmosphere prevailed throughout heating and cooling. In

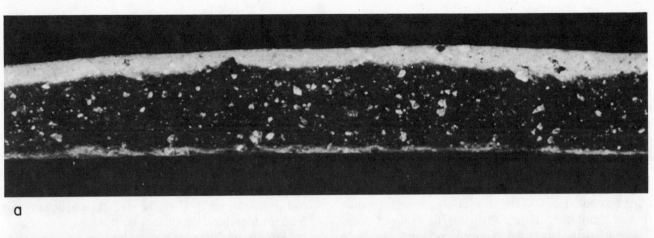

Fig. 105. Cross sections showing firing effects. **a,** Fine-textured clay, sharp core margins. The vessel was reduced, then cooled rapidly in air. The oxidized zone is wider on the exterior, indicating the interior was either cooled more quickly or (more likely) was less accessible to air. **b,** Coarse-textured clay, diffuse core margins. The vessel was reduced, then cooled slowly in air.

practice, the atmosphere during cooling may be different than during heating. The rate of cooling can contribute markedly to the removal or deposition of carbon.

In open firing, two methods of cooling have been observed among traditional potters. In one, the vessel is left in the setting. In this situation, the outer surfaces and possibly also the inner surfaces will almost certainly be covered with ash, unburned charcoal, and unburned fuel. The atmosphere will therefore be non-oxidizing. Provided this atmosphere is maintained

until the temperature drops to about 350°C, the surfaces will be blackened by deposition of carbon. If deposition occurred earlier during firing, the blackened surfaces will be maintained.

The second alternative is to remove the vessel and allow it to cool in air. In this case, the surface will be oxidized during cooling. This has no effect if the pottery is already oxidized. If it was originally reduced and blackened by carbon deposition, a thin layer of "natural" clay color will form adjacent to the surface (Figs. 104-9, 10; 105). This layer will have a very sharp interior margin. With fine-pored clays, it may be only a millimeter wide and consequently might be misidentified as a slip. With coarser-pored clays, the layer will be thicker, but the sharply defined internal margin remains characteristic. The presence of this sharply defined oxidized zone adjacent to the surface is diagnostic of open firing followed by very rapid cooling in air.

It is difficult or impossible to produce a very sharply defined oxidized surface layer in a kiln. Kilns must be cooled slowly and slow cooling causes formation of a broader, more diffuse-edged, oxidized zone adjacent to the surface. Reduced cooling in kilns is also slow and the surfaces of vessels are blackened by carbon deposition.

Effects of Changing Atmospheres.
A cross section implying a succession of oxidizing and reducing atmospheres during firing is shown in Figure 104-11. Assuming an open firing, the stages would have been:

(1) Heating under reducing or non-oxidizing conditions, preserving a dark core of unburned organics.

(2) Oxidizing above about 600°C, removing organics adjacent to the surfaces but leaving the core unaffected.

(3) Reducing for a time sufficient for carbon deposition to blacken the surface but not to eliminate the oxidized zone.

(4) Removing the vessel from the fire and allowing it to cool rapidly in air so only the surface layer (about 1 mm thick) is oxidized.

A sherd showing a similar cross section can be interpreted as having been exposed to this sequence of conditions.

Specialized Studies.
The cases discussed above are generalized to emphasize the main principles involved and do not incorporate all the potential effects of organic material and carbon deposition. The utility of core and surface deposition effects for reconstructing firing procedures can be more fully exploited by controlled experiments (Matson 1963; Hodges 1962). Samples of clays likely to have been used by ancient potters can be fired under a variety of controlled conditions to produce standards for interpreting variations in the archeological ceramics.

Duma and Lengyel (1970) suggest that the electron microscope can be used to differentiate carbon deposited during firing from that derived from organic inclusions. This distinction cannot be made using optical microscopy or chemical analysis. Again, samples prepared under controlled conditions would serve as standards.

Mineralogy

Because minerals decompose, fuse, and change their crystalline structures at consistent temperatures, the mineralogy of a sherd can give an indication of the conditions of firing. The temperature and, in some cases, the original atmosphere can be inferred from thin sections. Rigby (1953) provides the data for identifying minerals in thin sections of ceramics. X-ray diffraction can be used when the size of inclusions is too small for identification in thin sections.

Effects of Temperature.
Although clay minerals decompose during firing, other minerals are present as inclusions. Since the temperatures of decomposition are known, the minerals remaining unaltered provide an indication of the maximum firing temperature.

Some minerals are formed only at high temperatures. Mullite, for example, does not begin to crystallize below about 950°C; its presence in traditional pottery bodies thus implies that the original temperature of firing exceeded this minimum.

Iron exists within the crystal structure of many minerals and is released when their structure breaks down. It reacts with chlorides at about 1000°C, forming iron chlorides, which are volatile and lighten the color by their dissipation (Zakharikov et al 1961). Reactions between iron, calcium, and silica are responsible for a sequence of changes in color that are correlated with temperature and atmosphere (Table 2; Matson 1971).

Effects of Atmosphere.
Iron oxides are indicators of firing atmosphere. In oxidizing atmospheres, Fe_2O_3 is produced, which is orange, red or brown. In reducing atmospheres above about 900°C, FeO or Fe_3O_3 are formed, which are gray or black. These states can be differentiated using Mossbauer spectroscopy (Hess and Perlman 1974).

Thermal Expansion

When fired pottery is heated, it expands until its original firing temperature is reached. If cooled from this temperature, it reverts to its original dimensions. If the original temperature is exceeded, however, it will begin to shrink. The firing temperature of ancient pottery can thus be estimated by establishing the point at which expansion ceases and contraction begins using a dilatometer. This instrument combines a means of heating a specimen and accurately recording temperature with a very sensitive device for measuring length (and hence expansion or contraction). A plotting device attached to the instrument produces a graph showing expansion as a function of temperature. Use of thermal expansion to assess original firing temperatures has been discussed by Roberts (1960) and Tite (1969).

There are several kinds of limitations on the use of this technique for determining the firing temperatures of ancient pottery:

(1) The maximum temperature measurable by most dilatometers is about 1000°C, so pottery fired to a higher temperature cannot be analyzed.

(2) The length and thickness requirements restrict availability of samples for analysis. For example, the apparatus used by Roberts (1960) employs samples 2.5 × 1.0 × 1.0 cm, meaning that only sherds thicker than 1.0 cm could be analyzed. Other apparatus, used in my unpublished studies, requires samples 10 cm long and at least 5 mm thick. These can be obtained only from large vessels. Since large vessels may be fired differently than small ones, the results must be interpreted with caution.

(3) The composition of some wares may cause misleading results. The behavior of calcium carbonate variants, which decompose in the range of the original firing temperatures, and hydrous micas are examples. Impurities incorporated in the pores during burial can also affect the results, as can moisture absorbed during burial.

(4) The rate at which the samples are heated in the dilatometer may be different from the original rate, and corrections must be applied for accurate results.

Color

The colors of pottery immediately after firing can be altered or masked by processes occurring during the subsequent history of the vessel. The surface color is most likely to change, the subsurface color next, and the core least. In descriptions, it is essential to indicate whether the surface, subsurface or core color is being described. If these vary, all three should be reported. The color is usually determined by comparing specimens with standards provided by the Munsell Soil Color Charts.

A classification based on color alone is culturally and technologically meaningless because pottery from the same tradition, the same potter, the same firing, and even the same vessel can vary considerably (Fig. 109). Color can provide useful information, however, if correlated with other attributes. One approach is to subdivide an assemblage according to attributes of shape, decoration, materials, forming, and firing, and then determine whether there is a correlation between any of these groups and color. If not, the explanation may be provided by modification during use or post-use history, or variations in firing conditions. The latter alternative is unlikely if other physical properties indicate that firing conditions were relatively constant.

The second approach is experimental and involves refiring samples from the assemblage being studied under a range of controlled conditions and observing the colors produced. For maximum utility, sherds selected should be the lowest fired and large enough to be broken into 8 or 10 pieces. One is kept as a record of the original color and each of the others is fired to a different temperature, half under oxidizing and half under reducing (not carbon deposition) conditions. Temperature increments of 100°C are convenient. Comparing the colors of the refired pieces with the sherds in the original assemblage will establish which have changed most during use, disposal or burial. Caution should be exercised in inferring original firing temperatures from these comparisons, however, unless other kinds of evidence are available.

If samples of clay have been collected near the site, these should be wetted to a plastic condition, kneaded to homogeneity, dried, and fired to a range of temperatures in oxidizing and reducing atmospheres. The colors produced can be compared with those of the excavated pottery. This exercise is obviously more significant if the sources of materials used by ancient potters are known and the samples of clay are taken from these sources.

The common colors of pottery and the range of firing conditions responsible for them have been summarized by Shepard (1968:106).

Variations on Newly Fired Pottery. Three main classes of color are observable on newly fired pottery: surface color, subsurface color, and core color.

Surface color or colors reflect the mineralogical content of the clay as modified by firing treatment, coatings (e.g., slips, pigments, efflorescence of soluble salts), and finishing techniques (e.g., burnishing, polishing).

Subsurface color, revealed by scraping the surface sufficiently to remove all deposits, is also dependent on mineralogy and firing treatment. The subsurface color can be thought of as the "natural" fired color of the body.

Core color reflects the presence or absence of a difference in firing conditions at the surface and the center of the wall.

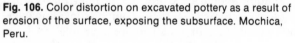

Fig. 106. Color distortion on excavated pottery as a result of erosion of the surface, exposing the subsurface. Mochica, Peru.

Fig. 107. Color distortion on excavated pottery as a consequence of exposure to distinct depositional conditions. Shepard Cord-marked, Maryland.

Variations on Excavated Pottery. The colors of excavated pottery have usually been modified from those of the newly fired vessel. The surface is more likely to have changed, making it least reliable as an indicator of firing conditions. Among the factors responsible for "discoloration" are:

(1) Mechanical effects, such as erosion (Fig. 106) and abrasion ("use wear"), which change the light reflectance of the surface and hence the apparent color. The original color of the surface gives way to the subsurface color as wear progresses.

(2) Deposits during use, such as staining by contents, accumulation from contents, staining from the environment (such as smoke-filled rooms), build-up of carbon during heating on an open fire, and adherence of material during partial burial while in use (particularly large storage and water jars).

(3) Post-usage treatment, including secondary use (such as incorporation as a building material) and disposal practices (Fig. 107). Again, surface deposits accumulate.

(4) Burial deposit, including adhesion of soil, precipitation from chemicals in percolating water, and effects of bacterial and other organic activity (Fig. 108). These deposits are the first observed by archeologists as the sherds are excavated and the most likely to be modified during washing, drying, and transport.

(5) Leaching during burial. Iron can be dissolved from pottery by acidic ground water, causing the color to become progressively lighter with time. Calcium carbonate is also readily dissolved by acids and its removal can alter color especially if the particles are very fine.

Although it is far more difficult for solid material to penetrate into the core, soluble substances may be introduced into the pores while in solution and remain when the moisture evaporates. Some leaching may also occur if acidic ground water has access to the subsurface. In general, however, the color of the core is unlikely to be affected by processes other than heating.

Variations on Single Vessels. The presence on a single vessel of a range of colors that includes (in Munsell color notation) reddish brown, light red, pink, pale yellow, yellow, white, olive-brown olive, and dark olive suggests that the original body contained calcareous minerals and salts. Pottery incorporating these materials commonly has a surface "skin" distinct in color from the subsurface and a range of hues that are a function of firing, changing consistently with temperature if materials, firing rates, and atmospheres are constant. This combination is commonly encountered in the Near East.

Differential access to air during firing and cooling can cause considerable variation in the surface color over a single vessel. Abrupt contrasts are produced by "fire clouding," or the formation of black areas (Fig. 109).

Fig. 108. Fine dark-blue lines caused by contact with roots interfere with the painted design. Napo culture, eastern Ecuador.

Fig. 109. Color variation on a single vessel resulting from uneven distribution of air during firing. Kintiel Ruin, Arizona.

Hardness

In general, everything else being equal, the hardness of pottery increases with firing temperature. In practice, everything else is never equal. Slips and organic coatings may or may not be applied, variations in salinity may create irregular deposits, and nonuniform conditions of disposal can cause differential weathering. Because the fabric is usually heterogeneous because of the uneven distribution of minerals, hardness may also differ according to which part of a sherd is tested. The range of variation produced by such factors may exceed that resulting from the original conditions of firing. Measurements by different individuals using the Moh mineral hardness scale are also subject to disagreement. All these factors reduce the utility of "scratch hardness" as a criterion for inferring ancient firing practices, although it may be useful for estimating the general level of technology represented by an archeological ceramic complex.

The variation in surface scratch hardness among vessels made by traditional potters has seldom been studied. Matson (1971) examined the relationship between scratch hardness and firing temperature for Seleucia clays. When firing temperature was below 900°C, predictions based on hardness had an accuracy of ± 200°C. Between 900° and 1170°C, accuracy improved to ± 100°C. These results led Matson (1971:70) to conclude that "differences in scratch hardness are not of diagnostic value in estimating firing temperature" for the materials he studied. If more studies of

this kind were done, it might be possible to establish closer correlations between hardness, rate and temperature of firing, and materials used.

Fracture

This property has not been used systematically for estimating firing temperatures. Like hardness, it is simple to evaluate but imprecise. General conclusions can be drawn by attempting to break a sherd with fingers or pliers. If it breaks easily with a friable edge, it was probably fired below about 750°C. If it is brittle and very difficult to break even with pliers, and the fractured surface is conchoidal with a "glassy" appearance, the firing temperature was at least 1100°C. An intermediate type of fracture, with an uneven edge characterized by irregular elevations and depressions, can represent any temperature between about 700° and 1200°C. The principal value of observing fracture is to isolate "unusual" sherds for further study.

Porosity

The relationship between firing temperature and apparent porosity for two hypothetical bodies is shown in Figure 110. As firing progresses, water and combustible or volatile constituents are driven off, causing apparent porosity to increase until point D, where decomposition of the clay minerals is complete. It then remains relatively constant until point V, when vit-

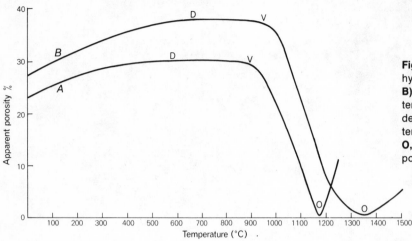

Fig. 110. Apparent porosity of two hypothetical typical clay bodies (**A and B**) as a function of temperature. **D,** temperature at which clay-mineral decomposition is complete. **V,** temperature at which vitrification begins. **O,** temperature at which apparent porosity reaches zero.

rification begins. As glass forms, pores are sealed gradually and apparent porosity decreases. This decrease continues until the temperature is high enough that the glass becomes fluid and the gas in the sealed pores expands, causing bloating. If temperature continues to increase, the fabric becomes distorted and fractured, and apparent porosity again begins to increase.

Unfortunately, most ancient and traditional unglazed pottery is fired to temperatures between points D and V, where apparent porosity is stable. Between the beginning of vitrification (V) and minimum apparent porosity (O), there is definite covariation between temperature and apparent porosity. Its utility for estimating firing temperatures from sherds is diminished, however, by the narrow range (± 100°C), which is less than the variation within most kilns (temperatures above 1000°C are unlikely to be reached in open firings). Confusion may arise in interpreting specimens fired above minimum porosity to the point of bloating.

In the example (Fig. 110 A), an apparent porosity of 10 percent can be equivalent to a firing temperature of either 1100° or 1240°C. This ambiguity is likely to occur only with high-fired wares, such as stonewares and porcelains.

Taking all this into account, it is obvious that apparent porosity rarely provides useful indications of original firing temperature. If the technique is to be attempted, samples of clays known to have been used must be fired to a range of temperatures to provide standards with which the sherds can be compared. This involves producing a graph like Figure 110, showing the relationship between firing temperature and apparent porosity.

An indication of the rate of temperature rise during the original firing may be obtainable from pore-size distribution (Sanders 1973). As with determinations of apparent porosity, however, these results may be distorted by deposition of material in the pores of the pottery during burial.

7 Applications of Technological Approaches

The preceding chapters describe attributes and techniques for reconstructing part or all of the sequence of events in the production of pottery. This chapter applies some of the procedures to real archeological situations. The following summaries are not intended as general models, but as examples of how I have approached two kinds of problems: (1) a general technological study of pottery excavated on Motupore Island in Papua New Guinea and (2) the reconstruction of forming techniques used to make Late Bronze Age storage jars excavated in Palestine.

CASE 1: ANALYZING THE POTTERY FROM MOTUPORE ISLAND, PAPUA NEW GUINEA

The Site

The site on which this case study focuses is on Motupore Island in Bootless Bay, 15 km east of Port Moresby, the administrative capital of Papua New Guinea. Motupore Island is a steep-sided, submerged hilltop with a sandspit about 1.6 hectares in extent at its northwest tip (Fig. 111). This sandspit creates a small sheltered bay and constitutes the only flat land on the island. It also provides the only evidence of prehistoric habitation.

At the time of European contact, Bootless Bay was a frontier between the Eastern and Western Motu. The last Western Motu village was (and still is) at the western end of the bay and the last Eastern Motu village was (and is now) at the eastern end of the bay. The central area is not permanently occupied and is fished mainly by Eastern Motu. Numerous sites have been encountered around the bay (Fig. 112). They suggest a build-up of population beginning about 500 years ago, followed by a rapid depopulation about 300 years ago (Allen, pers. commun.).

A series of radiocarbon dates, coupled with other archeological evidence, suggests that the site was continuously occupied between about 800 and 300 years ago by a single group. These people are considered by the excavator to have arrived at the island adapted to an extreme maritime subsistence pattern and with a developed pottery technology (Allen 1977a). They appear to have established trading relations with inland dwellers soon after their arrival.

The site is rich in material remains, including burials, post-holes, faunal remains, stone and shell artifacts, and pottery. Although less than two percent of the area has been excavated, more than 800,000 sherds have been recovered. Midden deposits in one part of the site are more than 4 meters deep, with pottery comprising the bulk of the accumulation.

Several specialists are analyzing various categories of material, including faunal remains and human burials. The study of the pottery is also still in process, so the following discussion presents initial results rather than final conclusions. As such, it may provide the reader with more insight into how at least one ceramic technologist proceeds. It should be noted that I did not become involved in the project until after excavations were completed. Some differences in the approach to sampling of materials that might have resulted from earlier collaboration will be mentioned where appropriate.

Fig. 111. Looking across the northwest tip of Motupore Island toward the mainland coast of Papua New Guinea. An archeological site is located on the flat area.

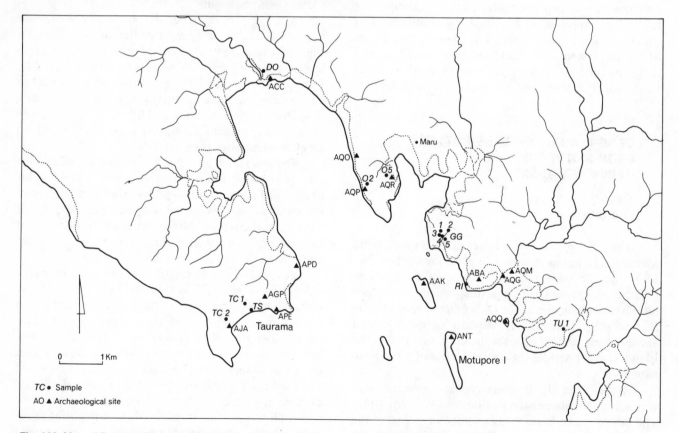

Fig. 112. Map of Bootless Bay, showing the locations of archeological sites (triangles) and sources of raw materials for making pottery (circles).

The Research Problems

The pottery available for study consisted of a sample from the 800,000 sherds excavated. The archeologists saved all stylistically distinctive sherds, such as rims and sherds with painted or plastic decoration. The remainder was counted and weighed, and then dumped on a suitable spot away from the excavations.

Morphologically, the sherds represented two basic shapes: (1) globular jars with restricted necks and everted to vertical rims, corresponding in general to water, cooking, and storage vessels recorded ethnographically, and (2) open bowls, the use of which is also noted in ethnographic accounts.

A change in decoration was evident through time. Painted globular vessels were relatively common in the lower levels, but disappeared from the assemblage late in the occupation. Shell-impressed and combed decoration were also early. Later vessels were incised or impressed, but not with a shell (Fig. 113).

Stylistically, the archeological pottery is related to modern or ethnographically recorded Motu pottery. Groupings obtained by the initial typological studies were inadequate for differentiating the Motupore ceramics from other sites in the vicinity or even within larger cultural units. Obviously, efforts to identify the sources of vessels could not employ stylistic criteria (Rye and Allen 1976). Considering that the Motu traded some 30,000 vessels annually, this situation was not surprising (Allen 1977b:437–8).

A major aim of the technological analysis of the pottery was therefore to derive methods for differentiating pottery from different sources and identifying the sources. If distinctive trends could be discerned in materials used during occupation of the site, these would be helpful. Isolation of changes in techniques and process sequences was another aim because it seemed unlikely that they would be identical at other sites.

Another important problem was to determine whether pottery production became increasingly specialized. It has been suggested that long-distance trading is relatively recent on the south Papuan coast (Allen 1977a:398). Since pottery was a major item of trade, increasingly localized specialization would be circumstantial evidence of involvement. This evidence could be sought in aspects of pottery production such as raw materials (range of materials used decreasing with time), forming techniques (range of techniques narrowing and process sequences simplifying), firing (techniques increasingly standardized), and types of vessels (number of forms decreasing and standardization increasing). Quantification of these factors would add substantially to the evidence for simplification in decoration, which is readily observable but difficult to measure and potentially attributable to cultural influences other than increasing trading activity.

To recognize possible changes, it was necessary to establish the general technological characteristics of the pottery from the Motupore site. This initial stage of the research is the main focus of this case study.

Studies of Materials

Four main lines of inquiry have been followed and completed: (1) a field survey of all sources of raw materials in the Bootless Bay area; (2) an evaluation of the relative suitability of materials from the sources for making pottery; (3) a general investigation of the effects of using shell (or calcite) as temper, and (4) a mineralogical study of sherds from Motupore and nearby sites.

Field Survey. The attempt to identify the origins of the pottery at the Motupore site required samples from the local clay deposits so the mineralogical composition of the sherds could be compared with that of the local raw materials. Even if it proved relatively easy to determine which sources were exploited, it would also be of interest to know which were not used because this would allow assessing the criteria for selection.

It was decided to combine the search for materials with a search for additional habitation sites around Bootless Bay. Although some sites were known, no systematic survey or surface collections had been made. Comparison of the mineralogy of samples of sherds from each site might allow identification of manufacturing sites; if many sherds with a distinctive set of materials occurred at a site near the source of those materials and few occurred elsewhere, then it could be inferred that the pottery was manufactured at the site. Wasters and other evidence of manufacturing would support this conclusion.

Because of the short time available, the survey was limited to a strip about 200–300 meters wide along the shore. This was considered a reasonable restriction because ethnographic information indicated the Motu lived on the coast. Their gardens were also generally very close to the shore. The survey was conducted from a small boat, starting at one end of the bay and landing wherever possible. Extensive mangrove prevented access along a considerable portion of the

Fig. 113. Types of decoration on archeological pottery from Motupore Island. **a–b,** Painting. **c–d,** Shell impression and combing. **e,** Coarse incision. **f,** Applied coil with impressions.

coastline. This restriction on landing may have been similar during the time of occupation of Motupore Island, but this has not yet been confirmed. Narrow belts of mangrove (up to about 3 or 4 meters) are made passable by present-day inhabitants by annual clearing with an axe.

Thirteen archeological sites were discovered (Fig. 112). Between 30 and 100 sherds were collected from each new site, and were chosen to represent the range of color, body texture, wall thickness, and stylistic variation. Sherds were not collected from previously reported sites because these were available for examination.

Samples of sand were taken from all accessible occurrences. Apart from beach sand from the sandspit on Motupore Island, only three deposits were found: TS, DO, and R1. R1 consisted of fine black beach sand with most particles smaller than one millimeter in maximum dimension. The deposit was sampled by coring to a depth of about 30 cm at several points along and across the beach. The cores were mixed and quartered to give a sample of about 5 kilograms. A similar procedure was used for a similar deposit at Dogura (DO).

Sand from the Motupore beach and from Taurama (TS) was sampled using a different technique. Cores taken down to 1.5 meters showed that only a zone about 10 cm in maximum thickness provided sand fine enough for making pottery (particles smaller than about 5 mm). Shell fragments up to 70 cm across (from giant clams) occurred below this depth. The samples for study were consequently collected from the surface, mixed, and quartered to provide 5 kilograms from each location.

All the samples of clay (TC1, TC2, DO, O2, O5, Maru, GG1–5, and TU1) were taken by identical techniques. An auger was used to core to a depth of about 1.5 meters. Material from the surface that contained many roots and plant fragments was rejected. As the depth increased, the clay usually contained increasing amounts of coarse rock fragments. Below the point where these exceeded about 5 mm in maximum dimension, collecting ceased. The sample from the intermediate zone was reduced to about 5 kilograms after thorough mixing.

Field checks of workability were made at each deposit to assess the suitability of the clay for making pottery.

Temper. The presence of shell in the Motupore pottery raised several technological questions: (1) Considering that calcium carbonate in any form is troublesome, not only placing an upper limit on firing temperature but creating the danger that vessels may disintegrate soon after firing, why would potters use it? (2) Why have calcite and shell been used in many parts of the world specifically for cooking pots or other vessels heated during use? (3) How have the Papuan and other potters who use calcium carbonate prevented post-firing damage from the hydration of CaO?

It has been suggested that the enhancement of resistance to thermal shock makes calcite beneficial in vessels intended for cooking and heating (Rye 1976:116–7). The thermal expansion of calcite up to 600°C (which is the maximum temperature likely to be achieved in cooking fires) is very similar to that of average clays. Experiments comparing the thermal shock resistance given by various tempers, including calcite, are not yet complete.

If calcite (or shell) is a beneficial addition for cooking pots, how is it used successfully? Before any experimental work was started, it was noted in the literature on brickmaking that lime spalling, which constitutes destruction by hydration of CaO, could be counteracted by adding common salt (NaCl) to the clay before forming. Also, many Melanesian potters have been observed to use seawater to wet the clay for making pottery, suggesting it was the source of salts that inhibited post-firing damage of the vessels.

Two series of experimental mixtures were prepared, one using seawater and the other freshwater. Each consisted of clay and beach sand obtained by me from present-day Papuan coastal pottery-making centers. Mixtures at 5 percent intervals were prepared, ranging from 100 percent clay and no sand to 60 percent clay and 40 percent sand. Mixtures containing more than 40 percent sand had insufficient workability. Each mixture was formed into numerous small briquettes, one of which was fired to each 100°C interval between 650° and 1050°C. This embraces the potential range of Melanesian firing temperatures.

After firing, the briquettes were stored and left untouched for about two months so that any damage by post-firing hydration of CaO could be observed. The results varied for different combinations, but those made using seawater suffered damage that was less severe and restricted to a narrower range of temperature than those made with freshwater (Fig. 114). For example, 90 briquettes were made from materials obtained on or near Motupore Island. Of the 45 combinations prepared using salt water, 37 survived; of the 45 prepared using freshwater, only 14 remained undamaged two months after firing. Most of the post-

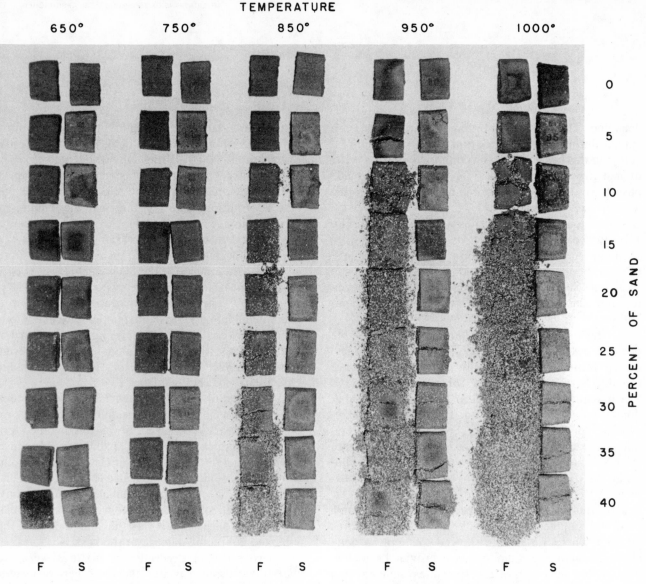

TEMPERATURE

| 650° | 750° | 850° | 950° | 1000° |

PERCENT OF SAND: 0, 5, 10, 15, 20, 25, 30, 35, 40

F S   F S   F S   F S   F S

Fig. 114. Briquettes prepared using standard proportions of clay and shell-rich sand, and fired to the same range of temperatures. In each pair, the row on the left was moistened with fresh water and the row on the right was moistened with sea water. Damage by post-firing hydration has been more severe for the samples prepared using fresh water and fired to higher temperatures.

firing damage occurred with the samples having high beach-sand content and fired to high temperatures.

In summary, to produce successful pottery using bodies with a high content of shell (beach sand), potters would need to: (1) wet the clay with seawater, (2) fire at relatively low temperatures, and (3) use relatively low proportions of beach sand to clay (For more details, see Rye 1976). The latter two constraints conflict with two general technological principles: (1) the highest possible firing temperatures should be used to maximize strength, and (2) as much shell as possible should be used for the thermal-shock resistance benefits of calcite to be realized. Obviously then, potters who used these materials were walking a technological tightrope and required a very high order of skill and understanding of materials to produce successful pot-

tery. That the Motupore potters succeeded is obvious. Not only could they satisfy their own needs for vessels; they also produced enough surplus to use them as a major item of trade.

Mineralogy. Studies of mineralogy were aimed at answering the following questions: (1) Was there a significant variation in the use of materials during occupation of the Motupore site? (2) Could the sources of the materials be identified? (3) Could it be established that any of the pottery from Motupore was manufactured at other sites around the bay?

The first procedure was to chose a sample of 800 sherds that represented all levels in the excavations at Motupore, but were randomly selected within each level. A small piece was broken from each sherd and attached to cards, as recommended in Chapter 4 (Fig.

30). An attempt to classify the pottery on the basis of mineralogy observed on the small pieces proved unsuccessful. Some inclusions, such as shell, were easily recognizable, but most minerals could not be identified under a binocular microscope with any certainty. This meant that thin sections would be needed for reliable identification.

For thin-section studies, about 50 sherds were chosen from the 800-sherd sample. Again, each level in the site was represented, but selection was otherwise random. About 5 sherds from each of the other habitation sites around Bootless Bay were also selected for thin-sectioning. These were all from surface collections because no excavation had been done. Two other kinds of samples were also judged relevant: (1) sherds from Boera, a modern coastal village some 25 km to the west, where pottery is still made, and (2) examples from surface collections from the Papuan Gulf, the major area to which Motu pottery was exported according to ethnographic accounts. Finally, a few sherds were selected from other excavated Papuan sites.

Thin sections were prepared from each sherd and from each sample of raw material obtained during the survey of Bootless Bay. The technique for the raw materials was different from that used for the pottery. For the sands, a layer of epoxy resin was smeared on a glass slide and the sand sprinkled over it uniformly. The section was then ground to the desired thickness. For the clays, each sample was dried and put in a plastic vial. Epoxy resin was poured into the vial, which was placed in a vacuum chamber to insure complete impregnation of the clay. The vial (and the sample it contained) was then cut in half vertically. A second adjacent parallel cut produced a thin slice of the material. This slice was affixed to a glass slide, ground, and prepared in the standard manner. These thin sections made it possible to compare the mineralogy of the pottery from various locations with the source materials available in the region.

The thin sections were analyzed by a geologist, who found that all the clays were similar mineralogically, as were all the sands except the black sand from R1. Quantitative rather than qualitative distinctions permitted three groups of pottery to be recognized (Worthing, pers. commun.):

Group A, made using materials from Boera

Group B, made using Bootless Bay clay and R1 beach sand

Group C, made using Bootless Bay clay and shell-rich sand from TS or Motupore Island

The presence of pottery from Boera in the Bootless Bay sites suggests prehistoric contact between the two areas. None of the pottery from Bootless Bay corresponded to that excavated on Yule Island, some 150 km to the northwest (Vanderwal 1973), or Mailu Island, over 250 km to the east (Irwin 1977), although extensive pottery-manufacturing industries existed at both locations.

The similarity between the clays and some sands from sources around Bootless Bay illustrates the situation noted in Chapter 4, where microscopic techniques are inadequate for differentiating sources of materials in an area of geological similarity. Variations found in the sherds that have been analyzed are within the range characteristic of individual sand and clay deposits. Nevertheless, some conclusions can be drawn from the thin-section studies. The results are consistent with the suggestion that the pottery was made on Motupore Island. It may also have been made near the R1 sand deposit; there are at least four sites near this deposit. Pottery could also have been made at the Taurama site (TS).

The thin-section studies make it possible to identify two potentially fruitful lines of further investigation. One is to study the trace-element composition of sherds and raw materials to determine whether sherds can be matched with specific deposits. This might indicate which deposits were actually used. At this stage, only the black beach sand from R1 can be designated as a definite source. Another possibility is to sort a larger sample of sherds into Groups A, B, and C either by preparing more thin sections or by establishing criteria for recognizing the groups from sample chips using a binocular microscope. The availability of a larger sample will make results statistically reliable for recognizing changes in use of materials through time.

Suitability. The behavior of various mixtures of clay and sand from Bootless Bay sources was studied to assess the technological constraints on their use for making pottery; that is, which were the "best" and which would have been most troublesome? The experimental results could be compared with the combinations of materials actually used as a basis for understanding their selection and possibly explaining changes through time.

Two properties of the materials were investigated: (1) the workability of clay-sand mixtures in the plastic state, and (2) the firing and post-firing behaviors of the mixtures. Samples collected from all sources of clay and sand during the survey were included in the study.

The first step was to examine the grit content and

Table 4. Experimental assessment of workability and firing behavior of raw materials from sources around Bootless Bay, Papua New Guinea.

Clays	Grit Content	Sands	Bodies (3)	% Sand for workable mixtures	Workability grading (4)	Samples with firing damage /45	Samples with post-firing hydration damage /45	Total successful combinations /45	Total successful combinations %
(Clay	plus	sand	= body)						
TC1		TS	T1	0- 40	B	14	26	16	35.5
TC2	Excess	TS	T2	40+	C/U	10	9	0	0
DO		DO	D1	15- 40	U	9	0	27	60.0
O2	Excess	MS	O1	5- 35	U	0	14	18	40.0
O5	Excess	MS	I1	15- 25	U	9	21	14	31.1
TU1		MS	U1	0- 20	U	0	10	22	48.9
TU1		R1	U2	0- 20	U	0	0	25	55.6
Maru		MS	M1	0- 40	B	17	12	22	48.9
Maru		R1	M2	0- 40	B	29	0	15	33.3
GG1		MS	G1	10- 30	U	0	10	20	44.4
GG2		MS	G2	10- 30	U	0	10	18	40.0
GG3		MS	G3	10- 30	U	0	9	22	48.9
GG4		MS	G4	10- 30	U	0	11	17	37.8
GG5		MS	G5	10- 30	U	0	13	20	44.4
GG1		R1	GR1	10- 30	U	0	0	25	55.6
GG2		R1	GR2	5- 30	U	0	0	30	66.7
GG3		R1	GR3	5- 30	U	5	0	37	82.2
GG4		R1	GR4	10- 30	U	0	0	25	55.6

(1) Some samples are included in both categories.

(2) Summary of grit content, workability, and firing behavior.

(3) Bodies (T1, T2, etc.) were obtained by mixing clays (TC1, TC2, etc.) with sands (TS, DO, etc.); for example, clay GG2 was mixed with sand R1 to give a series of 9 bodies, all designated GR2. For each specific mixture in the series, the clay/sand proportions varied by 5 percent, ranging from 100 percent clay/0 sand to 60 percent clay/40 percent sand.

(4) B = best combinations. U = usable combinations. C = unusable combinations. Total number of combinations = 45 (9 clay/sand mixtures × 5 firing temperatures)

dry strength of each sample of clay. The presence of coarse grit (inclusions larger than 5 mm) was an indication that the clay would have required handpicking to remove these particles. Such a clay would presumably be less desirable than one with fine grit that required no handpicking, other variables being equal.

Mixtures of clays and sands were then prepared. Each clay was mixed with one or two sands that occurred near the clay deposit. The mixtures represented increments of 5 percent between 60 and 100 percent clay (expressed alternatively as between 40 and 0 percent sand) and were prepared by weight. This resulted in 9 mixtures for each specific clay-sand combination.

The dry mixtures were moistened with sufficient seawater to bring them to a workable plastic condition and an assessment of workability was made by me, as a skilled potter, because no instruments adequately describe the suitability of clays for a range of plastic forming techniques. Each mixture was formed into a bar, which was cut to produce 5 briquettes. One of these was fired to each of the following temperatures: 650°, 750°, 850°, 950°, and 1050° C. Each briquette was inspected for firing damage (cracking, spalling) before being placed in a drawer and left for 2 months, during which it was examined periodically for damage from CaO hydration. The results of these experiments are summarized in Table 4.

Three clays (TC2, O2, and O5) had a relatively high content of large grit, which would require laborious handpicking to remove. As dug, they would be suitable only for making large thick-walled vessels, such as the sago storage jars used by the Motu.

The workability assessment indicated whether or not tempering would be required. Some clays had suitable workability without adding sand, although temper might be required to achieve suitable fired properties. These were TC1, a red clay that was workable at any sand concentration from 0 up to 40 percent; TU1, a clay workable at any sand concentration up to 40 percent; and Maru red clay, workable at any sand concentration up to 40 percent. All the other clays were unworkable without adding sand, so would require tempering.

Some briquettes were damaged during heating; these mixtures would be unsuitable for use in an open firing where the temperature rises rapidly. Some briquettes containing shell (added as beach sand) were damaged by post-firing hydration of CaO. Any vessel made from these mixtures would disintegrate a relatively short time after firing, unless fired within a narrow range of temperature. None of the mixtures containing black beach sand from R1 displayed hydration damage.

Forty-five combinations of materials and 5 firing temperatures were tested for each clay-sand mixture (9 different proportions, 5 firing temperatures). The number of usable combinations was determined by eliminating the bodies with unsuitable workability or exhibiting firing or post-firing damage (Table 4). The best all-around results were obtained mixing GG clays (from the mainland immediately adjacent to Motupore Island) with R1 sand. Body GR3, for example, had 82.2 percent usable combinations. Other bodies that produced high numbers of usable combinations were D1 (60.0 percent) and U2 (55.6 percent). All other bodies had less than 50 percent usable combinations. Significantly, the clays with best workability exhibited poor firing behavior.

Preliminary Interpretations. Various inferences can be drawn from these experiments, and predictive models of material usage can be developed.

From the technological point of view, the best materials are those offering the greatest chance of producing successful vessels. These are the materials insensitive to variations in proportions and to fluctuations in firing temperature. The experiments permit the materials to be ranked (Table 4) from GR3 (82.2 percent successful combinations) down to I1 (31.1 percent usable combinations). The best materials allow the greatest human error and require least sensitivity of control. The "worst" materials can be used only if very skilled control is exercised; otherwise, a large proportion of vessels would not survive for use or incorporation into the trading network so important to the Motu.

These data suggest the following hypotheses:

(1) If a large number of vessels were destined for trade, potters would tend to favor the materials likely to give the highest yield.

(2) When the area was first settled, they would be confronted with a new set of sources and would probably start off using relatively unsatisfactory materials. As the resources became better known, the potters would tend to employ the best materials and the best combinations of these materials.

(3) Similarly, if a particular clay required tempering, the potters would gradually discover the best clay-sand proportions. Conversely, if the clay could be used without tempering, even if they added temper at first, they would eventually simplify the procedure by eliminating it.

These predictions can be refined further. If, for example, bodies with shell temper are functionally more successful for cooking pots, it would be expected that the potters would eventually choose the best combination of a shelly sand and a clay. Thus, functional requirements can be fed into the model and predictions about functional restraints applied to the materials used.

Locational considerations can also be introduced. The best clay and the best sand, from the viewpoint of

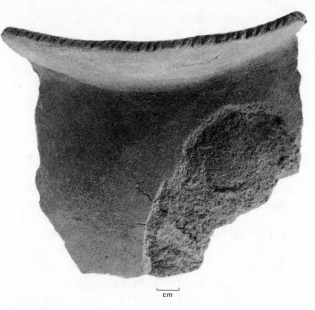

Fig. 115. Waster from the Motupore site, exhibiting low-temperature spalling implying too rapid heating during firing.

successfully produced vessels, both occur very near Motupore Island. It is not possible to infer that the people chose the location because it was accessible to excellent raw materials, but it can be assumed that if this advantage was not obvious initially it would soon be recognized. The GG clays are some 5 minutes by canoe from the island and about 100 meters from the landing point. Shelly beach sand occurs on the island and the very desirable black sand (R1) is a very short canoe trip away on the mainland.

There is some clear evidence that pottery was made on Motupore Island. The analysis of materials suggests this and the presence of wasters (Fig. 115) implies firing was done at the site. No wasters were found on nearby habitation sites (ABA, AQG, AQM). Large middens on the very small island AQQ have not been excavated, but the fact that this island is farther from the sources of raw materials makes its role as a manufacturing center unlikely.

Predictive models developed from experimental studies of materials must be tested against the archeological evidence. When the trace-element analyses of materials and sherds are completed, it will be possible to identify which materials were actually used. Changes through time can be observed and compared with the predictions. The predictions about tempering practices and possibly about the functions of vessels can be checked against the archeological remains. The results will help us begin to understand how the prehistoric potters of Bootless Bay exploited their resources.

Studies of Forming

An initial examination of the pottery assemblage from Motupore Island revealed two major obstacles to

Fig. 116. Sherd from the Motupore site with anvil impressions on the interior.

reconstructing forming process sequences. First, the sample of sherds was selected by the archeologist for stylistic and morphological attributes. This meant that sherds with unusual fracture patterns and other evidence of forming techniques were unlikely to be represented. The second and more serious difficulty was that most of the surface evidence of forming technique was difficult to interpret or had been obliterated by later operations, such as smoothing. As a result, it was decided to use X-rays. Different forming techniques should produce distinctive orientations of inclusions, which could be seen in the radiographs (Rye 1977).

Establishing Standards. The first stage of investigation was to collect pottery made by Papuan traditional potters and to record in detail their forming techniques. Vessels from collections made in Melanesia by other ethnographers were included. Since the forming techniques were known, the preferred orientation of inclusions revealed by the X-radiographs could be recognized, establishing a reference against which unknown archeological vessels could be compared. All the major forming techniques employed by traditional Melanesian potters were represented: drawing, coiling, beating, beater and anvil, pinching, and various methods of rotation.

Analyzing Sherds. Once the standards were available, a sample of about 300 sherds from the Motupore excavations was selected for initial examination. The main basis for selection was size; it was anticipated that larger sherds would facilitate recognition of preferred orientation and the initial trials showed this to be the case. Within the minimum size, an attempt was made to include sherds representing as many vessel shapes as possible. No distinction was made between rims, bases, and body sherds; all were considered equally relevant.

The sherds were sorted first according to thickness. All those on the same radiograph must have the same thickness to insure uniform exposure (Rye 1977:210). Film 14 by 17 inches (35.6 by 43.2 cm) was used, allowing up to 10 sherds to be exposed on each film.

The following information was tabulated for each sherd: site, level, and sherd number; particle-size distribution of inclusions; preferred orientation; fracture; visual description (including any attributes useful for inferring forming techniques), and a "diagnosis" of forming techniques. The techniques were arranged in a coherent process sequence for each sherd.

Groups of Process Sequences. Seven groups of process sequences were distinguished. The first two correlate with globular vessels; the others were used to produce open bowls. The groups have the following characteristics:

Group 1. Ball of clay drawn upward to form thick walls. Rim formed and smoothed by pinching combined with rotation. Walls and rounded base formed using a beater on the exterior opposed by the potter's other hand on the interior (fingertip impressions common on the interior walls).

Group 2. Same as Group 1, except that during beating an anvil was used on the interior to oppose the force of the blows (Fig. 116).

Group 3. Initial form produced by pinching. Rim formed and smoothed by pinching combined with rotation. Both surfaces scraped; interior then smoothed.

Group 4. Initial form produced by pinching. Rim formed and smoothed by pinching combined with rotation. Interior smoothed with fingers while clay still soft. Exterior scraped, then smoothed.

Group 5. Base pinched and drawn. Coils added to rim to increase height. Rim formed and smoothed by pinching combined with rotation. Interior and exterior smeared to bond coils, then smoothed.

Group 6. General form produced by coiling. Rim formed and smoothed by pinching and rotating between fingers. Interior and exterior scraped, then smoothed.

Group 7. General form produced by coiling. Rim formed and smoothed by pinching and rotating between fingers. Interior and exterior scraped; interior then smoothed.

Comparison of these groups shows that some are very similar. Groups 1 and 2 are identical except for the type of "anvil" used on the interior. Groups 3 and 4 are similar except for the extent of smoothing of the surface; Groups 6 and 7 are similarly related. Only Group 5 is distinct. The process sequences can therefore be combined into four major categories, with minor variations in three of these. The variations are important because they produce vessels with distinctive appearances; the difference between a scraped and a smoothed surface is visually very obvious.

The process sequence represented by Group 2 is identical to that I observed among present-day potters in Boera, some 30 km from Motupore. No observations have been made of techniques for making bowls. The bowl form so common in archeological sites appears to have been replaced by metal, plastic, and imported glazed ceramic vessels.

Chronological Differences. In order to establish whether changes in process sequences occurred through time in the Motupore site, the distributions of sherds in each group were examined by stratigraphic level. The frequencies of the sherds assigned to each group were calculated in two ways: (1) as a percentage of the total sherds in each level and (2) as a percentage of the sherds in the group (Table 5). In Level II, for example, 70 percent of the sherds belonged to Group 2; these represent 12.5 percent of the total number in Group 2.

Statistical analyses have not been attempted because of the inadequate size of the samples from some groups and stratigraphic levels, but some interpretations are suggested by the data:

Group 1 is much less common than Group 2, from which it differs only in the substitution of the potter's fingers for an anvil. This implies that Group 2 is the primary process sequence and Group 1 a minor variant.

Group 5, which represents a distinctive technique, contains only 3 sherds, which come from Levels I and III. Their rarity makes it desirable to include these sherds in studies of materials to determine if they were made elsewhere. If they were imported, the contact appears to have occurred late during the occupation, but the sample is too small for this to be certain.

If all the pottery in the sample was made on Motupore Island, the high frequency of Group 2 vessels might be interpreted as indicating this forming process was the most common. This inference is suspect, however, because larger vessels produce larger sherds and the sample was selected on the basis of sherd size, introducing a possible bias.

The data suggest the number of process sequences used to form bowls increased. If Groups 1 and 2 are combined and Groups 3-7 are combined, the ratios of bowls to jars remains relatively constant. Although the relative proportions of bowls and globular vessels do not change significantly, the relative distributions of bowl-forming process sequences change considerably. The Group 4 sequence is the predominant or only method in Levels VI through IX. Group 7 appears first in Level VII and Group 6 in Level VI. These patterns may indicate that potters were using more specialized techniques to produce bowls, but whether the differences in surface finish that distinguish related groups reflect changing esthetic tastes or functional specialization cannot be established at present.

These preliminary results are sufficient to demon-

Table 5. Relative frequencies of forming process sequence groups by stratigraphic level at the Motupore site, Papua New Guinea. N = size of sample; Arabic numbers = percentage of total in level; Italic numbers = percentage of total in group.

Forming Sequence Groups	Stratigraphic Levels										
	I	II	III	IV	V	VI	VII	VIII	IX	X	N
1	0	0	18.2	0	0	0	0	36.4	0	45.4	
	0	*0*	*4.4*	*0*	*0*	*0*	*0*	*6.8*	*0*	*35.7*	11
2	8.3	12.5	16.7	6.0	3.0	10.7	7.7	28.0	1.7	5.4	
	56.0	*70.0*	*62.2*	*76.9*	*83.3*	*69.2*	*65.0*	*79.7*	*60.0*	*64.3*	168
3	6.7	13.3	13.3	0	0	13.3	26.7	26.7	0	0	
	4.0	*6.7*	*4.4*	*0*	*0*	*7.6*	*20.0*	*6.8*	*0*	*0*	15
4	16.7	8.3	20.8	8.3	0	12.5	8.3	16.7	8.3	0	
	16.0	*6.7*	*11.1*	*15.4*	*0*	*11.5*	*10.0*	*6.8*	*40.0*	*0*	24
5	33.3	0	66.7	0	0	0	0	0	0	0	
	4.0	*0*	*4.4*	*0*	*0*	*0*	*0*	*0*	*0*	*0*	3
6	29.4	23.5	23.5	5.9	5.9	11.8	0	0	0	0	
	20.0	*13.3*	*8.9*	*7.7*	*16.7*	*7.7*	*0*	*0*	*0*	*0*	17
7	0	20.0	40.0	0	0	20.0	20.0	0	0	0	
	0	*3.3*	*4.4*	*0*	*0*	*3.8*	*5.0*	*0*	*0*	*0*	5
N =	25	30	45	13	6	26	20	59	5	14	243

strate that using X-ray techniques for observing preferred orientation of inclusions greatly expands the potential for forming studies. Whereas initial inspection allowed reconstruction of forming techniques for only about 10 percent of the sherds, the use of radiographs increased the figure to about 85 percent. The basic requirement for more detailed studies is samples of statistically reliable sizes.

Studies of Firing

Several lines of investigation have been initiated, but with disappointing results.

Color. The first criterion employed was color. Considering that when salt or salt water is mixed with bodies, the range of fired colors correlates with temperature, the attempt was made to sort sherds likely to contain salt according to color. These groups could be compared with control samples fired to known temperatures. Color variations on each sherd were too great, however, to permit reliable grouping. This difficulty was compounded because surface color was often modified by effects of use or burial. A further restriction on color as a criterion was that sherds unlikely to have contained salt could not be classified.

Dilatometer Measurements. Sherds were chosen for dilatometer measurements on the basis of size because the dilatometer sample must be a 5 by 5 cm square about 5 mm thick. Suitable samples of this size could only be cut from large sherds. Sherds previously used in studying materials and forming techniques were preferred because the results could be correlated. Only about 20 samples could be accepted by the institution that made the dilatometer measurements.

Again, the results were disappointing. Dilatometer readings were taken up to maximum temperatures of about 775° to 800°C. Two samples of pottery (not from Motupore Island) fired to a known temperature were used as experimental controls; these showed a clear change from expansion to contraction near this temperature. The Motupore samples all showed continuous expansion, indicating they had been fired originally above 800°C. Readings must be taken at higher temperatures to establish the actual firing temperatures.

The dilatometer technique cannot be regarded as routine for several reasons: (1) the large sherds required are not always available; (2) the time necessary for each measurement is long (up to 12 hours), and (3) the cost of the equipment is greater than can be afforded by most archeology departments.

Firing Cores. The remaining line of investigation is a study of firing cores. The sample chips (Fig. 30) used for identifying inclusions will be used for a preliminary study, which will be expanded if the results are promising. Firing cores will provide indications of the variability in firing atmosphere and rates of cooling of vessels of the same form, but will not indicate the firing temperatures.

Conclusion

This case study illustrates some of the potential of technological studies of pottery, as well as some of the difficulties. The interpretations raise questions that are not strictly technological and thus advance the study of prehistoric people, occasionally in unexpected ways. Studies of other archeological ceramics will not necessarily proceed along similar lines, but will be conditioned by the nature of the assemblage and the equipment and expertise available. The present study was unusual in that some general problems had to be solved before newly developed techniques could be applied on a routine basis.

CASE 2: RECONSTRUCTING THE FORMING PROCESS SEQUENCE OF STORAGE JARS FROM PALESTINE

The Late Bronze Age storage jars examined in this study were selected on the basis of similarity in shape. No measurements were taken; jars of about the same size and form were studied (Fig. 117).

Reconstructing the process sequence began using one jar that was relatively complete. Examination indicated that the sequence included primary forming and one or more stages of drying, and might include secondary forming, which would be subsequent to primary forming. Because all jars had handles, the sequence must also include their application; this had to follow primary forming (because handles cannot be applied until a form exists). Slip had been applied and since it covered the handles as well as the body, its application must have come after the handles were attached. Brushwork overlay the slip, so it was subsequent to slipping. The brushwork was very crisp and sharp in outline, indicating it was done when the vessel was dry.

A five-stage sequence could be inferred from these initial observations: (1) primary forming, (2) ap-

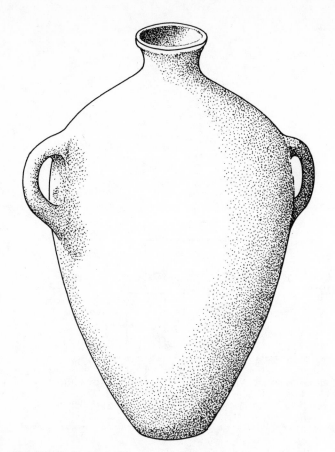

Fig. 117. Typical Late Bronze Age "Canaanite" storage jar from Palestine.

plying handles, (3) applying slip. (4) drying, and (5) applying brushwork decoration.

Evidence was then sought for additional stages and for elaborating those already observed. The interior of the vessel showed rhythmic grooves running from near the base to the rim, indicating that primary forming was by throwing on the potter's wheel. The absence of evidence that the rim or neck had been formed separately implied the vessel was thrown in one piece. Their size (between 40 and 60 cm high) made it unlikely they were thrown from the hump. Each was most likely thrown from one lump of clay placed on the wheelhead, although no evidence remained to prove this interpretation.

The next step was to look for evidence of removal from the wheel. None existed on the exterior. A slight bulge on the interior had no corresponding depression on the outer wall. This suggested slight deformation of the vessel while lifting it when it was in a plastic condition. It also suggested material had been removed from the exterior and the walls had originally been thicker. The question of how the vessel was removed was deferred.

Examination of the base showed traces of grit drag-lines on the exterior. Also, wall thickness was slightly eccentric. The interior showed no modification from its initial forming. These attributes, along with the slight bulge on the lower inner wall, suggested the vessel had been turned. This would involve drying from the plastic condition to leather hard before placing it upside down on the wheelhead. A chuck or other device would have been needed for support during turning, but no evidence of this could be found. The uneven thickness of the wall implied the vessel was replaced slightly off-center from the original throwing axis. The fact that grit drag-marks continued beneath the handles indicated that turning was completed before they were applied.

The bases of other vessels in the sample were examined for evidence of removal. The attributes suggested several methods were employed for completing the base. Some vessels had been turned and all these had a wall thickness at the base approximately the same as the body. Vessels showing no evidence of turning had base thicknesses 2 or 3 times greater than the walls. The interiors of some bases showed compression ridges, indicating pressure from outside. The base was reduced sufficiently by squeezing that the vessel would have fallen from the wheelhead had this been done at an early stage of throwing. The ridges were therefore judged to correlate with the end of throwing. The conclusion was that these vessels were removed from the wheel by squeezing and narrowing the base sufficiently that they could be lifted free. The "cutting" was done with the hands rather than a tool. This method of removal would have left a rough, pointed base. In order to create a uniform and strong base, the potters allowed the vessels to dry to leather hard so they could be supported upside down on the wheelhead.

The cross section of a base showed discontinuous preferred orientation of voids and a slight hollow section, indicating that clay had been added. Clay protruding into the interior of some bases implied a hole had been pushed through from the outside. This evidence led to the following reconstruction: These particular vessels were replaced upside down on the wheelhead after drying to leather hard. They would have been supported by a chuck, and the absence of marks indicated the shoulder was relatively firm when this was done. The base, being thicker, would still be relatively soft. A hole could therefore be poked through and, with the wheel revolving, the base could be thinned and refined from the irregular shape produced by removal with the hands. A coil of clay was then placed on the exterior and, with the wheel still revolving, thrown inwards to reclose the hole. Evidence of this coil consisted of eccentricity between

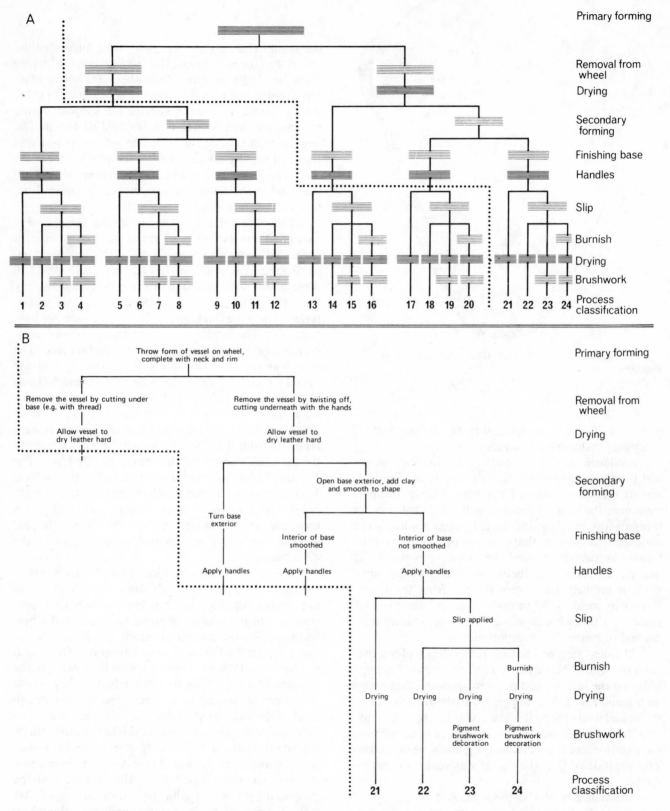

Fig. 118. Forming process sequences reconstructed for Late Bronze Age storage jars. The differences between the 24 variations are diagramed at the top (A). The details distinguishing the categories above the dotted line on A are specified at the bottom (B).

the base and upper walls and a join line where it was blended into the original form. In some cases, the vessel had been removed from the wheel and the inside of the newly formed base was smoothed with the fingers. In other cases, there had been no finishing of the interior.

Putting all this together, it became clear that two methods had been used for completing the bases: turning and adding clay. The method of finishing was obviously related to the method of removal from the wheel.

The forming process sequence classification (Fig. 118) was obtained after complete study of all the storage jars. Once this classification was available, a series of questions could be raised. Why were there two methods of completing the bases? Was the function of the two groups of jars different, one requiring thin walls and the other a thick heavy base? Do the jars represent two different traditions? Is one technique earlier than the other, the later one having technological or other advantages? Was one group of jars made locally and the other imported, perhaps filled with some commodity not obtainable in the area? Was there some mineralogical distinction between clays used for the two different base-finishing techniques?

These questions illustrate an important consequence of analyzing forming techniques. The analysis is not an end in itself, but raises questions that can be expressed as hypotheses for further investigations. These provide a deeper insight into past cultures than would be obtained by stopping when the technological analysis was complete.

Appendix

Two sets of guidelines are provided for recording the behavior of potters. They identify the significant kinds of information in the form of a checklist, which can be used for reference or as a basis for designing forms applicable to a specific group. Some of the categories are irrelevant to indigenous potters, who obtain their own raw materials and make vessels for their own use; they should be included, however, in studies of traditional potters, who may purchase some or all of their materials and who usually sell their products.

1. Pottery Technology Data Sheet and Checklist

PERSONAL DATA

Name of potter _____ Sex _____

Address _____ Age _____

Caste, tribe or ethnic affiliation _____

Languages spoken _____ Literate: Yes/No

Religion _____

Training (where, when, who) _____

Assistants: Casual/Seasonal/Permanent

Number _____ Sex _____ Rates of pay _____

Hours of work _____

Tasks _____

GENERAL INFORMATION

Other potters in village or district _____

Name _____ Caste/Tribe _____ Sex _____ Age _____

Wares same or different _____

Population of village or district _____

Apprentices _____

Number _____ Sex _____ Age _____

Age at recruitment _____ Age at conclusion _____

Method of recruitment _____

Marketing

Who buys _____ Where sold _____

Area of distribution _____

Method of transportation _____

SOURCES OF CLAY (expand on additional sheets as needed)

General geological observations

Kind of deposit

Thickness of overburden/why rejected

Method of digging

Depth of excavation/why no deeper

Does potter recognize different grades?

Does he/she put them to different uses? If so, what?

How is homogeneity achieved?

Samples taken and identifying numbers

Who started using the deposit? When? Why?

Who else uses the deposit? For what?

Why does the potter prefer this deposit?

Who owns the deposit?

Terms of use (lease, kinship, etc.)

PREPARATION OF CLAY/PREPARATION OF BODY
The following details should be described and photographed:
Methods of crushing and grinding
Methods of separation
Stages of addition or removal of water
Methods of determining the proportions of materials
Variations in non-plastic (temper), under what conditions, why?
Methods of combining and mixing clays and non-plastics
Who performs each phase of the work
A sample of water used should be collected for salinity tests

PREPARATION AND APPLICATION OF GLAZES, SLIPS, AND PIGMENTS
The following details should be described and photographed:
Methods of crushing and grinding
Methods of determining proportions of materials; specific proportions
Methods of separation
Methods of combining and mixing; methods of holding in suspension
Methods of application and stage when applied
Samples of each kind of material should be collected and given complete identification

TECHNIQUES AND PROCESSES OF MANUFACTURE
The following details should be described and photographed:
Methods of forming, joining, drying, including techniques specific to each potter
Role of assistants
Equipment and tools, including materials, sources, functions, and longevity
Potter's wheel
    Sketch of construction
    Name and construction of each part
    Materials
    Type of bearing; type used prior to adopting modern bearings
    Flywheel dimensions, construction, weight; dimensional relationship of
        flywheel to seat to wheelhead
Kiln
    Materials used in construction and their sources
    Type of mortar, source, preparation, where used
    How built, by whom
    Repairs: where required, how often, life expectancy of kiln
    Construction of arches, domes or other kinds of spans
    Sketch construction, specifying dimensions of chamber, area of floor. thickness
        of walls, size of door, location and dimensions of firebox, location and
        dimensions of all flame inlet flues, names of all parts
    Provide sectional views to show flame path rise and span of arches

FIRING PROCEDURES
The following details should be described and photographed:
Stages of the operation in sequential order
Role of assistants
Form of preheating employed; temperature reached
Kiln firing
    Number of vessels typically fired together
    Disposition of vessels; use of shelves and props; location of vessels of different sizes
    Special precautions to prevent glazed vessels from fusing together
    Fuel added when, where, how; type of fuel
    Hottest and coolest parts of kiln; how temperature is judged by potter; thermocouple meas-
        urements of variation in time and space
    Stages in firing: starting, watersmoking, reaching maximum temperature, variation in type or
        amount of fuel, variation of access of air and how accomplished
    Conclusion of firing; method of ascertaining completion; how terminated
    Firing losses; disposal of wasters
    Frequency of firing; special firings
    Amount of clay consumed per firing
Non-kiln firing
    Describe any permanent structures
    Techniques of preheating vessels
    Setting of vessels and fuel
    Reason for selecting locale of firing
    Time of day
    Criteria for judging completion of firing
    Number of vessels fired simultaneously and arrangement
    Kind and amount of fuel
    Damage during firing; number of vessels, kind of damage
    Disposal of wasters

GENERAL OBSERVATIONS
Specify local units of weight and measurement; the same name may be employed differently in different
    regions; provide metric equivalents
Record local currency, exchange value, barter or exchange arrangements made by potters
Sketch layout of each potter's workshop, showing location of kiln, raw materials, fuel, potter's wheel,
    glazing area, etc.
Map location of workshop in relation to the village and living quarters of the potter; specify other
    industries associated
Inquire when pottery is made, including seasonality, correlation with other kinds of activities of the potter
    or the community (such as planting, harvesting, ceremonies)
Describe the range of wares produced by each potter; for each, give name, size of vessels, function, by
    whom used, price if sold, number produced per day/season/month. Photograph examples with a
    scale in each picture
Note local markets, range of pottery sold, where it originates, reason for imports if present
Record range of wares in a typical household, lifespan of vessels, uses, restrictions on use
If ritual pottery is made, note special rules and prohibitions regarding manufacture, use, user, and
    disposal
Record the potter's opinion of his work compared to that of others, basis for evaluation, who is better,
    who is worse
Have methods changed during the memory of living potters? How?
Have tools changed? When? Why? What tools were previously used? How?

2. Raw Materials Data Sheet and Checklist

Data	Clay	Non-plastics	Slip
Location of deposit or supplier			
Distance of source from site of manufacture			
Frequency of acquisition			
Amount obtained each time			
Time expended by potter			
Assistants			
Cost/use of transport and assistants			
Method of transport			
Amount used per Day Week Month Season Year			
Amount used per firing			
Size of reserve stockpile			
Number of potters using source			
Other uses of raw material			

Literature Cited

Aitken, M.J.
  1975 Physics and Archaeology. Second Revised Edition. Oxford University Press, Oxford.
Al Kital, R. A., L. H. Chan and E. V. Sayre
  1969 Neutron Activation Analysis of Pottery Sherds from Hajar Bin Humeid and Related Areas. In Hajar Bin Humeid: Investigations at a Pre-Islamic Site in South Arabia, by Gus W. Van Beek et al, pp. 387–398. The Johns Hopkins Press, Baltimore.
Allan, J. W.
  1973 Abū'L-Qāsim's Treatise on Ceramics. Iran, Journal of the British Institute of Persian Studies, Volume 11, pp. 111–120.
Allen, J.
  1977a Sea Traffic, Trade and Expanding Horizons. In Sunda and Sahul: Prehistoric Studies in Southeast Asia, Melanesia and Australia, edited by J. Allen, J. Golson and R. Jones, pp. 387–417. Academic Press, London.
  1977b Fishing for Wallabies: Trade as a Mechanism for Social Interaction, Integration and Elaboration on the Central Papuan coast. In The Evolution of Social Systems, edited by J. Friedman and M. S. Rowlands, pp. 419–455. Duckworth and Co., London.
Amiran, R.
  1969 Ancient Pottery of the Holy Land. Massada Press, Jerusalem.
Arnold, D. E.
  1971 Ethnomineralogy of Ticul, Yucatan Potters: Etics and Emics. American Antiquity, Volume 36(1), pp. 20–40.
  1972 Mineralogical Analyses of Ceramic Materials from Quinua, Department of Ayacucho, Peru. Archaeometry, Volume 14(1), pp. 93–102.
  1974 Some Principles for Paste Analyses and Interpretation: A Preliminary Formulation. Journal of the Steward Anthropological Society, Volume 6(1), pp. 33–47.
  1975 Ceramic Ecology of the Ayacucho Basin, Peru: Implications for Prehistory. Current Anthropology, Volume 16(2), pp. 183–194.
Attas, M., L. Yaffe and J. M. Fossey
  1977 Neutron Activation Analysis of Early Bronze Age Pottery from Lake Vouliagméni, Perakhora, Central Greece. Archaeometry, Volume 19(1), pp. 33–44.
Bieber Jr., A. M., D. W. Brooks, G. Harbottle and E. V. Sayre
  1976 Application of Multivariate Techniques to Analytical Data on Aegean Ceramics. Archaeometry, Volume 18(1), pp. 59–74.
Bonham, Lawrence C. and J. H. Spotts
  1971 Measurement of Grain Orientation. In Procedures in Sedimentary Petrology, edited by R. E. Carver, pp. 285–312. John Wiley and Sons, New York.
Borst, R. L. and W. D. Keller
  1969 Scanning Electron Micrographs of API Reference Clay Minerals and other Selected Samples. In Proceedings of the International Clay Conference 1969, Volume 1, edited by Lisa Heller, pp. 871–901. Israel Universities Press, Jerusalem.
Brill, R. H.
  1970 The Chemical Interpretation of the Texts. In Glass and Glassmaking in Ancient Mesopotamia, by A. Oppenheim et al., pp. 105–128. The Corning Museum of Glass, Corning, New York.
Budworth, D. W.
  1970 An Introduction to Ceramic Science. Pergamon Press, Oxford.
Burton, W.
  1906 Porcelain, Its Nature, Art and Manufacture. Batsford, London.

Cardew, Michael
1969 Pioneer Pottery. Longmans, Green and Co., London.
Carroll, Dorothy
1962 The Clay Minerals. In Sedimentary Petrography, Fourth Revised Edition, Volume II, edited by H. B. Milner, pp. 288–371. George Allen and Unwin, London.
Carver, Robert E. (Ed.)
1971 Procedures in Sedimentary Petrology. John Wiley and Sons, New York.
Cesareo, R., F. V. Frazzoli, C. Mancini, S. Sciuti, M. Marabelli, P. Mora, P. Rotondi and G. Urbani
1972 Non-destructive Analysis of Chemical Elements in Paintings and Enamels. Archaeometry, Volume 14(1), pp. 65–78.
Cornwall, I. W.
1958 Soils for the Archaeologist. Phoenix, London.
Cox, G. A. and A. M. Pollard
1977 X-ray Fluorescence Analysis of Ancient Glass: The Importance of Sample Preparation. Archaeometry, Volume 19(1), pp. 45–54.
de Bruin, M., P. J. B. Korthoven, A. J. v. d. Steen, J. P. W. Houtman and R. P. W. Duin
1976 The Use of Trace Element Concentrations in the Identification of Objects. Archaeometry, Volume 18(1), pp. 75–84.
Demont, Micheline and P. Centlivres
1967 Poteries et potiers d'Afghanistan. Extrait du Bulletin Annuel du Musée et Insitut d'Ethnographie de la Ville de Genève, No. 10, pp. 23–67.
Duma, G.
1972 Phosphate Content of Ancient Pots as Indication of Use. Current Anthropology, Volume 13(1), pp. 127–130.
Duma, G. and I. Lengyel
1970 Mesocstat Pots Containing Red Blood Pigment (haemoglobin). Acta Archaeologica Academie Scientiarium Hungaricae, Volume 22, pp. 69–93.
Ellen, R. F. and I. C. Glover
1974 Pottery Manufacture and Trade in the Central Moluccas, Indonesia: the Modern Situation and the Historical Implications. Man (N.S.), Volume 9, pp. 353–379.
Folk, R. L.
1968 Petrology of Sedimentary Rocks. Hemphills, Austin, Texas.
Forbes, R. J.
1958 Studies in Ancient Technology. Volume VI. E. J. Brill, Leiden.
Fournier, Robert
1973 Illustrated Dictionary of Practical Pottery. Van Nostrand Reinhold Company, New York.
Franken, H. J. (with Kalsbeek, J.)
1969 Excavation at Tell Deir'Alla, Volume 1: A Stratigraphic and Analytical Study of the Iron Age Pottery. H. J. Brill, Leiden.
1974 In Search of the Jericho Potters. North-Holland Ceramic Studies in Archaeology, Volume 1, Leiden.
Freeth, S. J.
1967 A Chemical Study of Some Bronze Age Sherds. Archaeometry, Volume 10, pp. 104–119.
Glock, A. E.
1975 Homo Faber: The Pot and the Potter at Taanach.
Bulletin of the American Schools of Oriental Research, Number 219, pp. 9–28.
Grim, Ralph E.
1962 Applied Clay Mineralogy. McGraw-Hill Book Co., New York.
1968 Clay Mineralogy. Second Edition. McGraw-Hill Book Co., New York.
Hall, E. T., F. Schweizer and P. A. Toller
1973 X-ray Fluorescence Analysis of Museum Objects: A New Instrument. Archaeometry, Volume 15(1), pp. 53–78.
Hamer, Frank
1975 The Potter's Dictionary of Materials and Techniques. Pitman Publishing, London.
Hampe, R. and A. Winter
1962 Bei Töpfern and Töperferinnen in Kreta, Messenien and Zypern. Romisch-Germanisches Zentral Museum zu Mainz, Mainz.
Harbottle, G.
1970 Neutron Activation Analysis of Potsherds from Knossos and Mycenae. Archaeometry, Volume 12(1), pp. 23–34.
Hedges, R. E. M.
1976 Pre-Islamic Glazes in Mesopotamia-Nippur. Archaeometry, Volume 18(2), pp. 209–213.
Hedges, R. and P. Moorey
1975 Pre-Islamic Ceramic Glazes at Kish and Nineveh in Iraq. Archaeometry, Volume 17(1), pp. 25–43.
Hess, J. and I. Perlman
1974 Mössbauer Spectra of Iron in Ceramics and their Relation to Pottery Colours. Archaeometry, Volume 16(2), pp. 137–152.
Hodges, H. W. M.
1962 Thin Sections of Prehistoric Pottery: An Empirical Study. University of London Bulletin of the Institute of Archaeology No. 3, pp. 58–68.
Hughes, M. J., M. R. Cowell and P. T. Craddock
1976 Atomic Absorption Techniques in Archaeology. Archaeometry, Volume 18(1), pp. 19–38.
Hurley, William M.
1979 Prehistoric Cordage. Manuals on Archeology, 3. Taraxacum, Washington.
I. I. C. (The International Institute for Conservation of Historic and Artistic Works)
1975 Conservation in Archaeology and the Applied Arts. Preprints of the Contributions to the Stockholm Congress 2–6 June 1975. The International Institute for Conservation of Historic and Artistic Works, London.
Irwin, G. J.
1977 The Emergence of Mailu. Unpublished Ph.D. thesis. Department of Prehistory, Research School of Pacific Studies, Australian National University, Canberra.
Jizba, Zdenck V.
1971 Mathematical Analysis of Grain Orientation. In Procedures in Sedimentary Technology, edited by R. E. Carver, pp. 313–333. John Wiley and Sons, New York.
Kelso, J. L. and J. P. Thorley
1943 The Potter's Technique at Tell Beit Mirsim, Particularly in Stratum A. In The Excavation of Tell Beit Mirsim, Volume III, pp. 86–142. The Annual of the American Schools of Oriental Research, New Haven.

Lauer, P. K.

1970 Amphlett Islands' Pottery Trade and the Kula. Mankind, Volume 7(3), pp. 165–176.

1974 Pottery Traditions in the D'Entrecasteaux Islands of Papua. Anthropology Museum, University of Queensland. Occasional Papers in Anthropology, No. 3.

Leach, Bernard

1962 A Potter's Book. Faber and Faber, London.

Leigh, David et al.

1972 First Aid for Finds. Rescue Publication No. 1. Rescue and University of Southhampton, Southhampton.

Linné, Sigvald

1925 The Technique of South American Ceramics. Goteborg, Sweden.

1931 Contribution à l'étude de la ceramique sudaméricaine. Revista Instituto Etnología, Universidad Nacional de Tucuman, Argentina, Volume 2, Entrega 2, pp. 199–232.

Litto, G.

1976 South American Folk Pottery. Watson-Guptill Publications, New York.

Lucas, A.

1962 Ancient Egyptian Materials and Industries. Fourth Edition. Edward Arnold, London.

Matson, Frederick R.

1943 Technological Notes on the Pottery. In The Green Glazed Pottery, Nicholas Toll. The Excavations at Dura Europos, Final Report IV, Part 1, Fasicle 1, pp. 81–95. Yale University Press, New Haven.

1951 Ceramic Technology as an Aid to Cultural Interpretation: Techniques and Problems. In Essays on Archaeological Methods. Proceedings of a Conference Held under Auspices of the Viking Fund (March 1950), edited by J. B. Griffin. Anthropological Papers No. 8, Museum of Anthropology, University of Michigan.

1952 The Contribution of Technical Ceramic Studies to American Archaeology. In Prehistoric Pottery of the Eastern United States, No. 2, pp. 1–7. Museum of Anthropology, University of Michigan.

1956 Techniques of the Early Bronze Potters at Tarsus. Appendix in Excavations at Gözlü Kule, Tarsus, by Hetty Goldman. From the Neolithic through the Bronze Age, Volume 2, pp. 352–361. Princeton University Press.

1960a The Quantitative Study of Ceramic Materials. In The Application of Quantitative Methods in Archaeology, edited by R. F. Heizer and S. F. Cook. Viking Fund Publications in Anthropology, No. 28, pp. 34–59. Aldine Publishing Co., Chicago.

1960b Specialized Ceramic Studies and Radioactive-Carbon Techniques. In Prehistoric Investigations in Iraqi Kurdistan, by R. B. Braidwood and B. Howe. Studies in Ancient Oriental Civilization, No. 31, pp. 63–70. The Oriental Institute of the University of Chicago. The University of Chicago Press, Chicago.

1963 Some Aspects of Ceramic Technology. In Science in Archaeology, edited by D. Brothwell and E. Higgs, pp. 489–498. Thames and Hudson, London.

1965a Ceramic Ecology: An Approach to the Study of the Early Cultures of the Near East. In Ceramics and Man, edited by F. R. Matson. Viking Fund Publications in Anthropology, No. 41, pp. 202–217. Aldine Publishing Co., Chicago.

1965b Ceramic Queries. In Ceramics and Man, edited by F. R. Matson. Viking Fund Publications in Anthropology, No. 41, pp. 277–287. Aldine Publishing Co., Chicago.

1966 Power and Fuel Resources in the Ancient Near East. Advancement of Science, Volume 23, pp. 146–153.

1971 The Study of Temperatures Used in Firing Ancient Mesopotamian Pottery. In Science and Archaeology, edited by R. Brill, pp. 65–79. The Massachusetts Institute of Technology Press, Cambridge, Mass.

1972 Ceramic Studies. In The Minnesota Messenian Expedition: Reconstructing a Bronze Age Regional Environment, edited by W. A. McDonald and G. R. Rapp, Jr., pp. 200–224. The University of Minnesota Press, Minneapolis.

Matson, Frederick R., Editor

1965 Ceramics and Man. Viking Fund Publications in Anthropology, No. 41. Aldine Publishing Co., Chicago.

Mayes, P.

1961 The Firing of a Pottery Kiln of a Romano-British Type at Boston Lincolnshire. Archaeometry, Volume 4, pp. 4–18.

1962 The Firing of a Second Pottery Kiln of Romano-British Type at Boston, Lincolnshire. Archaeometry, Volume 5, pp. 80–86.

Meggers, B. J. and C. Evans

1957 Archeological Investigations at the Mouth of the Amazon. Bureau of American Ethnology Bulletin 167, Washington, D.C.

Nicklin, Keith

1971 Stability and Innovation in Pottery Manufacture. World Archaeology, Volume 3(1), pp. 13–98.

Olsen, F. L.

1973 The Kiln Book. Keramos Books, Bassett, California.

Parmelee, C. W.

1951 Ceramic Glazes. Revised Second Edition. Industrial Publications, Chicago.

Peacock, D. P. S.

1967 The Heavy Mineral Analysis of Pottery: A Preliminary Report. Archaeometry, Volume 10, pp. 97–100.

1970 The Scientific Analysis of Ancient Ceramics: A Review. World Archaeology, Volume 1(3), pp. 375–389.

Perlman, I. and F. Asaro

1969 Pottery Analysis by Neutron Activation. Archaeometry, Volume 11, pp. 21–52.

Piccolpasso, C. C.

1934 The Three Books of the Potter's Art. Translated by B. Rackham and A. Van de Put. The Victoria and Albert Museum, London.

Plenderleith, H. J. and A. Werner
  1971   The Conservation of Antiquities and Works of Art. Second Edition. Oxford University Press, Oxford.
Poole, A. B. and L. R. Finch
  1972   The Utilization of Trace Chemical Composition to Correlate British Post-Medieval Pottery with European Kiln Site Materials. Archaeometry, Volume 14(1), pp. 79–92.
Renfrew, Jane M.
  1973   Palaeoethnobotany. The Prehistoric Food Plants of the Near East and Europe. Methuen and Co., London.
Rhodes, D.
  1968   Kilns: Design, Construction and Operation. Chilton Book Co., Philadelphia.
Rigby, G. R.
  1953   The Thin-Section Mineralogy of Ceramic Materials. Second edition. The British Ceramic Research Association.
Roberts, G.
  1960   X-ray Microanalyser. Archaeometry, Volume 3, pp. 36–37.
Rosenthal, Ernst
  1954   Pottery and Ceramics. Revised edition. Penguin Books, Harmondsworth, Middlesex.
Rye, O. S.
  1974   Technological Analysis of Pottery-Making Materials and Procedures. Hombre y Cultura, Volume 2(5), pp. 41–62.
  1976   Keeping Your Temper Under Control: Materials and the Manufacture of Papuan Pottery. Archaeology and Physical Anthropology in Oceania, Volume 11(2), pp. 106–137.
  1977   Pottery Manufacturing Techniques: X-ray Studies. Archaeometry, Volume 19(2), pp. 205–211.
Rye, O. S. and J. Allen
  1976   New Approaches to Papuan Pottery Analysis. Prétirage: IX Congress, Union Internationale des Sciences Préhistoriques et Protohistoriques. Colloque XXII: La Préhistoire Océanienne, pp. 198–222.
Rye, O. S. and C. Evans
  1976   Traditional Pottery Techniques of Pakistan: Field and Laboratory Studies. Smithsonian Contributions to Anthropology, No. 21. Smithsonian Institution Press, Washington.
Salmang, Hermann
  1961   Ceramics. Butterworths, London.
Sanders, Herbert H.
  1972   The World of Japanese Ceramics. Seventh Printing. Kodansha International, Tokyo.
Sanders, H. P.
  1973   Pore Size Distribution Determinations in Neolithic, Iron Age, Roman and Other Pottery. Archaeometry, Volume 15(1), pp. 159–161.
Saraswati, Baidyanath and N. K. Behura
  1966   Pottery Techniques in Peasant India. Memoir No. 13 (1964). Anthropological Survey of India, Calcutta.
Searle, Alfred B. and Rex W. Grimshaw
  1959   The Chemistry and Physics of Clays and Other Ceramic Materials. Third edition. Interscience Publishers, New York.
Shepard, Anna
  1968   Ceramics for the Archaeologist. Sixth printing. Carnegie Institution of Washington, Publication Number 609, Washington, D.C.
Skinner, B. J.
  1966   Thermal Expansion. In Handbook of Physical Constants. Revised edition, edited by S. Clark, pp. 75–96. The Geological Society of America Inc., New York.
Smith, R. H.
  1972   The Sectioning of Potsherds as an Archaeological Method. Berytus, Volume 21, pp. 39–53.
Stanislawski, M. B.
  1977   Ethnoarchaeology of Hopi and Hopi-Tewa Pottery Making: Styles of Learning. In Experimental Archaeology, edited by D. Ingersoll, J. Yellen and W. MacDonald, pp. 378–409. Columbia University Press, New York.
Textoris, D. A.
  1971   Grain-size Measurement in Thin-Section. In Procedures in Sedimentary Petrology, edited by R. E. Carver, pp. 95–107. John Wiley and Sons, New York.
Tite, M. S.
  1969   Determination of the Firing Temperature of Ancient Ceramics by Measurement of Thermal Expansion: A Reassessment. Archaeometry, Volume 11, pp. 131–144.
Vanderwal, R. L.
  1973   Prehistoric Studies in Central Coastal Papua. Unpublished Ph.D. thesis. Department of Prehistory, Research School of Pacific Studies, Australian National University, Canberra.
Wertime, T. A.
  1973   Pyrotechnology: Man's First Industrial Uses of Fire. American Scientist, Volume 61(6), pp. 670.
Williams, J. and D. A. Jenkins
  1976   The Use of Petrographic, Heavy Mineral and Arc Spectrographic Techniques in Assessing the Provenance of Sediments Used in Ceramics. In Geoarchaeology, edited by D. A. Davidson and M. L. Shackley, pp. 115–135. Duckworth, London.
Wulff, Hans E.
  1966   The Traditional Crafts of Persia. The Massachusetts Institute of Technology Press, Cambridge, Massachusetts.
Zacharikov, N. A., N. V. Lesovoi and N. G. Mitin
  1961   Firing Porcelain in a Gaseous, Whitening Atmosphere. Translation from Steklo i Keramika, Volume 18(2), pp. 15–19. Ceramics and Glass, Volume 18.

Glossary

Additive. Any material mixed with clay to improve its un-fired or fired properties.

Anvil. A tool with a convex face held against the interior wall of a vessel to oppose the blows of a beater against the exterior.

Bagwall. A wall inside a downdraft kiln over which the flame from the firebox travels before moving down through the chamber (Fig. 89).

Beater. A tool applied with sharp blows over the exterior to shape plastic or leather-hard vessels; used alone or with an anvil on the interior (Fig. 69).

Biscuit. Ceramic ware that has undergone the first firing be-fore glazing; unglazed ware that has been fired once.

Bloating. Increase in porosity and pore size in a ceramic body that has vitrified as a result of extreme overfiring (Fig. 94).

Bloom. Synonym for efflorescence.

Body. Clay or a blend of clay and temper suitable for forming vessels. Applicable to the unfired and fired states. Fired body is synonymous with fabric and paste.

Bone dry. Stage of drying when no further water is lost to the atmosphere under natural conditions.

Calcining. Heating a rock, mineral, etc. in a furnace or kiln to a temperature below its fusion or sintering point. De-composition may result (as with limestone) or stresses may develop due to expansion and contraction of min-erals, making the material easier to crush.

Centering. Applying pressure to a lump of clay on the wheelhead to position it for even rotation (Fig. 59 b).

Chamber. The enclosed portion of a kiln where pottery ves-sels are placed for firing (Figs. 88, 89).

Chuck. A device made from fired or unfired clay for attach-ing a leather-hard or dry vessel to a potter's wheel so its form may be modified (Figs. 44, 74 d–e).

Colloidal water. Water molecules loosely attached to clay-mineral crystals.

Colorant. An element or compound that contributes to a ceramic composition.

Core. See Firing core.

Crazing. A network of fine cracks in a glaze.

Dilatometer. Instrument used to measure the expansion of a piece of pottery as it is heated.

Downdraft kiln. A kiln in which the flame travels from the firebox over a bagwall before passing down through the chamber to flues and chimney (Fig. 89).

Dunting. Type of cracking caused by cooling vessels too rapidly after firing (Figs. 101, 102).

Dust pressing. Forming ceramic objects by forcing nearly dry powder into a metal mold.

Efflorescence. The process by which soluble salts in solution in the wall of a vessel are deposited on the surface dur-ing evaporation of the water; also, the surface coating so produced.

Elemental analysis. Determining the chemical elements present in a substance (qualitative) and their relative amounts (quantitative).

Eutectic. The composition with the lowest melting point in a series of blends of ceramic materials.

Fabric. The constituents of fired pottery, including matrix, inclusions (solids and voids), pores, and glass, but excluding surface coatings.

Facet. A flat area on the surface of a vessel formed by cut-ting away material or by beating (Figs. 73, 116).

Fault. An undesirable change occurring during forming, dry-ing or firing (such as a crack).

Firebox. The enclosed section of a kiln where fuel is burned (Figs. 88, 89).

Fire cloud. A dark area on the surface of a vessel caused by incorporation of carbon in the pores during firing (Fig. 109).

Firecracking. A network of fine cracks on the surface of an unglazed vessel, caused by fast firing (Figs. 98, 99).

Firing. Heating pottery to a temperature high enough to cause permanent destruction of the clay minerals; rendering pottery hard and durable by heating; heating and cooling in a kiln.

Firing core. A zone of contrasting color in the cross section of a vessel wall, caused by and indicative of variations in atmosphere and rate of heating and cooling during firing (Figs. 104, 105).

Firing loss. The number of vessels damaged during firing, expressed as a percentage of the total number of vessels in the firing.

Flue. An opening or passage for hot gases within a kiln.

Flux. A material in a clay body, slip, glaze or other ceramic composition that promotes or increases vitrification.

Friable. Crumbly, easily eroded, poorly bonded.

Frit. A mixture of materials that has been fused by heating, used as an ingredient of glazes.

Fusible. Materials that form glasses when heated to normal pottery firing temperatures.

Glaze. A coating of glass fused to the surface of a ceramic vessel (Fig. 36).

Grit. Coarse particles in clays (see Inclusions).

Grit drag-marks. Lines caused by dragging inclusions across the surface with a tool (Figs. 71–73, 75).

Grog. Crushed pottery used as an additive to clay.

Inclusion. Any constituent of a fired pottery vessel or fragment that was not originally a clay mineral, such as voids, plant remains, rock fragments, temper, etc.

Interstitial water. Water occupying interstices (spaces) between mineral grains in clay.

Kneading. Mixing plastic clay or body to distribute minerals, organic materials, and water evenly and to eliminate air pockets and voids (Figs. 9, 22 c)

Leather hard. Stage of drying when plasticity is minimal but water content is still sufficient to allow some kinds of modifications; stage intermediate between plastic and bone dry (Fig. 11).

Macroporosity. The presence of pores visible to the naked eye in a fired pottery fabric.

Matrix. The part of a pottery fabric originally composed of clay minerals.

Neutral. Atmosphere during firing when the ratio of air to fuel is optimum, with neither an excess of air or fuel.

Non-plastic. Any material present in a clay body that exhibits no plasticity, whether occurring naturally or added by the potter.

Normal fracture. Fracture perpendicular to the vessel wall.

Overfiring. Increasing the temperature or duration of firing above the optimum for a particular ceramic composition (body, glaze, slip, etc.).

Oxidizing. Atmosphere during firing in which the amount of oxygen is more than required to combust the fuel.

Paddle. Synonym for beater.

Parting agent. A material, such as sand, ash, or powdered clay, sprinkled over the surface on which the plastic clay is worked to prevent sticking (Figs. 9, 10).

Paste. Fired body; synonym for fabric.

Permeability. The property that allows fluids to pass through ceramics, measured as the amount of liquid passing through a given thickness of ceramic in a given time.

Pigment. A material, generally a mixture of minerals, painted onto a piece of pottery before or after firing to produce a contrasting color.

Pinching. Technique of hand-building vessels by squeezing the clay, usually between fingers and thumb (Figs. 52, 53).

Plastic. The condition when clay can be transformed into a new shape without tearing or breaking.

Plasticity. The property of clay that allows change of shape when pressure is applied and retention of the new shape when the pressure is removed.

Porosity. The amount of space in a fabric occupied by pores.

Preheating. Heating vessels prior to setting for firing to remove remaining free moisture (Fig. 90).

Primary clay. Clay in association with the parent rock from which it was formed by weathering.

Pyrometer. The instrument that indicates the temperature to which a thermocouple has been heated (Fig. 5).

Reducing. Atmosphere during firing in which carbon monoxide is present because insufficient oxygen is available to combust the fuel.

Refractory. The condition of being able to withstand high temperature without fusing.

Rehydration. The reforming of a clay mineral by taking up water in the crystal after this water has been driven off by heating.

Residual clay. Clay weathered in situ, associated with the parent rock from which it has formed.

Ring building. Synonym for coiling.

Scratch hardness. The relative hardness of pottery compared with standard minerals of known hardness (Moh's scale). Any material can be scratched by a mineral that is harder, but is unmarked by one that is softer.

Secondary clay. A clay moved from its original place of formation by erosion and redeposited.

Secondary forming. The stage during which the final vessel form is produced. Subsequent operations involve only changes in surface texture or adding surface coatings.

Setting. Placing vessels in a kiln for firing; also, the entire arrangement of vessels in a kiln or open firing.

Silica inversion. The change in the molecular structure of crystalline quartz at 573°C.

Sintering. The bonding of a ceramic mass during firing without vitrification.

Slag. Glassy material formed in a kiln as a by-product of heating.

Slaking. Exposing dry or semi-dry clay to water to cause lumps to disintegrate (Fig. 19).

Slip. A fluid suspension of clay or clay-body in water; a non-vitreous coating applied to a pottery vessel. The term is applicable both before and after firing.

Slip casting. A method of forming ceramic vessels by pouring slip into a plaster mold, allowing a layer adjacent to the mold to dry (forming the vessel), and then pouring off the excess.

Slurry. A viscous suspension of clay in water (Fig. 11).

Soaking. The stage of firing in a kiln when the temperature is kept constant (usually at the maximum temperature).

Souring. Storing a clay body in plastic condition for a period of time sufficient to allow growth of bacteria and other organisms, which improve workability.

Squatting. Sagging or collapsing of a vessel during firing at high temperature (Fig. 94 a).

Stokehole. The opening in a kiln through which fuel is introduced.

Tempering. Adding non-plastic materials to clay to improve its workability or fired properties.

Texture. Surface quality of a vessel, judged by touch and sight and expressed as roughness, smoothness, irregularity or regularity.

Thermal expansion. Increase in the size (volume) of a ceramic body when heated.

Thermal shock resistance. The ability to withstand sudden changes in temperature or cycles of heating and cooling without damage, such as cracking.

Thermocouple. A junction of two metal wires of different compositions, which generates an electric current when heated.

Throwing. Forming vessels on a potter's wheel (Fig. 59).

Turning. Removing excess clay from a leather-hard vessel by shaving with a sharp-edged tool as the vessel revolves on a potter's wheel (Fig. 74).

Turntable. A disk or other device that can be revolved slowly by hand and supports a vessel being formed (Fig. 42 b).

Underfiring. Decreasing the temperature or time of firing below the optimum for a particular ceramic composition (body, slip, glaze, etc.).

Updraft kiln. A kiln in which the chamber is directly above the firebox (Fig. 88).

Vitreous. Containing fused or glassy material.

Vitrification. Formation of glass during heating.

Void. Open space in a pottery fabric (Fig. 23).

Volatilization. The process by which some elements are lost during firing by becoming gaseous.

Warping. Abnormal change in the shape of a vessel during drying or firing (Fig. 94).

Waste clay. Unfired body accumulated as a by-product of forming operations, which is collected for recycling.

Waster. Vessel damaged during the manufacturing process, particularly during firing; also, sherds from such vessels (Figs. 95, 97).

White dry. Stage of dryness of clays and bodies intermediate between leather-hard and bone dry.

Wiped. A surface with the appearance of having had a hand or a soft material passed over it while the clay was wet (Fig. 35).

Workability. The suitability of a plastic clay or body for forming pottery, as judged by its feel to the potter. Not synonymous with plasticity (a clay may be too plastic to be workable).

Analytical Table of Contents